Hard Times

THE AMERICAN WAYS SERIES

General Editor: John David Smith
Charles H. Stone Distinguished Professor of American History
University of North Carolina at Charlotte

From the long arcs of America's history, to the short timeframes that convey larger stories, American Ways provides concise, accessible topical histories informed by the latest scholarship and written by scholars who are both leading experts in their fields and polished writers.

Books in the series provide general readers and students with compelling introductions to America's social, cultural, political, and economic history, underscoring questions of class, gender, racial, and sectional diversity and inclusivity. The titles suggest the multiple ways that the past informs the present and shapes the future in often unforeseen ways.

CURRENT TITLES IN THE SERIES

HARD TIMES

Economic Depressions in America

Richard Striner

ROWMAN & LITTLEFIELD
Lanham • Boulder • New York • London

Published by Rowman & Littlefield
A wholly owned subsidiary of The Rowman & Littlefield Publishing Group, Inc.
4501 Forbes Boulevard, Suite 200, Lanham, Maryland 20706
www.rowman.com

Unit A, Whitacre Mews, 26-34 Stannary Street, London SE11 4AB

Copyright © 2018 by The Rowman & Littlefield Publishing Group, Inc.

British Library Cataloguing in Publication Information Available

Library of Congress Cataloging-in-Publication Data

Names: Striner, Richard, 1950– author.
Title: Hard times : economic depressions in America / Richard Striner.
Description: Lanham : Rowman & Littlefield, [2018] | Series: The American
   ways series | Includes bibliographical references and index.
Identifiers: LCCN 2018005996 (print) | LCCN 2018007136 (ebook) | ISBN
   9781442253247 (electronic) | ISBN 9781442253230 (cloth : alk. paper)
Subjects: LCSH: Depressions—History. | Business cycles—United
   States—History. | Financial crises—United States—History. | United
   States—Economic conditions.
Classification: LCC HB3743 (ebook) | LCC HB3743 .S887 2018 (print) | DDC
   338.5/42—dc23
LC record available at https://lccn.loc.gov/2018005996

Printed in the United States of America

To the memory of my father, the economist Herbert Striner, and also my grandfather, Harry Striner, who arrived in this country in 1912 and made good

Contents

Preface

AS I WRITE, THE CIRCUMSTANCES are conducive for a book about America's economic depressions because the tepid economy that Americans have been stuck with since 2008 qualifies, in the opinion of many, as a genuine depression. To be sure, most economists have called it a recession, and some of them have even declared that it ended several years ago.

Many of us question that latter proposition and wonder what kinds of standards are used by such economists when they define "recession" and "depression."

Anyone who studies economics is confronted at the outset by problems such as these because the facts of economic life are almost always in dispute. So far from being a "science," economics is a field that is fraught with epistemological, conceptual, and methodological difficulties, some of them insoluble. The database, for instance, is often incomplete and in some cases nonexistent, as in the case of the black market economy and the financial side of crime. The presuppositions of economic inquiry—and this is hardly a problem unique to the field of economics—are skewed by assumptions, some of which are at times quite arguable, depending upon one's point of view. Debates about economics are affected by the vested interests of participants; the force of opportunism makes the contentions that arise in the course of these debates dubious.

The human mind has a terrible propensity to overgeneralize, to create simplistic propositions and embrace them with fanatical intensity. For dogmatic personalities, economics has served as a channel for myth-based theory approximating religion, at least in the intensity of the convictions that arise.

Prefaces are places for authors to declare their sensibilities, and the statements that I have just set forth should reveal my own for what they are: those of a man who is willing to come to some conclusions about economics in the face of an evidence base that is sometimes hard to trust. We can never know the full truth about the content and scope of many marketplace exchanges, so we have to decide what sort of evidence seems credible and then educe from that evidence some patterns as the basis for generalizations—generalizations as responsible and defensible as we can make them.

So I will try to speak plainly in regard to the limits of what the evidence can teach us about hard times in America. The causes of certain economic contractions, for instance, seem clearer to me in some cases than in others, and whenever this occurs I will try to be as candid as my own point of view will permit.

What is my point of view?

I identify myself as a political independent. I have mixed feelings about the fluctuating content of right-wing and left-wing ideology. For that reason I represent no orthodoxy. I insist upon being the autonomous judge in regard to whatever I support or oppose.

I do have a very definite point of view—a skeptical point of view—in regard to many of the generalizations made by free market ideologists or "classical" economists. It seems obvious to me that society embodies chain reactions that often get out of control and overwhelm the power of individuals. Economic contractions can be usefully compared to epidemic illnesses: the process spreads out of control and then blameless individuals suffer. So when market forces, like contagions, get out of control and cause suffering, it seems clear to me that well-grounded forms of intervention are necessary and justified. This is only common sense.

I do not believe that economic hard times should be suffered in passivity.

And I believe that my point of view in regard to that matter should be placed before the reader at the outset.

Acknowledgments

I am proud to contribute this volume to the American Ways series. I want to thank my editors John David Smith and Jon Sisk for their helpful and astute contributions. That said, any errors in this work are my own. I have done my best in the preface and elsewhere to present my views for what they are. I encourage both economists and historians to consider those views on their merits.

Introduction

SOME AMERICANS HAVE BEEN LUCKY enough to have had no prolonged experience of hard times: the twentieth-century "Baby Boomers" encountered nothing worse than short recessions before they reached the age of retirement.

But for much of our history, depressions were a regular occurrence. And the pattern of prosperity and slump in economic life was so familiar (even seemingly predictable) that economists and others called it the "boom-and-bust cycle."

This book will explore the impacts of economic depressions on the people who had to live through them. The result for many was ruin: hard times drove some of the people in deepest despair right over the brink into suicide, family abandonment, or wandering homelessness. Others were driven into violent mob actions that could sometimes lead to deadly results.

But *Hard Times* will also show how privation could elicit inspirational messages: depressions were sometimes invoked as *providential* disasters that could chasten the wayward, clear away the rubbish of dysfunctional social arrangements, and usher in a matchless opportunity to build anew.

In the case of the Great Depression of the 1930s, a series of chapters will explore the impact of hard times on American politics, and one chapter is entirely devoted to American culture in the 1930s as shaped by the Depression.

Depressions can teach us a very great deal about American history in general. But people have often disputed the facts about depressions. And many of these disputes have been grounded in larger debates about economic life and how it works.

Several patterns in regard to American depressions seem worthy of comment. First, there was often a strong correlation between the onset of depressions and panics in the American financial sector. The panics of

1819, 1837, 1873, and 1893 were followed by depressions. This association of events led many to presume causality—that the panics were catalytic events that *caused* the chain reactions that followed. But sometimes this presumption has been doubted or disputed: some believe that the Wall Street Crash of 1929 was obviously involved in the onset of the depression that followed, but others have argued that the proof of this does not exist. Few, however, have disputed the cause-and-effect relationship between the banking crisis of 1930–1933 and the onset of the Great Depression.

Second, there was often an international dimension to America's depressions. But commentators have often disagreed on the nature and direction of global causality. In the case of the Great Depression of the 1930s, the argument can be made that the transoceanic chain reactions were in some ways reciprocal.

Third, in many of America's depressions, Americans disagreed about what (if anything) ought to have been done to ameliorate things. The tradition of ultra-libertarianism, for instance, prompted Democrats in the 1830s to oppose governmental intervention in the economy because one of their party's slogans at that time was "The Government that Governs Best, Governs Least." But the leaders of the opposition Whig Party advocated job-creating public works ("internal improvements" in the parlance of the times) that would ease unemployment and abet economic expansion.

Laissez-faire—the anti-government philosophy that emerged from the teachings of the eighteenth-century French Physiocrats—was taken up by classical liberals and then appropriated later by conservatives. It found its way into economic doctrine via the arguments of Adam Smith and others who contributed to the "classical" economic tradition in academia. Classical economists in the nineteenth century often claimed that the "boom-and-bust cycle" was equivalent to natural law: economies expanded and contracted and nothing could be done about it. This fatalistic outlook was also applied to the international component of depressions: pessimists concluded that no individual nation on its own could lift the curse of an economic depression because its patterns were international in scope.

In light of such beliefs, it is a somber commentary that Nazi Germany recovered from the Great Depression as hard times continued to ravage the United States, Great Britain, and many other nations.

Keynesian economists have attributed this result to Hitler's massive public works programs.

At this writing, the so-called Great Recession that began in 2008 has generated intense debates about policy between those who argue that government should have done much more to reverse the economic contraction and those who argue that government *worsened* the contraction.

What light can be shed upon disputes such as these by a study of historical patterns in America's experience of hard times? We shall see.

1

Hard Times from Colonial to Postrevolutionary America

THE AMERICAN ECONOMY CONTAINED an international dimension from the outset: the first seventeenth-century English colonies in North America were established to exist in a symbiotic relationship with the mother country. Virginia, established in 1607, was fundamentally a commercial venture, launched by the royally chartered Virginia Company of London. To be sure, Virginia was envisioned by some in *political* terms: as a New World extension of English power vis-à-vis the Spanish. But the Virginia Company (a joint stock company) was also set up to make a profit.

Early hopes to emulate the Spanish by finding gold and silver in Virginia were dashed, and so the leaders of the colony searched for a way to put Virginia on a paying basis. In 1612, success was attained with the planting of tobacco, thus launching the fateful plantation system in the American South.

The tobacco economy of Virginia and other plantation colonies would fluctuate according to the transatlantic market for the crop, and this meant that the tobacco colonies could fall into a slump when the market for tobacco diminished. An early boom in the 1610s ended rudely with the short-term saturation of the English market for the product that King James I had condemned as an obnoxious weed. Some early efforts to diversify the Virginia economy and encourage the building of towns—efforts intensified in the middle of the century by royal governor William Berkeley—led nowhere.

Some attempted to hammer out an agreement among planters to suspend production, perhaps for a year, thus creating a shortage that would drive up the price of tobacco, but Virginia planters could never maintain enough solidarity for such a plan to work. The problem was compounded by the fact that other plantation colonies such as Maryland would have to agree to participate in such a scheme. But Lord Baltimore was uncooperative.

By 1672 over ten million pounds of tobacco were reaching the port of London every year, and the price of the commodity was roughly half of what it had been a few decades earlier. Meanwhile, the discontent of poor whites in Virginia increased. Former indentured servants led a hardscrabble life on the Virginia frontier, and while a mixture of causes fueled the violent insurrection in 1676 known as Bacon's Rebellion, economic grievances played a role.

In the early New England colonies the situation was different, though still fundamentally grounded in transatlantic patterns. The Puritan Separatists in Plymouth colony desired to break away from England as much as they could, but the larger and more consequential Massachusetts Bay colony was dedicated at first to setting up an ideal Puritan commonwealth, one that could be adopted in England itself.

The mainstay of economic life in early New England derived from farming, fishing, and the basic trades, but the economy of Massachusetts expanded in the 1630s due to the need to build new homes and provide a host of services to new immigrants. Puritans kept on arriving from England during these years to participate in this "errand into the wilderness."

But in the 1640s, all of that changed. England was plunged into civil war and the flood of eager immigrants diminished to a trickle. The "Great Migration" was over. The predictable result was hard times—economic contraction. Massachusetts adapted to the crisis by developing a much larger mercantile economy based on trade with many other nations.

Over time, the role that was played by the Boston merchants was equaled or surpassed by the work of busy merchants in Philadelphia and New York.

From the seventeenth to the mid-eighteenth century, the economies of the English colonies were challenged by a fundamental hardship: the shortage of a circulating money supply. Coined money was scarce, and in 1695 Parliament made the situation worse by forbidding the exportation of coin beyond the British Isles. This restriction—though never completely effective—was nonetheless a very significant hindrance. The colonists were "cash poor" except for the foreign coins that were received from time to time in normal trade (or else brought to colonial ports by pirates who decided to spend their loot in town). The Bank of England was chartered by Parliament in 1694, but banking in America would not develop in any significant form for many years.

So the colonists exchanged goods and services through procedures that were tantamount to barter—but in this case with an intermediary form of monetary valuation. Colonial legislatures gradually established conversion ratios that set fixed rates for standard commodities (such as corn) in terms of pounds, shillings, and pence. Sometimes these commodities were given the status of legal tender under law, that is, they were a means of payment that *had* to be accepted by sellers. International trade was conducted largely through bills of exchange, based in warehouse receipts for commodities.

But slowly—very slowly—the stock of foreign coin built up on colonial shores through international trade. Most widely in use was the "Spanish dollar," an Anglicization of the German "thaler," a silver coin of the same size and weight as the Spanish one. Spanish dollars were also called "pieces of eight" because the coin's silver content was eight times the weight of the basic Spanish monetary unit of the time, the "real."

In 1720, a financial panic in England, resulting from a wave of reckless speculation known as the "South Sea Bubble," caused an economic contraction in the British Isles. One result was falling prices. American colonial merchants found that their wares brought far less return than they had expected when they first shipped the goods. And because the swap-like offsets of warehouse receipts were no longer enough to cover the balance of payments, the cash (such as it was) in the coffers of colonial merchants began flowing steadily outward toward Britain to make up the difference.

All of the colonies were affected to some extent by the hard times that followed. The Philadelphia merchants were especially hard hit, so they began to apply more pressure to their debtors, renters, and tenants to make up for their deficiency of revenue. They foreclosed, for instance, on working-class debts, and this led right away to predictable grievances, which in turn caused political upheaval in the colonial legislature.

But one of the major complaints, to quote one of the petitions, was the "want of a medium to buy and sell with."

In 1722, the governor of Pennsylvania wrote to the English authorities that "the people of this place are just now in a very great Ferment on Account that for some time past their usual Trade has stagnated for want of a sufficient currency of cash amongst themselves whereby to Exchange the produce of their Labour according to their accustomed Manner of Business." Consequently, "the Farmer brings his provision to Market but there is no Money to give for it, the ship Builder & Carpenter starve for want of Employment . . . the interest on Money is high, and the usurer grinds the Face of the Poor so that Lawsuits multiply, the Gaols are full," and the bill of complaints went on and on.

Various populistic remedies were proposed (or demanded) by protesters: prohibition on the export of gold and silver coins, laws to extend the legal tender status of commodities such as crops, limitations on interest, and a debt moratorium.

One far-sighted merchant named Francis Rawle proposed a scheme to create an economic expansion that would benefit everyone by increasing the money supply, and to do it in a manner that would inject new purchasing power into the Pennsylvania economy. Several colonies had been experimenting with the issuance of paper money by the colonial government itself, and the results had been mixed; the experiments had sometimes led to inflation, which meant that the notes would circulate at far less than their face value. Many were understandably suspicious of a monetary form that possessed no intrinsic value of its own as a commodity. But Rawle proposed that Pennsylvania should print legal tender money and lend it into circulation with real estate as the collateral. With collateral, the money would be "grounded" in a tangible form of real wealth.

In 1723, the governor and the colonial assembly took action on Rawle's proposal. An amount of legal tender currency worth £15,000 was created and lent at 5 percent interest, with mortgages on real estate and houses as collateral, and the loans were to be repaid in eight annual installments. After the loans were repaid, the currency would be destroyed.

The experiment was successful, and the legislature went on to create an additional £30,000 worth of legal tender currency that year.

In 1726, the Pennsylvania legislature reported that "the Face of our Affairs appeared entirely changed; Traders exerted themselves; the Produce of our Country came into Demand, and bore a Price, whereby the People were better enabled to pay the Proprietary's Quitrents, and answer other Demands; our City fill'd again with Inhabitants; Artificers found Employment; our British trade increased; and Strangers, from the Encouragement of finding ready Pay, resorted to us."

Indeed, the experiment succeeded so well that it caught the attention of Benjamin Franklin, who in 1729 wrote an influential pamphlet titled *A Modest Enquiry into the Nature and Necessity of a Paper Currency*. In the same year, the Pennsylvania legislature authorized another currency issue in response to another economic slump. Other colonies, such as New Jersey and Delaware, began to copy the method.

During the French and Indian War (1754–1763), Pennsylvania emitted more paper currency—"for the King's use"—to fulfill its wartime obligations. This time, however, the bills were designed to be redeemed later on in coin that would be obtained (hopefully) as revenue from taxes.

But from the very beginning, British policymakers had taken a dim view of paper currency, and the first Pennsylvania experiment was tolerated in London only because of the legislature's promise to destroy the currency after the loans had been repaid. After several decades, the British clamped down decisively. In 1764, Parliament, at the behest of the British Board of Trade, passed an act forbidding any further use of paper currency in the colonies. British merchants had complained about the practice, and the board proclaimed that paper money was inherently grounded in "fraud and injustice" because people were compelled to "receive that as lawfull money which has no real intrinsic value in itself."

Benjamin Franklin gave testimony in support of the Pennsylvania system but the members of the board were unimpressed: there was a powerful and widespread presumption that the only "honest" money was commodity money, an intermediary form of exchange with a value of its own.

The new British prohibition on colonial currency issues played a role in the hard times that followed during the 1760s, especially when coupled with the new imperial taxes—such as the 1765 Stamp Tax—that were levied in order to pay down the costs of the French and Indian War and to underwrite postwar expenses. These new taxes drew significant amounts of coined money from the colonists' purses, and though the taxes in question hit the upper classes harder, a contraction of the overall monetary base led to broader patterns of economic contraction that affected the working class as well.

Beyond the effects of this contraction of the money supply, no historical consensus exists in regard to the mix of other causes that produced this late colonial depression. For what it is worth, the balance of payments with the mother country was favorable throughout the period in question.

The period in question comprises the years of resistance and revolutionary agitation that led in the 1770s to the creation of the Continental Congress and America's Revolutionary War. And the economic effects of war itself deserve some commentary.

War is a double-edged sword in economic terms and it can lead to very different results: it can lead to economic expansion, economic contraction, or a poignant mixture of the two, depending on specifics. Total war can result in civilian austerity and privation as material resources get channeled into military operations. Yet mobilization, if successfully conducted, can also prompt massive forms of economic stimulation with the gains reflected not only in expanded production but also at times in the full employment of the workforce. It all depends on the specifics, especially if a war's destructive effects are meted out on the home front—or not.

The American Revolutionary War created another experience of hard times for many. But the overall economic effects of the war were mixed. Demand for war materiel stimulated output. Overseas trade patterns were disrupted and thwarted in some respects, but stimulated in others. Many European merchants were afraid at first of the risks of doing business with Americans, but others—especially after the consummation of the Franco-American alliance in 1778—saw new opportunities. Some American businesses were destroyed while others prospered. Some suffered privation, not least of all depending on the destructive vicissitudes of the military campaigns themselves.

One of the most fundamental economic factors of the war was the financial side of the revolution, for the Continental Congress, which lacked the power to levy taxes, turned with gusto to the method of issuing paper money. And this new American experiment with government-created money led to mixed economic results. Unlike the colonial Pennsylvania currency, the "continental currency" that was emitted by the Continental Congress depreciated during the revolution and high inflation rates made market transactions precarious. On the other hand, it is doubtful whether the American Revolution could have been paid for without these new currency issues.

As usual the stock of coined money was relatively small. So Congress created new "credit" for itself through two related expedients, both of which amounted to deficit spending: (1) it sold bonds on the international market and (2) the new paper money that the Continental Congress created was in and of itself a form of borrowing.

The continental currency bills were promises to pay: they would be backed by coin and, after their redemption in cold hard cash, they would be destroyed. In the meantime, they could be spent directly into use. They were legal tender.

And yet the timing and circumstances for the bills' redemption in coin were left vague. The text that was printed on the bills could vary, but here is a representative sample: "This bill entitles the Bearer to receive three Spanish milled dollars according to the Resolution of the Congress, held at Philadelphia, the 10th of May 1775."

Because the bills were grounded in a promise to pay in silver coin, their reputation would stand or fall depending on the expectation for such cash redemption. But the expectations were negative. Not only was coin in its nature a scarce American commodity but the power of Congress to consummate redemption in coin would also be dependent on battlefield results. And to make matters worse, the British were emitting a blizzard of counterfeit currency to make the reputation of the "Continentals" plummet further. Consequently, the continental currency circulated as often as not at a miniscule fraction of its face value, the result being price inflation.

The issue of money creation as a factor in American depressions would recur in subsequent episodes of hard times.

Both the economic and political consequences of the American Revolution set the stage for the first economic depression in the history of the new American nation—the depression of 1785–1786.

The newly independent United States was free of any direct British economic controls. American merchants could trade with whomever they wished, and they could do it under the best terms they could negotiate. But many foreign trade partners were leery of signing commercial treaties with the United States as such because while the first constitution of the United States—whose complete title was Articles of Confederation and Perpetual Union—bound the thirteen states together in perpetuity, such "perpetual union" might in fact be impossible to sustain if the United States should break up into thirteen separate sovereignties.

Indeed, some American leaders were inclined to believe that the states were *already* separate nations, though bound together in a "Union" that constituted an *alliance* rather than a full national polity. The Articles of Confederation described the "perpetual union" as a "firm league of friendship," and Article II of the document stated that "each state retains its sovereignty, freedom, and independence, and every power, jurisdiction, and right, which is not by this Confederation expressly delegated to the United States, in Congress assembled." Each of the individual states within the union was free to negotiate its own separate trade agreements and to impose its own separate import duties.

The "United States" as such and each of the separate thirteen states were encumbered by immense amounts of public debt. The Confederation Congress, like the earlier Continental Congress, lacked the power to tax, and elected leaders at the state level were leery of imposing taxes on citizens who had previously rebelled against British taxes. The continental dollars of the revolution were worthless, and it remained to be seen whether any United States bond would ever be redeemed. Coined money was quickly drained away by foreign creditors.

Then the British decided to make things harder for the newly independent republic by imposing economic restrictions on American trade. In particular, an Order in Council limited United States commerce with the British West Indies to trade that was carried in British-owned and British-built ships, manned by British crews.

The West Indies played a fundamental role in the transoceanic "triangular trade" that was vital for American commerce. In one variation of the trade, distilled rum was shipped by New England or New York merchants to Europe, where it was sold in exchange for manufactured goods, which in turn were swapped for slaves in Africa. The slaves would be sold in the West Indies for sugar, which, when converted to molasses, would be sold for distillation into rum. This trading sequence was continuous and self-sustaining. Tobacco from the southern American states provided an alternative commodity for the triangular trade.

The British Order in Council was sweeping in its economic effects on America because the West Indies would be closed to American shipping. Many cried out for American retaliation against Britain, especially in the form of tariffs (import taxes) to be placed on British goods that were transported to America in British-owned ships.

The demand for British-manufactured goods in America was keen, and so the imposition of import duties on British goods seemed at first to offer a handy way to send a stern message to the British, at least if the tariffs succeeded in putting a damper on British sales. Alternatively, for those who were willing to pay the customs duties in order to obtain British wares, the taxation would bring in much-needed revenue for the state in question. It appeared to be a win-win proposition at first: almost any result would bring a kind of economic benefit to America.

But the Confederation Congress lacked the power to impose tariffs. So the separate states began to levy such tariffs, whereupon the weakness of the new American union began to manifest itself right away, for the states could not maintain solidarity. The elected leaders of some states could not resist the opportunity to bring more trade to their ports by lowering their tariffs in competition with their neighbor states. And so the states began to undercut one another's policies. It was not very long before some state legislatures began to pass retaliatory measures against other states, and this began to have a crippling effect on interstate commerce.

Some retaliatory measures against the British went beyond the imposition of punitive customs duties. Massachusetts and Rhode Island, for example, prohibited British ships from loading in their ports. And this new trade war with Britain had disastrous effects on the New England mercantile economy: exports to Britain of lumber, fish, and farm products from the northeastern states plummeted. An economic contraction in New England had begun by 1785.

Into this increasingly chaotic situation came the expedient of new currency issues because the legislatures of several states began to issue new paper money that would constitute legal tender for the payment of taxes, including customs duties, but would not be legal tender in other transactions. Much of this currency soon became worthless. Other issues of currency were given full legal tender status, but the monetary experiment that had succeeded so well in Pennsylvania from the 1720s through the 1750s—the lending of currency into circulation with real estate as the collateral—was not repeated. So the new issues of legal tender currency were not linked to any form of tangible wealth.

Consequently, the state-issued legal tender currency of the 1780s depreciated disastrously or failed altogether when no one would accept the bills in payment. Even some local attempts to force the acceptance of such bills at face value through vigilante action or the threat of fines were unsuccessful. So the monetary logjam worsened and fed on itself.

These currency failures did not usher in an inflationary trend (as one might suppose) for several reasons. In the first place, the growing economic contraction led to huge counter-pressures that drove prices down. Besides, because many of the new bills were not legal tender in all transactions, their role in many marketplace transactions was irrelevant. Put differently, there was no fluctuation in the value of these bills because they had no value at all. In many cases even bills with full legal tender status were not accepted by anyone, regardless of what the law required. Laws that cannot be enforced become farcical.

Deflation—an overall drop in prices—was reflected in the 1780s by means of the monetary conversion ratios, the ledger entries set down as buyers and sellers exchanged commodities directly. Sellers lowered their asking prices when they found no takers due to the overall slump in the market, as reflected in the reduced purchasing power of buyers.

Farmers began to destroy their crops in the hope of forcing prices back up. But their actions were largely ineffective. The growing deficiency of farmers' revenue made rural Americans increasingly unable to pay their debts.

The situation was especially severe in Massachusetts where the legislature had refused to countenance a paper money issue or to make farm commodities legal tender in the payment of debts. Creditors in Boston and other coastal towns began to foreclose on the farmers' mortgages—to take their land away from them—and to prosecute debtors who lacked any tangible assets as a warning to others. The jails of Massachusetts began to be filled with debtors.

The result, in 1786 and 1787, was a violent episode of civil unrest: Shays's Rebellion. It began in the summer of 1786 when the Massachusetts legislature adjourned without responding to pleas from indebted farmers for various forms of relief. Angry town selectmen from the western part of the state called county-wide "conventions," which proceeded to call for radical changes in the state government, including a new state constitution, a drastically restructured legislature, and reform of the judicial system. In the meantime, citizen militias reminiscent of the early years of the American Revolution showed up in various towns to prevent the courts from conducting debt foreclosures. Comparable events began to unfold in New Hampshire and Vermont.

Massachusetts governor James Bowdoin called out the state militia to suppress these "treasonable proceedings," and Samuel Adams demanded that rebels under a republican form of government should face the death penalty. While draconian justice was demanded by many wealthy men of affairs in Massachusetts, several well-to-do citizens sided with the rebels. Chief Justice William Whiting of the Berkshire County Court in a broadside that bore the pen name "Gracchus"—in memory of the ancient Roman patricians Tiberius and Gaius Gracchus, who sided with the destitute as Roman politics approached class war in the second century BC—proclaimed that most of the state's wealthy leaders were nothing better than "overgrown Plunderers" who deserved to be disobeyed.

Governor Bowdoin called the legislature into emergency session, and the lawmakers offered some concessions to the rebels—including provisions to allow them to pay back taxes in goods and offering pardon to those who would submit to legitimate authority. But the legislature also threatened jail and whipping to those who remained outside the law.

In January 1787, rebel militiamen under the leadership of a farmer named Daniel Shays of Pelham, Massachusetts—a veteran of the Revolutionary War—attacked the U.S. arsenal at Springfield with the purpose of seizing its weapons. A privately funded state militia fended off the attackers, and then more state troops under the command of General Benjamin Lincoln, another Revolutionary War veteran, pursued the Shaysites. Lincoln's troops conducted a surprise attack on the rebels' camp in Petersham, Massachusetts, on the night of February 3–4. Some of the rebel leaders escaped into neighboring states, from which they conducted raids into Massachusetts for months afterward.

By the summer of 1787, it was over. Fourteen of the rebel leaders, including Shays, were condemned to be executed for treason, but John Hancock, after he was elected governor in April, pardoned them, and then the new legislature passed laws to cut taxes and impose a debt moratorium.

Hard times in the new American nation had brought at least one state to the brink of a civil war with overtones of class war in the 1780s. Far away in France, Thomas Jefferson reacted to these events with the nonchalant observation that "the tree of liberty must be refreshed from time to time with the blood of patriots and tyrants." But other American leaders such as James Madison and George Washington feared that the rebellion might spread to other states and even signify the demise of the American experiment.

So they pushed for amendments to the Articles of Confederation that would grant the U.S. government stronger powers, including the economic powers to tax, to coin money, to "pay the debts" of the United States, and to regulate interstate commerce. The result, of course, was the drafting of the federal Constitution of 1787, which, among its negative provisions, forbade the states to issue money or make separate agreements with other nations.

2

Hard Times and the Financial Panics of 1819 and 1837

HERE'S A PROPOSITION THAT OUGHT to be self-evident: healthy economies result from a mixture of social forces that are brought into successful alignment.

In strong economies, the following factors are present: access to raw materials, tangible production assets (such as fertile farmland and state-of-the-art factories) that are preconditions for creating goods and services, a competent workforce, sufficient purchasing power to create an ample customer base for the purchase of goods and services, an adequate money supply, and a process of spending for investment that is self-sustaining, self-reinforcing, dynamic, and grounded in the creation of goods and services rather than in mere speculation for its own sake (gambling).

When any of these necessary forces are missing or weak, economic problems will occur. All of these factors in economic life are important.

Does this need arguing?

It does. For while economies are complicated things, ideology—especially the sort of ideology that often flows from a political agenda—generates endless oversimplifications that preclude intelligent analysis of the many different things that go wrong from time to time in the marketplace. It is well to keep the full array of economic factors in mind as we study depressions and recessions.

Far too many participants in debates about economics—from ordinary street-corner smart alecks to winners of the Nobel Prize in Economics—oversimplify economic life by overemphasizing one single variable in the economic process. The late Milton Friedman and his followers, for instance, through the theory that they called "monetarism," argued (or implied through the nature and tone of their rhetoric) that the slow and steady growth of a nation's money supply is somehow more important to economic health than anything else. It is easy to disprove such oversimplifications.

Still, it is obvious that an *adequate* money supply is a crucial precondition for investment. It is also obvious that the particular system of money and banking that developed in the course of American history could, when it became dysfunctional, trigger a chain reaction that affected almost all of the other forces in the economy.

Put bluntly, there is truth in the notion that financial panics played a fundamental role in causing most American depressions. It is therefore time to examine in detail the evolution of early American finance in relation to some nineteenth-century depressions.

COINAGE AND FRACTIONAL RESERVE BANKING

The previous chapter explained the nature of the monetary problems in colonial America: the shortage of coin forced a system of exchange that was based on commodity swaps, as reflected in warehouse receipts and ledger entries that recorded them. Experiments in the direct creation of legal tender paper money by government—extremely important experiments from the standpoint of world economic history—left a mixed record, with the programs of Pennsylvania and the middle colonies succeeding quite well from the 1720s to the 1750s, but with subsequent experiments during the 1770s and 1780s giving "paper money" a bad name.

From the 1780s onward, a new system of money creation was developed through the advent of commercial banking in America. Moreover Congress, in the Coinage Act of 1792, created the United States Mint. Through the conjunction of these two activities—the minting of coins and the business of commercial banking—a new monetary system arose. And to understand American finance, it is crucial to understand the working mechanics of this new system.

Coins in this period were produced through a process that no longer exists. The coins that were circulating in early America (and elsewhere) consisted entirely of precious metal—they were either solid gold or solid silver. All government mints around the world were set up at the time to receive any bullion that wealthy individuals might wish to have coined.

This was a voluntary proposition; no one had to bring their gold or silver to the mint. But when people did decide to have their precious metal coined, the process was simple and straightforward: the gold or silver was melted, stamped into standard-measure coins, and given back. And that was how coins entered circulation.

Though created under law by the sovereign state, these coins were private property. The possessors of the coins were the owners of the gold or silver they contained. People were quite free at their discretion to have their coins melted down again so they could be shipped abroad for recoinage by other nations. This would happen if the size of the coins no longer reflected the market value of gold and silver as commodities. If the gold in a gold dollar, for instance, was worth more (when melted down and sold) than the market value of a dollar—as reflected in a dollar's purchasing power, which declined when inflation occurred—then it made no sense for the owner of the gold to keep it coined in the form of a dollar. "Money brokers" facilitated the melting, shipping, and international recoinage of gold and silver.

Thus nations were competing with each other all the time for a limited amount of gold or silver. Under law, the size of the coins could be altered to reflect the current market value of the precious metal they contained. In the United States, however, it took an act of Congress to do this. Based upon the recommendation of Treasury Secretary Alexander Hamilton, the original "mint ratio" was set at fifteen to one, which meant that every silver dollar contained fifteen times as much precious metal as a gold dollar. Gold was more valuable than silver, so it took fewer ounces of gold to make a dollar.

Precious metal coins were thus the basis for the legal tender money supply, not only in the United States but in all Western nations.

The obvious advantage of such precious metal coinage was that everyone accepted the coins because their value as a means of exchange flowed directly from the value of their contents. But the disadvantage of a money supply that was based on silver and gold was that the scarcity of these attractive metals—one of the very things that gave them their international value as "treasure"—made it hard to create a money supply that would always be large enough to sustain the needs of trade. Many nations found themselves recurrently "cash poor" due to shortages of circulating coinage.

In the seventeenth century, money lenders found a way to fill this unfortunate gap in the size of the "circulating medium." And the method they conceived became the basis for modern commercial banking.

The business of lending money at interest began in ancient times and it continued through the Middle Ages. Sometimes money lenders would lend out the money that other people had deposited with them. This became the basis for modern banking, though a stunning new twist was added by the middle of the seventeenth century. No one knows who thought of this technique, but it amounted to a trick (a legal trick) through which the bankers were actually able to create a great deal of the money that they lent. It appears from the historical record that gold-smiths in London and Holland were the ones who developed the trick.

It worked like this: goldsmiths had strongboxes that they used to pro-tect their gold from thieves. Over time, they began to offer customers the use of their strongboxes for the storage of gold coin, and they charged a fee for this service. When people deposited coin for safekeeping, they received a piece of paper in return that amounted to a receipt. Before long these pieces of paper bore the following statement: "Payable to the bearer on demand."

Goldsmiths began to lend some of the gold that they received and of course they charged interest on these loans. But they had to be absolutely certain to keep enough of their customers' deposits on hand to be able to disburse the gold "on demand" when their customers needed it.

And then—historians would certainly love to know who thought of this first—the goldsmiths began to notice an interesting fact: the paper receipts that they were giving their depositors were actually circulating in market transactions. They were serving as a means of payment (a financial shortcut, in effect) when people accepted them. And then the trick sug-gested itself: what if the goldsmiths began to print up bills that would *look exactly like the deposit receipts*—a veritable blizzard of such bills, a blizzard so large it would *exceed the stock of coin that they had received*—and then *try to make loans in the form of these bills* and see if they could get away with it?

They got away with it.

This was the beginning of the modern commercial banking business, a business set up (in effect) to manufacture money in the form of "bank notes." Bankers received a steady flow of coin deposits and they gave the depositors receipt notes that bore the statement "payable to the bearer on demand." These accounts were known as "demand accounts" and the deposits were "demand deposits."

When the bankers made loans, they gave the borrowers bank notes, notes that were *not* receipts for cash deposits. Each of these bank notes bore the very same statement that appeared on the deposit receipts—a statement that explicitly assured the bearer that he or she could get cash in exchange for the note on demand. The bank notes that were issued as deposit receipts and the bank notes that were lent into circulation were identical in appearance. But their origins were different, even though many people understandably thought otherwise.

It was a trick.

Many presumed that there was an exact correspondence—a one-to-one correspondence—between the bank notes that were emitted by the bank and the value of the coin that the bank had taken in. People frequently believed that the face value of every single bank note corresponded to precisely the same amount of cash, which had been deposited in the bank and then stored in the vault or else lent to a borrower.

But this was an illusion. The cash deposits, to be sure, were often kept as a "reserve" that would be used by the bankers (during "bankers' hours") to redeem any bank notes presented at the teller's window. But there were always more bank notes circulating than the value of the cash reserve that was "backing" them. The bankers were conducting a high-stakes gambling operation: they figured it was highly unlikely that every single person in possession of one of their notes would come storming into the bank at the very same moment demanding cash.

And the banker's calculation was on average correct—except when a panic broke out and caused a "run on the bank" that would drive the bank in question "into default."

When that happened, the bankers would have to try to borrow enough cash (at interest) from another bank to satisfy their panicky depositors. Any bank that was nearing default had a huge "liquidity" problem; it had to find a way to turn its paying assets (investments or loans in its portfolio) into cash or else find a way to borrow cash quickly. But if the bankers found themselves unable to borrow more cash (or else call in enough loans to generate sufficient quick cash), then the bank would become "insolvent," which would mean that its balance sheet liabilities were greater than its assets.

What happened after that would depend on the banking laws that were on the books—and whether or not these laws were effectively enforced. Sometimes the law would permit a "bank holiday"—a time-out period in which the bank could close its doors and "suspend specie payments" (coin was often called "specie" in financial jargon) as it tried to reorganize its affairs. In some jurisdictions this practice was not permitted, but the banking laws were not always enforced (especially if the bankers had political influence). Sometimes the bank would suspend *full* specie payment but exchange bank notes for coin at a *fraction* of their face value. This could surely be held to be a breach of contract, but the remedies under civil law could be difficult to use. In any case, the notes would then circulate at a depreciated value.

If the law did not permit bank holidays, then the insolvent bank would fail—go bankrupt—and the people who were using its notes as a means of exchange were left in the lurch.

The bank's remaining assets would be sold ("liquidated") and doled out to creditors, according to varying procedures that were specified in state and local laws.

For this reason there was widespread and deep-seated distrust of bankers in the United States for many years. Thomas Jefferson once told John Adams that he had "ever been the enemy of banks; not of those discounting [that is, lending] for cash but of those foisting their own paper into circulation." He complained that he had been "derided as a Maniac by the tribe of bank-mongers, who were seeking to filch from the public their swindling."

Many people shared Jefferson's opinion; they regarded banking as fraudulent. They found it outrageous that bankers in effect were creating the money that they lent—not official money, not legal tender money, not the sort of money that anyone was forced under law to accept in payment of a debt. But when people did accept these circulating notes as payment of a debt (or as payment for purchases), the notes began to serve as a form of genuine purchasing power, a surrogate for coined money that added to the operational money supply of the nation. In time, economists began to call this juggling act "fractional reserve banking" because the cash deposits that were held by the bank were but a fraction of the much larger "circulating medium" that the bank was creating through its day-to-day lending operations.

People like Jefferson believed that only cold hard cash—real coin of the realm that was created at the mint by the government—should constitute money. Indeed, many believed that "paper money" of *any* kind was a fraud. The very same suspicion that had been created by the legal tender paper money created by the Continental Congress during the American Revolution was aroused by the private sector paper money that banks were creating in America. The fear was identical: when push came to shove, the paper bills might never be redeemed in real coin.

But commercial banking in the early American republic had some powerful champions. As early as 1780, the financier Robert Morris succeeded in getting a charter for a "Bank of Pennsylvania." A year later, he succeeded in getting the very same bank reorganized as the "Bank of North America," set up with a charter that was granted by the Confederation Congress. The bank was set up in part to make loans to the U.S. government.

Under the federal Constitution, a far more powerful bank—the first Bank of the United States—was chartered in 1791 at the behest of Treasury Secretary Alexander Hamilton. It was modeled on the Bank of England, which had been chartered by Parliament in 1694.

Hamilton argued that as long as any bank kept sufficient reserves and stayed solvent, its lending operations were a blessing to the business community and indeed to everyone else. He wrote that "the money which a merchant keeps in his chest, waiting for a favorable opportunity to employ it, produces nothing till that opportunity arrives. But if . . . he either deposits it in a bank, or invests it in the stock of a bank . . . [his money] is a fund upon which himself and others can borrow to a much larger amount. It is a well established fact, that banks in good credit, can circulate a far greater sum than the actual quantum of their capital in gold and silver."

Congress found Hamilton's reasoning persuasive enough to create the first Bank of the United States in 1791. Its capital came through the sale of bank stock to the tune of $10 million. The federal government bought 20 percent of this stock, and the bank was authorized to issue notes equivalent to the size of its stock subscription, that is, $10 million. The bank's charter was granted for a twenty-year term, and the charter would have to be renewed when its term ran out.

The charter of this Bank of the United State lapsed in 1811. Its enemies in Congress complained that a significant amount of the bank's stock had been purchased by foreigners. After the charter expired, a wealthy Philadelphia merchant named Stephen Girard purchased most of the stock, and the bank continued to function as "Girard's Bank."

In 1816, Congress chartered a second Bank of the United States. With its headquarters in Philadelphia, this second bank received a twenty-year charter and it was capitalized at $35 million, with the federal government purchasing 20 percent of the stock. Leading proponents of the bank were Henry Clay of Kentucky and John C. Calhoun of South Carolina. One of the principal arguments that was used by the bank's supporters was the fact that federal finances during the War of 1812 had been crippled by the absence of a strong central bank that could serve the U.S. government as the Bank of England served Britain.

Meanwhile, thousands of commercial banks across the country had been chartered at the state level. Banking laws varied from one state to another, and the laws of some states permitted banks to be operated recklessly. Banks often kept very little coin on reserve and they were therefore vulnerable if a bank panic should erupt. Some banks, called "wildcat" banks, kept almost nothing on reserve; they were fly-by-night operations whose owners were sometimes little better than bandits.

THE PANIC OF 1819

A severe banking panic occurred in 1819, and the ensuing depression in America lasted approximately four years.

The problem started with overspeculation in land throughout the trans-Appalachian West. For several years after the Napoleonic Wars, food shortages in Europe put a premium on American agricultural commodities. The price of cotton, for example, stood at roughly 20 cents a pound in 1815. By January 1818 the price had surged to 33.5 cents a pound. Thousands of planters and farmers raced to expand their production by acquiring more land. Commercial banks extended lavish credit to facilitate (and take advantage of) the boom. They often made loans without requiring a down payment and without sufficient collateral.

By the end of 1818, the European agricultural sector was recovering fast, and so the price of American goods began to plummet. By the middle of 1819, the price of cotton had dwindled to 15 cents a pound.

Farmers and planters found their revenue slipping away. And as they struggled to make ends meet, the payments on their bank loans became burdensome. Some of them started to default on their loans, which put commercial banks in danger of default or even insolvency.

Then the second Bank of the United States began to worsen the contraction. One of the policies that the bank had adopted under the leadership of Langdon Cheves (a lawyer from South Carolina) was to return any bank notes that it received from other banks for redemption in coin. As a consequence, commercial banks with scanty reserves began to default. To avoid insolvency, the banks that survived began to foreclose on the land that served as collateral for real estate loans.

As thousands of planters and farmers lost their lands, they were forced into bankruptcy. And their catastrophe ramified across the economy, exerting a contraction that began to reduce the business of manufacturers and merchants. Workers began to suffer layoffs in many cities. In 1820 a tenth of the people residing in New York City were receiving some sort of poor relief, and the total level of unemployment in the United States was estimated by some to be as high as 500,000.

Across the country, farmers and workers lobbied their state legislatures for debt moratoriums or "stay laws" that would stop foreclosures and put an end to imprisonment for debt. Ten states adopted such laws. Others who were stricken by the new depression turned their wrath on bankers, protesting the practices that allowed banks to issue paper bank notes that could plummet to a fraction of their face value in market transactions when people refused to accept them at full face value. Most of all, the resentment of bankers was focused on the second Bank of the United States, whose policies had made it the owner—through foreclosure—of vast amounts of unproductive real estate. Thomas Hart Benton of Missouri complained that the bank had become "the engrossing proprietor of whole towns." The Planters' Bank of Savannah charged that the Bank of the United States "came here to destroy our very substance. Ships, plantations, Negroes, wharves, stores, all the sources of wealth in the state" had been taken over "by this all-consuming power." Many began to demand that the financial "monster" in Philadelphia should be dismantled.

The policies of the bank in this particular crisis were arguably misguided, or at least one-sided. For while in ordinary times the bank's policy of returning commercial bank notes to the banks of issue could exert a necessary and salutary deterrent effect on the temptations of wildcat banking, in a time of economic contraction a central bank can serve as a "lender of last resort," making loans that will shore up threatened financial institutions in order to give them time to reorganize and recover.

In the absence of such central banking policies, there remained another method for reversing the economic contraction that began with the Panic of 1819: public works that would generate employment and create an economic expansion. This was not at all an abstract or theoretical proposition at the time, for proposals for such "internal improvements" were rife in Washington during the presidency of James Monroe.

After the War of 1812, many members of Congress called for the construction of roads and canals that would provide a better infrastructure for national defense in any future wars. John C. Calhoun of South Carolina, who was serving as secretary of war under Monroe, bade Congress to "bind the Republic together with a perfect system of roads and canals." Henry Clay of Kentucky called for a "chain of turnpikes, roads and canals from Passamoquody to New Orleans." In 1824, Congress passed a General Survey Act to pave the way for such projects and vested the U.S. Army Corps of Engineers with responsibility for river and harbor improvements. Newly elected president John Quincy Adams called in 1825 for a massive public works program.

But the consensus for federal "internal improvements" broke down, and years later—looking back in 1837 upon the stimulating effect that such a program might have brought to depression-ridden America during the 1820s—Adams ruefully reflected that his program, if adopted, "would have afforded high wages and constant employment to hundreds of thousands of laborers," and that "every dollar expended would have repaid itself fourfold."

There were several reasons why support for "internal improvements" waned at the federal level after 1825.

For one thing, the leaders of the slaveholding South became opposed to any strong forms of federal action. The reason was simple: they feared that a strong federal government might fall into the hands of abolitionists. The Missouri Compromise of 1820–1821 divided up the Louisiana Purchase territory in a manner that would have barred the institution of slavery from entering most of the land in question. From that point on, defenders of slavery confronted a worst-case scenario of a Union containing a super-majority of free states—a Union in which the slave state bloc in Congress would lack the power to stop anti-slavery legislation or prevent the enforcement of federal anti-slavery laws. So they vowed to prevent any strong and decisive federal action, action that could constitute a threat to "states' rights" over time.

The second reason why support for public works declined in Washington was the rise to preeminence of Andrew Jackson and the Democratic Party. Jackson was a believer in minimal government on ideological grounds. As president, he vetoed bills that were passed by Congress to fund internal improvements. Jackson was also an enemy of banks and a determined supporter of "sound money." By the 1830s, when "Jacksonian Democracy" was riding high, the opponents of paper money in America were known as "hard money men" and "Locofocos."

THE PANIC OF 1837

Jackson was one of the people who blamed the second Bank of the United States for the Panic of 1819 and the hard times that followed. After his election to the presidency in 1828, he made it known that he would oppose the rechartering of the bank when its charter expired in 1836.

When Jackson ran for reelection in 1832, his opponent Henry Clay persuaded Nicholas Biddle (who had succeeded Langdon Cheves as president of the Bank of the United States in 1822) to press Congress to provide the bank with a new charter immediately—four years before its charter would expire. Clay believed that a majority in Congress would support the measure and that Jackson might very well bow to such support for the bank in the middle of an election year. But when the bill passed Congress, Jackson vetoed it, condemning the bank as an unconstitutional and elitist affront to "the humble members of society—the farmers, mechanics, and laborers—who have neither the time nor the means of securing like favors for themselves."

After Jackson won reelection, he continued his attack upon the bank, vowing to destroy it. He directed the Treasury Department to withdraw all federal deposits from the bank. But he had to fire two successive secretaries of the treasury in order to get his directive carried out. On his third attempt, he shifted another cabinet member, Roger Taney, to the

Treasury Department (Taney had been serving as attorney general), and Taney enforced Jackson's order with gusto. Federal funds were redeposited in a number of state-chartered banks (which Jackson's critics called his "pet" banks).

The destruction of the second Bank of the United States left the United States with no central bank when the next financial panic happened in 1837. In the meantime, Nicholas Biddle got the Bank of the United States rechartered at the state level and it continued to exist (under Biddle's leadership) as the United States Bank of Pennsylvania until it failed in 1841.

Some causes of the Panic of 1837 were comparable to the causes of the Panic of 1819. State-chartered banks were more numerous. And without the discipline imposed by the ever-weakening second Bank of the United States, these state-chartered banks became reckless. By 1837, their circulating notes had an overall face value of roughly $22 million, but the bank notes were backed by merely $2 million of cash reserves.

With public works thwarted at the federal level, state lawmakers and policymakers pushed them at the state level. Some of the projects were financed by bond sales, especially to British investors. But other projects were carried out by state-chartered companies with shaky business plans and shaky management structures, companies that all too often received their very own bank charters to finance the projects in question. Many of these banks were set up on "wildcat" principles.

A major fact of life at the time was that the federal government owned millions of acres of public land in the western territories—lands that had been acquired from the British and the French (the Louisiana Purchase) and from Native American tribes—and the land was for sale. Federal land sales brought in great amounts of revenue and also played a key role in many aspects of American economic life.

Land speculation was rife in the West and the federal government was doing such a "land office business" that land sales surged from approximately four million acres in 1835 to over twenty million acres in 1836. Many of these sales were made possible by loans from the wildcat banks.

And then Andrew Jackson did two things in rapid succession that burst the speculative bubble and triggered the worst bank panic to date in American history. First, he supported a bill to turn the federal government's financial surplus (largely accrued from the boom in land sales) over to the states. This meant that the federal funds that Jackson had moved from the Bank of the United States to the state-chartered banks (his "pet" banks) would have to be paid out. This reduced the deposits of the banks in question, thus reducing their power to withstand a financial crisis. Second, Jackson issued a directive known as the "specie circular" in July 1836—a directive stipulating that only specie (coined cash) would thenceforth be accepted for the purchase of federal lands. This measure prompted land speculators to get rid of their bank notes in a hurry. They raced to convert them into cold hard cash, and the result in one state after another was a series of "bank runs" that drove shaky banks into default.

As Jackson waltzed his way out of the White House—he was not running for another term in 1836—he turned over to his hapless successor Martin Van Buren a financial sector that was low on reserves, pushed hard to the brink of insolvency, and without the presence of a central bank that could serve as a lender of last resort.

There was also an international dimension to the Panic of 1837, and historians have argued for a very long time about whether domestic or transatlantic causes should be given more weight in explaining what happened. Crop failures in 1835 had made it harder for American farmers to pay their creditors. As American exports of farm commodities decreased, British merchants and bankers began to demand more payment in specie to remedy the growing balance of payments deficiency. Meanwhile, British credit had been tightening for other reasons. In 1836, the Bank of England raised interest rates in order to attract more cash deposits. This action forced American banks to raise their own interest rates, which put a damper on credit.

The crop failures began to raise farm prices, and protests began to erupt among the urban poor. In February 1837, hard money agitators in New York called a rally to protest the higher prices. They blamed paper money for inflation, and then, as the crowd became angry, someone yelled "Hart's Flour Store!" A mob converged upon the store of Eli Hart and Company and wrecked the establishment. When Mayor Cornelius Lawrence tried to stop the rioters, he was pelted with stones. The mob went on to attack food warehouses until the city's police finally got the riot under control.

In the same month, Senator Thomas Hart Benton of Missouri drew President-Elect Van Buren aside in the U.S. Capitol and told him that

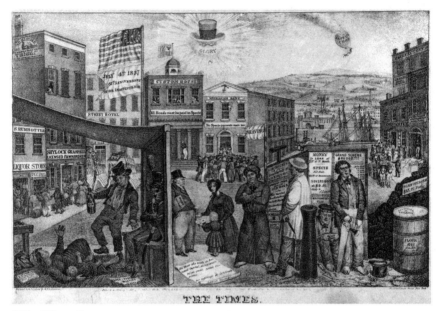

"The Times."
This 1837 cartoon print by Edward Williams Clay depicts scenes of misery and economic breakdown caused by the Panic of 1837.
Source: Courtesy of the Library of Congress.

America was in danger of financial collapse. "Your friends think you a little exalted in the head on that subject," Van Buren quipped with a smile. Benton recalled that he muttered, almost under his breath, "You will soon feel the thunderbolt."

As the prices of food commodities surged, the price of cotton fell, and cotton sales on the international market were critical not only to the economies of the Southern states but also to the American mercantile economy.

On May 10, 1837, New York banks suspended specie payments, as the local law permitted them to do. Banks in other major cities followed suit within a week. A huge economic contraction set in, and though Van Buren tried to reverse some of Jackson's worst decisions—he withdrew the specie circular and delayed the last disbursement of the federal surplus from state-chartered banks—the damage had been done. Indeed, Van Buren pushed a brand new scheme that would place the federal government's revenues beyond the reach of any bank—a scheme to establish "subtreasuries" (branch offices of the U.S. Treasury Department) that would store the federal government's revenues, thereby reducing them to idle funds.

The idea of a complete "divorce" between government and banking had been promoted by writers such as William M. Gouge, who in June 1837 published an influential polemic titled *Inquiry into the Expediency of Dispensing with Bank Agency and Bank Paper in the Fiscal Concerns of the United States.*

A fitful recovery trend—supported in part by attempts by Nicholas Biddle to stimulate bank reinvestments and sell more American cotton in Europe—sputtered out in 1838 when foreign investments turned sour and the growing balance of payments deficit caused Britain to demand more payments in cash, which drained more specie out of the country. Another financial panic struck in 1839. Van Buren's "subtreasury" plan passed Congress in 1840, but Van Buren faced a hopeless task as he tried to campaign for reelection. Hard times made the fate of this presidential incumbent comparable to the fate that would remove Herbert Hoover from office in 1932.

The depression that followed the Panic of 1837 led to waves of land foreclosures, business failures, falling prices, and the loss of tens of thousands of jobs in the nation's cities. American urban culture in the 1830s had been plagued by violence—Baltimore, for instance, was often called "mobtown" during the period—and the new economic grievances worsened this situation tremendously. Nine states defaulted on their debts, and several state constitutions were amended to prohibit the states from borrowing money. This put a damper on further public works spending—spending that might (if responsibly carried out) have served as an economic stimulus. And when the states defaulted on their bonds, foreign investors became quite leery of making further investments in America.

In all, this latest spell of hard times lasted for approximately six years before it finally ran its course.

3

The Panics of 1873 and 1893—And Hard Times in Between

IN POST–CIVIL WAR AMERICA, two depressions were triggered by panics that occurred precisely twenty years apart: the Panics of 1873 and 1893. And coinciding with these two depressions was a period of hard times in certain regions and among certain groups, an extended period of localized suffering that started in the 1870s, continued through the overall recovery period of the 1880s, and then worsened significantly in the 1890s. Consequently, the story of hard times in Gilded Age America is complicated.

For reasons that will soon become clear, it is necessary to begin this chapter with an update on the evolution of money and banking. Two important developments occurred from the Civil War onward: (1) the intermittent tradition of government-created paper money was revived on a very large scale in the course of the Civil War and then extended in subsequent decades by Gilded Age "Greenbackers" and (2) the system of fractional reserve banking became more powerful and also more vulnerable when the practice of making loans in the form of paper bank notes was supplanted by a new and more subtle technique, the creation of checking accounts.

GREENBACKS AND CHECKING ACCOUNTS

The legal tender paper money created by the Confederacy in the Civil War became legendary for its worthlessness: the rate of inflation in the Confederate states reached approximately 9,000 percent. But the legal tender paper money created by the Republican Congress during the Lincoln administration had an inflation rate of roughly 80 percent—double-digit inflation for sure, yet the comparison to the Confederate experiment speaks for itself.

The United States Notes, created and spent into use, were authorized by the Legal Tender Act, introduced in Congress by Rep. Elbridge G. Spaulding of New York and passed on February 25, 1862. In addition to this act, two subsequent legal tender acts—passed by Congress on July 11, 1862, and March 3, 1863—resulted in a currency issue that, by the end of the Civil War, totaled approximately $430 million.

Like the continental currency of the Revolutionary War, the United States Notes were promises to pay. On the front of each note was the statement that "the United States will pay the bearer" the face value of the note. Unlike bank notes, however, these currency notes did *not* bear the statement "payable to the bearer on demand." Instead, like the earlier continental currency, the United States Notes contained no statement at all in regard to the timing or circumstances for redemption in coin. But it was generally understood that the issuance of these notes was an emergency measure, a temporary expedient—that after military victory, the notes would be redeemed in due course.

On the back of each note was a statement that was printed in green ink, for which reason the United States Notes were popularly known as "Greenbacks." The statement limited the legal tender force of the notes as follows: "This note is a legal tender for all debts public and private except duties on imports and interest on the public debt; and is receivable in payment of all loans made to the United States." This meant, among other things, that the Greenbacks had to be accepted by banks when their borrowers chose to repay their loans in United States Notes. It also meant that the government had to accept the notes for the payment of internal taxes and for purchases of war bonds (but not for the payment of tariffs or import duties). The *purchasers* of war bonds—who were lending their money to the government—would be obliged to accept the notes as repayment when the bonds matured, but with a caveat created to serve as an incentive for the purchase of the bonds: the *interest* on these interest-bearing bonds would have to be paid in gold.

All of these provisions, of course, would be void at such time as the Greenbacks themselves were redeemed in gold coin and then destroyed.

After the Civil War, the redemption of the Greenbacks was advocated by a wide range of American political leaders, both Republicans and Democrats. But as early as 1865, proposals were made to keep the Greenbacks in permanent circulation. A gradual redemption policy was authorized by Congress in December 1865, but then the policy was halted in 1868 due to economic conditions. Among other things, the Greenbacks were proving themselves to be useful for federal finance.

It is important to understand that before the twentieth century there was no federal budgetary process of the kind that we are used to. Congress would appropriate funds, and then the members of Congress and the leaders of the executive branch would wait, cross their fingers, and hope that the incoming tax and land sales revenues would be enough to cover the spending that Congress had approved.

When revenues were insufficient, the treasury would have to fill the gap through deficit spending, that is, through the sale of bonds.

But the Greenbacks changed this calculation. When the treasury received any payments in the form of Greenbacks—and when these payments created a financial surplus in the fiscal year in question—the notes, instead of being destroyed, could be stored away by the treasury in a reserve fund and spent back into circulation in subsequent fiscal years when the incoming revenues were insufficient to cover congressional appropriations.

In 1875, Congress passed the Specie Payment Resumption Act, which required the treasury to begin redeeming the remaining Greenbacks in gold beginning on the first business day of 1879. But in 1878, the Democrats in Congress pushed through a contradictory bill ("An Act To Forbid The Further Retirement of United States Legal Tender Notes") that made the treasury keep the remaining quantum of Greenbacks in circulation *indefinitely*—and the circulating United States Notes at that time had a collective face value of $346,681,016. Could these two laws be reconciled? Yes, and what happened was both interesting and simple.

The treasury established a "gold reserve" totaling $100 million for the redemption of Greenbacks. The gold came into the treasury from a number of revenue sources: import duties, land sale receipts, and bond sales. When people presented Greenbacks for redemption at any of the local "subtreasury" offices around the country, the office would receive the legal tender bills and immediately swap them for gold dollar coins. But the United States Notes would be retained by the treasury branch instead of being destroyed. They would be stored and in later years spent back out into circulation whenever such spending was consistent with congressional appropriations.

This meant that approximately $347 million of legal tender money from the Civil War era had been added indefinitely to the overall money supply of the United States. And because the Greenbacks could be redeemed at any time in gold at treasury offices by 1879, they held their value. And this point is extremely important. The depreciation that occurred in the course of the Civil War—an 80 percent inflation rate—abated by the 1880s. A one-dollar United States Note at the time possessed as much purchasing power as a one-dollar gold coin, and this would continue to be the case as long as the redemption policy held good.

In light of these facts, economic reformers began to propose in the 1870s that the government should create new issues of legal tender currency. In 1876, for example, a new "Greenback-Labor Party" nominated Peter Cooper of New York (the founder of the famed Cooper Union school) for the presidency. In the decades to follow, reformers would advocate a number of very interesting measures designed to relieve depressions through projects that would be financed by new legal tender currency issues.

Meanwhile, fractional reserve money creation by commercial banks evolved through a quantum leap.

During the Civil War, the Republican Congress passed measures intended to make commercial banking more reliable and safer. In 1863, Congress created a system of federally chartered "National Banks," and the bank charters were granted according to a *quid pro quo*. Each national bank would be allowed to operate on the principle of fractional reserves and to lend out National Bank Notes printed by the Treasury Department. The limit of this bank note issue was preliminarily set at $300 million. But in return for the bank charter and the privilege of lending the government-printed notes, each bank had to purchase a stipulated amount of federal war bonds and place these bonds on deposit with the Treasury Department, where they would serve as both a real and symbolic reserve. Each National Bank Note bore the following statements: "National Currency," "Secured by United States Bonds deposited with the Treasurer of the United States," and . . . "Payable to the Bearer on Demand."

It was clearly the intention of the Civil War Republican Congress to create a new, dependable, and federally regulated system of commercial banks. And to help establish the "National Currency" of these banks as a standard-issue circulating medium, Congress in 1865 levied a stiff tax on the notes that were issued by state-chartered commercial banks. Put bluntly, Congress hoped to drive these notes out of circulation so that the new, safe "National Currency" would make future bank panics unlikely.

But it was not to be. Commercial bankers at the state level figured out a new way to create new money out of thin air in the process of lending. By the 1870s, they began to switch from the process of making loans in the form of bank notes to making loans in the form of "checking accounts."

It is hard to overstate the importance of this development.

Many people who still write checks in the digital age of the twenty-first century make a common and understandable presumption: they presume that their checking accounts are nothing more than a process for spending out deposits that have been received by the bank at the teller's window or else through direct electronic deposits. The situation in the Gilded Age was comparable.

In the Gilded Age, it is likely that a great many people presumed that every single check—a directive to pay out money to a stipulated person or firm—was backed by a cash deposit in the very same amount.

But it was not so. The new technique of fractional reserve banking worked as follows: borrowers who applied for a loan would go through the usual routine in which the bank would check on the proposed collateral, the projected long-term income, the business plan and market expectations (in the case of commercial loans), and so forth. If the loan was approved, the borrower would be given a checkbook and told that the loan had been "credited" to their newly created checking account. To spend the loan, they would simply write checks, and then the bank would redeem these checks on demand when they were presented to be "cleared."

But where did this "credit," which had been "deposited" to the borrower's new checking account, come from in the first place? It came from thin air—from out of nothing. Within a generation, the word "deposit" in the lexicon of bankers and economists had become a euphemism for deposits that had been created *out of nothing* and then lent into circulation via *checking accounts*. No one could safely presume that a check was a representation of a *cash* deposit as opposed to a *credit* "deposit."

Once checking accounts had begun to replace the use of bank notes in transactions, the realities of this process slipped away from the common understanding of citizens. By the 1930s, Yale economist Irving Fisher tried to enlighten a lay audience as follows: "When a bank grants me a $1,000 loan," he wrote, "and so adds $1,000 to my checking deposit, that $1,000 of 'money that I have in the bank' is new. It was freshly manufactured by the bank out of my loan and written by pen and ink on the stub of my check book and on the books of the bank. . . . Except for these pen and ink records, this 'money' has no real physical existence." He qualified the assertion as follows: "Sometimes a little actual cash passes through the teller's window in one direction or another. . . . But typically and for the most part, checking deposits are manufactured out of loans."

It was in the Gilded Age that this new method of fractional reserve money creation was pioneered and within a few decades the "National Currency" bank notes of the national banks were dwarfed in volume by checks—directives to pay. And because checks were designed to be returned to the bank routinely for clearance—instead of continuing to circulate as routine pocket currency, like the notes of reputable banks—fractional reserve banking became more volatile and dangerous. It became much easier for a bank to slip into default when the barrage of checks presented for clearance exceeded its cash reserves.

Of course it was easier for banks to make good if a check was deposited in the account of the person to whom it was made out; "clearing-houses" were set up to expedite this process through ledger offsets. But whenever checks were presented at the teller's window for cash, the bank would have to pay out.

THE PANIC OF 1873

The next depression in American history began, like the two that preceded it, with a financial panic. The Panic of 1873 centered on the collapse of a prominent bank, the house of Jay Cooke & Company in New York. Cooke's establishment was an "investment bank," a rising form of financial enterprise that traded in stocks and corporate securities. By the end of the 1870s, another investment bank, the house of John Pierpont Morgan, became a titanic institution that consolidated many corporations into unified aggregates called "trusts." The rise of investment banking was an important Gilded Age development.

But the Panic of 1873 was a complex affair and historians continue to argue—as they continue to argue in regard to the Panic of 1837—about which causes were the most important and whether the international dimensions were as important as the domestic. It seems likely that these arguments will never be resolved because the evidence itself is unsatisfactory. Some cause-and-effect sequences in this panic seem obvious, but others can only be inferred. Some of the events were perhaps international coincidences, but possibly there were also causal linkages of which the evidence vanished long ago as the day-to-day records of many corporations in different countries were discarded. To this day, when historians are hired to write corporate histories, the eventual accounts that they produce will only be as good as the corporate archives.

This panic was indeed international in its scope, and so were the hard times that followed. In Britain, this depression continued well beyond the 1870s, whereas in the United States a substantial recovery occurred by 1879.

The Franco-Prussian War of 1870–1871 triggered economic changes and dislocations, not least of all due to the large war indemnity that France was forced to pay to newly unified Imperial Germany. Under the leadership of Otto von Bismarck, Germany began to change its minting procedure and, abandoning the widespread monetary policy of "bimetallism"—the open coinage at the mint of both gold and silver bullion—the Germans embraced "the gold standard." An international chain reaction ensued, with the gold standard quickly rising to European and international hegemony as one nation after another closed its mints to the further "free and unlimited coinage" of silver. Congress adopted this policy in the Coinage Act of 1873, and furious disputes have ensued ever since as to the significance (or insignificance) of this act in terms of macroeconomic effects, class interests, and political motivations.

The Panic of 1873 began in Europe well before the failure of Jay Cooke's bank in New York. The Austrian stock market crashed in May, and a German economic contraction began as well.

In America—as elsewhere—the banking crisis overlapped with problems in the railroad industry as well as the stock and bond markets. All of these problems, in turn, were to some extent derivative from a cultural trend of baleful significance in America: Gilded Age sleaze. A long sequence of corruption scandals poisoned American business and political affairs from the late 1860s through the 1870s. Malfeasance was rife, and deception lurked in many nooks and crannies of the business world and in government.

The railroad industry was plagued with fraud, mismanagement, conflict of interest, and white collar crime. Here is an example.

In 1872, the "Crédit Mobilier" scandal was exposed. It involved the huge Union Pacific Railroad, a company that Congress had chartered in 1862. Members of the Union Pacific board had been looting the company and their method is easy to comprehend. First, they set up a construction company that they called Crédit Mobilier, a company that was supposed to be completely independent of Union Pacific. But this was an illusion. Second, they arranged for this company to overcharge Union Pacific. Third, they pocketed the difference between what the construction of the railroad cost and what Union Pacific was billed. They could pocket the difference through the medium of stock dividends because they sat on the boards of both companies and owned stock in both companies. And the stock dividends of Crédit Mobilier were generous, due to its profits, which of course derived from fraud.

Here is another example of the way in which stocks became a medium for fraud.

"Stock watering" was a ploy that was used by tricksters to promote and sell stocks (ownership shares of publicly held corporations) whose par value was inflated far beyond the company's book value. Corporate law generally required that the par value of stock issues should not exceed the corporation's assets. That way, the shareholders would have a chance of recovering their investment if the company went out of business: its assets would be sold and the proceeds would be distributed—to creditors first and then to shareholders. Cornelius Vanderbilt was defrauded in the 1860s by speculators Jay Gould, Jim Fisk, and Daniel Drew, who sold him $7 million of watered stock in a war for control of the Erie Railroad in New York. Gould and his fellow crooks, who sat on the railroad's board, repeatedly expanded the size of the stock issue and Vanderbilt, in a vain attempt to gain control of the company, kept buying. After their shenanigans were exposed, the culprits fled across state lines. They hired thugs to prevent their extradition to New York and they also tried to use the Tammany Hall machine in New York City to bribe state legislators into making their actions legal. Eventually the affair was ended through an out-of-court deal in which Vanderbilt forced the crooks to buy back the watered stock.

Many railroads during the Gilded Age were run crookedly and many frauds and manipulations were being perpetrated on Wall Street. We will never know exactly how much corruption was going on because the most successful conspiracies are the ones that leave no traces.

In light of all this, it was only a matter of time—perhaps—before railroading, stock and bond speculation, and investment banking created a "perfect storm" of a financial panic like the one that erupted in 1873.

The bank of Jay Cooke and Company was founded in 1861. A commercial bank, it evolved very quickly into an investment bank as well: it invested in bonds and it became a principal agent for the marketing of Union war bonds during the Civil War. It pioneered the use of "wire transactions"—deals made by means of the telegraph. After the Civil War, the bank used its expertise in bond trading to do an international business in railroad bonds. Given the shakiness of the railroading business, a great many investors were leery of railroad stocks; they preferred the relatively greater security of bonded obligations.

In 1870, the new Northern Pacific Railroad Company made Cooke's bank its exclusive agent for international bond sales. But in 1873, the international sale of Northern Pacific bonds fell short of expectations. Cooke had been counting on the income from these bond sales to back up fractional reserve lending, and so when the bond sales fell short, the bank neared default and suspended specie payments on September 18, 1873.

This set off a stock market crash, which the *New York Times* reported as follows: "The brokers stood perfectly thunderstruck for a moment, and then there was a general run to notify the different houses of Wall Street of the failure. The brokers surged out of the Exchange, stumbling pell mell over one another in general confusion and reached their offices in race horse time. The members of the firms who were surprised by this announcement had no time to deliberate. The bear clique was already selling the market down in the Exchange, and prices were declining frightfully."

The panic was contagious: many figured that if Cooke's bank were shaky, who could say how many other banks were shaky? Other financiers such as Fisk and Hatch began to fail, and over a dozen financial houses unable to meet their obligations started to topple. To try to bolster confidence in the business community, the U.S. Treasury Department began to buy bonds, but by September 20 the New York Stock Exchange closed its doors for the first time in its history.

President Ulysses S. Grant and his new treasury secretary William Richardson came to New York to meet with Vanderbilt and other financiers. But after the treasury had purchased $13 million in bonds, Grant called it off.

The panic continued, and it lasted over a month. Over seventy members of the stock exchange and thousands of financial houses failed. The shock waves from the financial crisis spread outward over the country. Interest on railroad bonds went unpaid, and railroad construction was cut back drastically by 1874. Cotton and iron mills closed, and many workers were thrown out into the streets, unemployed. On January 13, 1874, police in New York used violence to break up a protest meeting of thousands of unemployed men in Tompkins Square Park.

A month earlier, a "Committee of Safety" had been organized by local protestors who demanded a city-wide public works campaign. City

"The Red Flag in New York."
This cartoon printed in *Frank Leslie's Illustrated Newspaper* on January 31, 1874, depicts the Tompkins Square Park riot in New York City in which police beat unemployed protesters.
Source: Courtesy of the Library of Congress.

officials refused to meet with the organizers, and so more radical factions urged protesters to descend on city hall. The original committee convinced the unemployed to assemble at Tompkins Square Park, where they had an assembly permit good for January 13. But unbeknownst to the marchers, the permit had been revoked the night before, so on that date a "riot" broke out—in actuality a police riot in which the protesters were beaten savagely by police on horseback.

In 1874, Congress voted to expand the issue of United States Notes because a contracted money supply was not compatible with economic expansion. But President Grant—arguably in over his head—vetoed the measure. As a compromise, Congress voted to limit the stock of United States Notes to $382 million. But in 1875, the Specie Payment Resumption Act—authorizing the unlimited redemption of United States Notes in gold coin on the first business day of January 1879—was pushed through Congress and Grant signed it.

Between 1874 and 1876, a new political party, at first called the Independent Party and then called the Greenback-Labor Party, appeared on the political landscape. After sponsoring a convention in Indianapolis in 1874, the party nominated Peter Cooper for the presidency in 1876. The "Greenbackers" called for the repeal of the Specie Payment Resumption Act and the issuance of more United States Notes. But the best that they could do was to prompt Congress to stabilize the note issue at approximately $347 million, the amount of bills outstanding in 1878. As previously noted, these notes could be swapped for gold coin beginning in 1879, but instead of being destroyed they would have to be spent into circulation again in support of congressional appropriations.

Hard times continued to ravage the United States. In 1877—the first year of the one-term presidency of Rutherford B. Hayes—a strike that before long was known as the "Great Railroad Strike" spread from one state to another. From West Virginia it spread to Pennsylvania, and then to the railway hubs of St. Louis and Chicago; lives were lost and millions of dollars in property were destroyed. Many strikers said that they did what they did because of wage cuts and layoffs.

In addition to outrage by supporters of law and order—and conservatives who defended property rights—the labor violence was condemned by a new breed of opinion makers among the intelligentsia: those who subscribed to the creed of "survival of the fittest." Though the creed would be dubbed "Social Darwinism," it was definitely not a creation of Charles Darwin the naturalist. The vision of life as a war between the "fit and the unfit" was derived to a significant extent from the internationally influential teachings of a British philosopher named Herbert Spencer, who succeeded in gaining a large cohort of American acolytes, such as the sociologist William Graham Sumner. Spencer and his followers generally deplored all attempts by reformers to make use of government. Such actions, they argued, would interfere with the stupendous and magnificent process of evolution.

These people seemed to be saying that the poor and destitute *inherently* got what they deserved and the results advanced the progress of the world.

But in 1879—as the American depression of the 1870s finally began to lift—a vastly influential book, one that would challenge the inevitability of suffering during hard times, began its literary career: *Progress and Poverty* by Henry George. The subtitle of the book read as follows: *An Inquiry into the Cause of Industrial Depressions and of Increase of Want with Increase of Wealth*. George argued that industrial progress ironically fostered suffering and that correction lay in a system of progressive taxation to provide the basis for appropriate relief measures. In particular, he recommended a master tax on increases in the value of land.

"Material progress," wrote George, "does not merely fail to relieve poverty—it actually produces it. This association of progress with poverty is the great enigma of our times." George's contention implied that depressions worsened an underlying situation. Social Darwinists, of course, saw no cause for alarm in the duality of poverty and progress: to them, it was nothing more than the salutary sorting out of the "fit and the unfit."

IMPACTED HARD TIMES IN THE SLUMS AND ON THE FARM

Even as the so-called boom-and-bust cycle worked its way through Gilded Age America, a condition of extended hard times in certain parts of the United States became a significant part of the American condition—one that accentuated the depressions of the 1870s and 1890s and proved largely resistant to the recoveries that followed them. Chronic hard times for certain "down-and-out" people loomed more and more in the popular imagination as what might well await any middle-class family if an economic chain reaction threw the breadwinner out of work.

The American underclass in the Gilded Age was both rural and urban in its nature.

What some were beginning to call the "farm problem" was related to some overall economic trends but it was also caused by circumstances particular to agriculture. And a growing crisis of poverty in urban slum districts got steadily worse in the 1880s and 1890s.

Urban poverty is certainly an age-old story but the conditions in American slums in the Gilded Age were appalling. Many of the slum dwellers were recently arrived and impoverished immigrants. Too often they were crammed into squalid "tenement houses"—a new residential building type designed to house as many people as possible in grossly substandard conditions. Light and ventilation were minimal and sanitary facilities were grossly inadequate or nonexistent. Whole families worked at home together in "sweat shops," living by piecework. The figures for disease and infant mortality in these tenement districts compared to some of the worst statistics anywhere on earth and the conditions on New York's Lower East Side were notorious. Conditions in the worker housing in American factory towns were often little better.

Urban poverty in the Gilded Age had its rural counterpart, and conditions in the post-Reconstruction South were especially bad. To replace chattel slavery, Southern planters instituted tenant farming—in which farmers would rent land on the plantation—and also "sharecropping," a system in which both black and white laborers would be paid in a "share of the crop" instead of wages. Because the crop would not be ready until the end of the growing season, the planters (often with the assistance of so-called furnishing merchants) would set up a company store to provide the sharecroppers and their families with food and supplies "on credit." At the end of the season, the ledger value of the goods furnished would be deducted from the value of the cropper's share of the harvest.

The hitch: dishonest planters and merchants often falsified and inflated the ledger value of the goods they had furnished, so the sharecroppers (many illiterate) were stuck in debt slavery—peonage—because their share of the crop was always lower in value than what they owed.

At least the planters were telling the truth when they told their field hands that the price of cotton was going down—it was. In fact, by the

1870s, farm prices were down across the board, and this trend of price deflation—part of a larger macroeconomic deflationary trend—made it hard for farmers in many parts of the country.

Part of the situation was the impact of industrialization on farming, both in terms of agricultural techniques and economic strategy.

New products for use in agriculture and new kinds of harvesting equipment made it possible for one man by the 1880s to do the work of many. Farm periodicals had been preaching a gospel of mass production: farmers were advised to think big, go West, buy land, plant in bulk, specialize in one cash crop, try for large-scale economies of production, ship by railroad, and get rich.

The problem was that bumper crops drove down the price of farm commodities through supply and demand. The result was steadily less revenue pound for pound.

Of course big industrialists also produced their goods in bulk, and then they often cut prices to benefit from volume sales. But manufacturers also enjoyed an advantage: they were in a better position to control their costs. In the big cities, where their factories were, they could often play the railroads off against each other to get low freight rates; indeed, railroads, facing major problems of cash flow and eager to compete with each other for the volume business of industrial shippers, would offer rebates. But farmers, and especially those on the Great Plains, were often at the mercy of a single railroad monopoly and they had to pay exorbitant shipping rates.

With farmers lacking options to control their costs, they often found themselves, in financial terms, "upside down": it cost them more to grow crops than they could make in sales. They were operating at a loss.

And they were also indebted, which meant that their plunging revenue made it harder for them to pay creditors, let alone to buy what they needed. The result was a massive trend of farm bankruptcies. Farmers lost their land, then slipped into the dusty byways of rural poverty. Some became homeless; they were "hobos" and "tramps." Some moved to the city and tried manual labor.

An additional turn of the screw for farmers was the fact that price deflation means that money increases in value, it buys much more: the purchasing power of money varies in inverse relationship with prices. And so deflation hit the farmers both coming and going, as it were: lower prices meant less income every month and higher money values meant that the farmers had to pay creditors in dollars more valuable than the ones they had borrowed in the first place.

One result of these rural hard times seems counterintuitive by the standards of our own day and age: in the 1870s and for decades thereafter, a movement arose in rural America to drive up prices in general—not just farm prices but *all* prices, thereby reducing the value of money. In other words, farmers and farm leaders actually sought to *create* macroeconomic inflation. There were many strategies for doing so. One of them was manipulating the value, size, or amount of coined money.

During the Gilded Age, a welter of new organizations was set up to advance the interests of farmers: the National Grange of the Order of the Patrons of Husbandry, for example ("The Grangers"), and a cluster of organizations that used some variation of the name "Farmers Alliance." Of the latter, the most important organization was founded in Texas during the 1870s. In the 1880s it spread through the South and beyond, into the Midwest, prairie states, and even into the Rocky Mountain West. It was known as the National Farmers Alliance and Industrial Union.

"Agrarian radicalism" during the 1880s and 1890s advocated sweeping reforms of various types: regulation of railroad rates, abolition of the national banks, progressive taxation, price inflation, and—perhaps most interesting of all—a federal program, to be paid for by means of a new legal tender currency issue, to help both the sharecroppers and landowning farmers get back on their feet again.

Essentially the brainchild of a self-taught Texas economist named Charles Macune, this particular plan was a scheme by which the sharecroppers could work themselves out of debt slavery through cooperative action. They would set up vast buying and selling cooperatives through which they could spurn the predatory "services" of the planters and furnishing merchants. They would do it by purchasing the goods they needed together, directly and in bulk, thus getting the lowest possible price. They would cut out the middlemen and cheats. Similarly, they would sell their shares of the crop together and in bulk to get the highest possible price. Instead of grappling with poverty alone and divided, the sharecroppers would adapt the techniques of mass organization and economies of scale for their own purposes.

The problem was finding the capital to jump start the scheme. So Macune and friends came up with a plan to have the federal government furnish the money as a loan. Collateral would be the crops, which—as an added benefit—would be pulled off market and stored, thus by happy coincidence reducing supply and driving up prices. Best of all, this plan would not cost the taxpayers anything. It would not cost anybody anything. It would be paid for via newly printed United States Notes: Greenbacks.

This extremely interesting new departure in the economic uses of legal tender currency—comparable, in its way, to the plan of Benjamin Franklin and Francis Rawle in colonial Pennsylvania to create paper money and lend it into use with a "grounding" in collateral—prefigured an even more interesting proposal for the use of Greenbacks during the depression of the 1890s.

Macune and his friends tried to get candidates for Congress to pledge themselves to support the plans of the "Alliancemen." But the politicians routinely reneged on such promises. And so, between 1890 and 1892, the National Farmers Alliance and Industrial Union transformed itself into a new political party. Once again, the idea was to cut out the middlemen and cheats—in this case cheating politicians.

The newly founded Populist Party set forth a vision of radical reform in its "Omaha Platform" of 1892 that would gradually transform the Democratic Party in the twentieth century and lay the groundwork for a significant amount of New Deal legislation during the Great Depression of the 1930s.

The Populist Party's "Omaha Platform" of 1892 was adopted in an election year. One year later, in 1893, a new financial panic would usher in the worst American depression to date.

THE PANIC OF 1893

Once again, we must pause for a brief but necessary update on monetary matters. As previously noted, the United States Mint was closed in 1873 to the further "free and unlimited coinage" of silver. Some have mistakenly written that silver was essentially "demonetized" in this act, but that was not the case: existing silver coins continued to circulate. But the United States, like most European nations at the time, was embracing the "gold standard," at least in this case to the extent of leaving the mint completely open to the further coinage of gold while excluding silver.

Throughout the Gilded Age, advocates of higher prices sought to create inflation by pushing alternative versions of "silver inflationism" on the theory that continued coinage of silver would cheapen the value of money. The reasons for this belief will be examined later in detail.

The simplest form of this advocacy was to demand repeal of the Coinage Act of 1873 and thus reinstitute the free coinage of silver. That never happened. And yet, with significant help from some silver mine owners who were seeking an outlet for their product, Democrats in Congress did find a way to reinstitute silver coinage on a *limited* basis.

In 1878, over the veto of President Hayes, the Democrats pushed through the Bland-Allison Act, which directed the U.S. Treasury to actually *purchase* stipulated amounts of silver and pay for the metal by means of printed "silver certificates," a new form of paper currency. The silver that was purchased would be coined at the mint, and the coins would be stored by the treasury. Anyone who wished to swap a $1 silver certificate for a brand new silver dollar could do so. Thus the money supply would be expanded.

The working assumption, which still carries weight in some economic circles, is the presupposition that a larger money supply will always (or almost always) devalue money, thus causing inflation, because money itself obeys the law of supply and demand. Such is the venerable "quantity theory of money." Renewed silver coinage (however achieved) would increase the money supply. And so would new issues of legal tender United States Notes.

In 1890, silver inflationists secured passage of the Sherman Silver Purchase Act, which increased the silver purchases beyond the limits of the earlier Bland-Allison Act. Under the terms of the Sherman Act, the paper currency that was used to pay for the silver could be redeemed in either gold or silver coin. And because the treasury opted to pay in gold, the silver that was purchased was stored as bullion rather than coined.

Enough (at least for a moment) about silver, silver coinage, and silver purchases. But the relevance of these points about silver both to the economics and the politics of the 1890s depression will now be set forth.

Based on the known facts, the Panic of 1893 was in some respects comparable to the panic that occurred twenty years earlier, except that in this case fears regarding the precious metal content of America's coinage were far more important as dynamic factors than they were in 1873.

Once again, there was an underlying international dimension. Despite an economic boom in the 1880s—notwithstanding the hard times that increasingly afflicted America's urban and rural underclass and notwithstanding a robust export trade (including massive agricultural exports)—Americans were net importers in overall terms, so a balance of payments deficit existed. Rather than demand that Americans ship gold across the ocean to make up the difference in ledger book accounts, European creditors were generally content to accept American securities, especially railroad bonds, in lieu of gold.

When some British investments in Argentina began to go sour in 1890, however, British investors and speculators began to sell off American bonds for gold, which caused some immediate negative effects in both the American bond market and stock market. A net outflow of gold from the United States occurred. In the meantime, the Baring Brothers banking house in Britain failed.

Under the terms of the 1890 Sherman Silver Purchase Act, the new legal tender currency (silver certificates) that the government used to pay for the silver was redeemable in either silver or gold at the discretion of the treasury. But the treasury officials chose as a matter of policy to redeem in gold. A relevant fact was that the value of silver as an international commodity had been steadily plummeting for years. This made it more difficult to establish a dependable ratio between the number of ounces that would constitute a silver dollar and the number of ounces in the weight of a gold dollar. For this and other reasons, the silver that was purchased by the treasury pursuant to the Sherman Act was, as previously noted, stored as bullion rather than coined.

Shaky market conditions in the United States between 1890 and 1893 led many who received the new silver certificates to take them straight to the nearest U.S. subtreasury office for redemption in gold coin. Thus began a great "gold drain" at the treasury that, by 1893, threatened to reduce the $100-million "gold reserve" that had been set aside for the redemption of Greenbacks (United States Notes). Soon after his inauguration in 1893, President Grover Cleveland called on Congress to repeal the Sherman Silver Purchase Act, and Congress complied. And in order to shore up the gold reserve, Cleveland turned to the strongest banks (such as the house of J. P. Morgan) so that Uncle Sam could borrow gold quickly.

The overall sequence of events that caused the Panic of 1893 is less clear in its financial details than the chain of events that caused the panic that ushered in the previous depression in the 1870s. Here are some known facts. On February 20, 1893, the Reading Railroad went into receivership. On May 5, 1893, the National Cordage Company, whose stocks possessed a high market value, failed. Then the Panic of 1893 was on. Banks suspended specie payments in many parts of the country, and 158 national banks had gone into default or failed outright by the end of the year. A huge credit contraction began, and one railroad after another went into bankruptcy: the Reading, the Northern Pacific, the Union Pacific, the Santa Fe, and the Erie.

The usual pattern of contraction set in: runs on banks, the shrinking away of the money supply, both visible and invisible—in other words, money created out of nothing via lending went right back up to its source, thin air, when banks could not redeem the many checks that their customers had written—business failures, layoffs, unemployment, and suffering. Meanwhile, the dynamics of this latest depression merged with the preexisting agitation and protest by the underclass.

Already in 1892—a year before the panic—Populist orator Ignatius Donnelly had spoken of "a nation brought to the verge of moral, political, and material ruin." The Populists' Omaha platform asserted that "the fruits of the toil of millions are boldly stolen to build up colossal fortunes for a few . . . and the possessors of those, in turn, despise the republic and endanger liberty. From the same prolific womb of governmental injustice we breed the two great classes—tramps and millionaires."

A year later, it seemed to many that class warfare was raging in America. Many noticed an eerie coincidence: 1893 was the centennial of the French Revolution's Reign of Terror. In 1894, a year that some people began to call "l'année terrible"—a phrase that was actually coined a few decades earlier in reference to the struggles of the Paris Commune of 1871—a strike shut down much of the nation's railroad infrastructure: the Pullman strike.

It began with a strike in a company town: Pullman, Illinois. Built to contain the factory and worker housing of the Pullman Palace Car Company, George Pullman created an industrial version of the debt slavery afflicting so many Southern sharecroppers: the salaries of Pullman's workers were usually not quite enough to enable them to pay what they owed to the company store. After several wage cuts with no reduction in the rent charged for company housing, the workers went on strike. And the strike spread when the members of a new interstate union, the American Railway Union (ARU), refused to work on trains containing cars manufactured by Pullman. This strike was in essence a boycott. In the midst of the worst depression in America to date, the interstate transportation infrastructure was shutting down.

President Grover Cleveland and his attorney general Richard Olney (a former railroad lawyer) broke the strike by classifying the ARU as a conspiracy in restraint of trade, per the terms of the Sherman Anti-Trust Act of 1890, which of course had been (supposedly) aimed at corporations, not unions. Cleveland also charged that the ARU was interfering in the delivery of United States mail. And so, by presidential order, the U.S. Army broke the strike by force. Eugene Victor

Marchers in "Coxey's Army" approaching Washington, D.C.
This photograph was published in *Frank Leslie's Illustrated Newspaper* on May 10, 1894.
Source: Courtesy of the Library of Congress.

Debs, the leader of the ARU, went to prison, where he became converted to socialism.

In 1894, the first great protest march on Washington occurred. The marchers were seeking to counteract the depression by creating public works jobs to ease unemployment and pump up consumer purchasing power. This powerful but eminently moderate idea was taken up by a maverick Ohio businessman named Jacob Coxey, who conceived of a $500 million "good roads bill" that Congress would fund through a new issue of . . . Greenbacks.

On a trip to Chicago, Coxey encountered a Populist organizer named Carl Browne, who was advocating a march of the unemployed on Washington, a "petition in boots" as Browne called it. The men joined forces: Browne moved into Coxey's home in Massillon, Ohio, and they organized their march, which they insisted had to be peaceful. Coxey arranged for a Populist member of the U.S. Senate, William Peffer of Kansas, to introduce the good roads bill. The marchers (some of whom called their movement the "Commonweal of Christ" while others called it "Coxey's Army") departed Massillon on Easter morning and arrived in Washington on May 1.

Coxey, Browne, and other leaders of the march were arrested for walking on the grass of the U.S. Capitol grounds. They spent twenty days in jail. Peffer's good roads bill went nowhere.

In this political environment, with only two years left before the elections of 1896, the leaders of the Populist Party saw their chance to initiate a brand new party system, to show up Grover Cleveland's Democratic Party (supposedly the organizational champion of the common man) as a hollow or corrupted vessel. The Populists had a chance to put the Democratic Party of Grover Cleveland out of business and take its place, much as the new Republican Party of 1854, with its anti-slavery impetus, destroyed the older Whig Party and took its place.

In the South, Populist organizers attempted to initiate a new class-based alliance that would cut across racial lines. Tom Watson of Georgia urged poor whites in his state to unite with poor blacks under Populist auspices. "You are made to hate each other," Watson told his white followers, "because upon that hatred rests the financial despotism that enslaves you both. You are beggared and blinded that you may not see how this race antagonism perpetuates a system that beggars both."

If events had shaken out differently, and if the Populists had made different strategic assumptions, the new party might well have found itself in a formidable position in 1896. But Populists fell victim to a fatal presupposition: they presumed that Cleveland's Democratic Party was worthless and hopelessly corrupt. They presumed that the Democrats would nominate a politician like Cleveland for the presidency in 1896. So they waited too long to hold their own nominating convention.

But they were wrong about the Democrats. A protest insurgency was raging in the Democratic Party, an insurgency of vast long-term consequences. For instance, in response to President Cleveland's action in breaking the Pullman strike, the Democratic governor of Illinois, John Peter Altgeld, snarled that "to laud Clevelandism on Jefferson's birthday is to sing a Te Deum in honor of Judas Iscariot on a Christmas morning."

The Democrats nominated a protest candidate in 1896, a former congressman from Nebraska named William Jennings Bryan. A spellbinding orator, Bryan brought down the house at the Democratic convention. In his unforgettable and charismatic speech, he turned his wrath upon his own party's indifference to mass suffering. "We have petitioned and our petitions have been scorned," he thundered; "we have entreated, and our entreaties have been disregarded. We have begged, and they have mocked when our calamity came. We beg no longer; we entreat no more; we petition no more. We defy them!"

The power of Bryan's speech was so great that even a Cleveland Democrat (according to one account of the convention) yanked the man next to him up on his feet and shouted "Yell, for God's sake, yell!"

But there was a big problem with Bryan's candidacy: he was a silver inflationist, and he regarded this principle as something of a political and economic panacea. He called for the repeal of the Coinage Act of 1873 (the "crime of '73") and he demanded the free and unlimited coinage of silver at the ratio of sixteen to one. That had been the mint ratio of silver to gold back in 1873: it had taken sixteen times as much precious metal to make a silver dollar as it took to make a gold dollar.

But silver had plummeted in value by 1896. When Bryan ran for the presidency, the market ratio of silver to gold was more like thirty-two to one. So this meant that if silver dollars were created through open mintage at the old ratio of 1873 (16-1), the money pool would be flooded in 1896 with millions of new dollars that, notwithstanding their face value, would contain roughly 50 cents' worth of precious metal apiece, though the coin would be legal tender for a dollar.

And this would lead to raging inflation. Undervalued gold dollars would be melted and shipped abroad for recoinage. Meanwhile prices would double for anyone proposing to pay with dollars worth 50 cents apiece.

For American inflationists, that would have been just fine. But inflationism, so strong in the agricultural heartland, was dead on arrival in the cities. Supporters of the Republican candidate William McKinley had a field day asking industrial workers if they wanted to see the value of their paychecks cut in half.

And the Populists? They found themselves in a classic dilemma: they confronted two stark choices and both of them were bad. They had waited too long to hold their own nominating convention. They figured the Democrats would nominate a stubborn defender of the status quo. But they figured wrong. And now the Democrats were stealing their thunder, and stealing it with a catastrophically self-defeating reform proposal.

So what were the Populists to do? Join forces with Bryan and sink to defeat or nominate their own candidate and thus split the reform vote?

Some Populists ("fusionists") argued that the party had no choice but to support Bryan; to do otherwise would guarantee McKinley's election. Others ("mid-roaders") argued that the party had to maintain its own distinct identity, promote its sweeping reform ideals, distance itself from Bryan's silver monomania, and live to fight another day. The fusionists won. The Populists endorsed Bryan but insisted that Tom Watson should occupy the vice presidential slot on the unified ticket.

Bryan ignored the Populists' nomination. But it didn't matter: McKinley won in a landslide. And in 1897, the first year of McKinley's presidency, the depression started to lift, and McKinley began to get the credit, which of course was wholly undeserved.

William McKinley was a very lucky man—until his luck ran out in 1901 when an assassin shot him dead.

4

Depressions and Policy Disputes in America, Circa 1720–1928

MORE AND MORE, PEOPLE WONDERED what ought to be done to prevent depressions. From the eighteenth century onward, an argument raged between the champions and opponents of government intervention. In America, those debates became particularly shrill as hard times kept ravaging the nation.

The intellectual history of these disputes sheds light on thinking in leadership circles regarding the challenges posed by depressions. Was preventive or remedial action by government justified? If so, how much action was justified?

LAISSEZ-FAIRE AND ITS EARLY CRITICS

The emergence of Newtonian physics was seen by many in the early eighteenth century as a milestone in history. "Nature and Nature's Laws lay hid in Night," wrote Alexander Pope circa 1730; "God said, *Let Newton be!* and All was Light." For many, Newtonian science led straight to some odd forms of pseudo-science—such as the appealing notion that the pattern of the heavens was somehow a model for humanity to copy.

This enticing idea (at least for some) led to maxims that might sound convincing at first, though on closer analysis most of them made no sense.

To demonstrate: In 1729, a minor and long-forgotten English writer, J. T. Desaguliers, wrote a verse tract titled *The Newtonian System of the World, the Best Model of Government*. There were several ways to apply the idea that celestial "balance" was somehow a "model of government," and one of them was to build a machinery of state whose "checks and balances" would correspond (vaguely) to the interplay of centrifugal and centripetal forces. Several participants at the Constitutional Convention of 1787 espoused this idea.

But there was another and simpler application of "Newtonian politics" that began to make the rounds within Enlightenment culture: the notion that a perfect balance *already* exists within human institutions. And this led to a predictable question: If so, how could anything go wrong? The answer was all too simple: government destroys society's harmony when well-intentioned but wrong-headed policymakers interfere. This was essentially the doctrine that was popularized by French Physiocrats Francois Quesnay and Vincent Gournay, who promoted the slogan "laissez-faire" and who advocated deregulation. And the Physiocratic argument profoundly influenced Adam Smith, who argued in his *Wealth of Nations* (1776) that the market's "invisible hand" would guide most economic transactions to satisfactory outcomes.

"Laissez-faire," roughly translated as the admonition to leave things alone, was the battle cry of the Physiocrats, whose disciples argued that society's natural harmony plays out to perfection except when deranged by governmental meddling.

By the middle of the nineteenth century, this intellectual tradition had profoundly shaped the emergence of "classical economics," whose adherents regarded themselves as "scientists" and who based their "science" on the notion that inflexible economic laws play out through invariable patterns. Some of the "laws" that were promulgated by these "political economists" (for so they were called at the time) were endlessly arguable: "Say's Law," for instance, laid down that "production" is always the source of economic "demand"—a notion that was updated in the 1970s and 1980s as "supply side economics"—or the so-called Iron Law of Wages, which asserts that wage levels devolve invariably downward toward the minimum for bare subsistence.

One might quickly infer from these facts that most of the early theories of the business cycle regarded it as a rigid and invariable fluctuation. Importantly, however, this was not always the case because the emergent field of economics contained a fair amount of intellectual diversity.

Many economic writers by the nineteenth century departed from the presuppositions of their "classical" peers, and some of them dissented vigorously from the doctrine of laissez-faire, from the theories of Adam Smith, and from other staples of emergent economic orthodoxy.

For example, in his *Nouveaux Principes d'économie politique* (1819), the French writer Jean Charles Léonard de Sismondi argued that depressions result from either "overproduction" or "underconsumption" (or both) and that such derangements in economic force might well be amenable to solutions. Sismondi also helped to pioneer the concept of the "business cycle," the pattern of alternating periods of economic expansion and contraction that confounded the vision of economic equilibrium that so many classical economists took for granted.

Importantly, most economic thinkers in America from the colonial period through the mid-nineteenth century tended to be interventionists—opponents of laissez-faire and economic fatalism. And some of these thinkers were hands-on policymakers.

Benjamin Franklin, as we have seen, advocated novel methods to inject purchasing power into stagnant economies through direct governmental money creation. Alexander Hamilton went out of his way to ridicule laissez-faire; the notion, he wrote, that "trade will regulate itself" was "one of those wild, speculative paradoxes, which have grown into credit among us, contrary to the uniform practice and sense of the most enlightened nations." Hamilton advocated governmentally sponsored infrastructure projects (especially roads and canals), observing that without such sponsorship by government, many "desirable enterprises might . . . not be undertaken for want of sufficient private capital, or when unexpected causes thwarted a prosperous flow of commerce." In other words, when private sector action is impeded (due to unexpected causes), the obvious remedy is government intervention.

Among American writers who identified themselves (or were identified by others) as "economists" in the decades before the Civil War, almost all were interventionists who advocated the building up of working-class purchasing power not only as an economic stimulant but also as a worthy goal in and of itself: Daniel Raymond (1786–1849), author of *Thoughts on Political Economy* (1820); Mathew Carey (1760–1839), author of *Essays on Political Economy* (1822), and his son Henry Charles Carey (1793–1879), author of the four-volume *Principles of Political Economy* (1837–1840). Most of these writers urged a public-private partnership between government and business, a partnership to build up prosperity and purchasing power in the manner that Hamilton had touted in his days as treasury secretary back in the 1790s.

Under the influence of such thinkers, political leaders such as John Quincy Adams, Henry Clay, and Abraham Lincoln advocated public works or "internal improvements" projects to be underwritten by government as economic stimulators.

THE CONTINUING DEVELOPMENT OF LAISSEZ-FAIRE THEORY AND RESPONSES FROM ITS LATER CRITICS

But governmental action in response to economic depressions was generally thwarted in the United States during the nineteenth century. The doctrine of laissez-faire grew stronger, notwithstanding the challenges by policymakers and elected leaders who were working in the Hamiltonian tradition. The reason that laissez-faire grew stronger in America was twofold: (1) it became an important standard doctrine of political ideology, first among the early liberals (on an international basis) and then later on among American conservatives, and (2) it received a new infusion of credibility from an updated form of ersatz science: "Social Darwinism."

It bears noting, of course, that extreme libertarianism was one of the fundamental impulses in the colonial radicalism of the 1760s that propelled the movement for American independence. An often bitter aversion toward government as such remains a part of America's political "genetic code" to this very day, and this fact must be constantly considered—kept firmly in mind—in regard to the various fluctuations of American political culture over time.

However, the creed of laissez-faire was also adopted by emergent liberalism—on both sides of the Atlantic—though conservatives would later on appropriate the doctrine through a process that intellectual historian Jacques Barzun once called "the great switch."

But the liberals embraced it first.

"I own I am not a friend to a very energetic government," wrote Thomas Jefferson in 1787; "it is always oppressive." In 1791, Thomas Paine wrote that "man, were he not corrupted by governments, is naturally the friend of man . . . and human nature is not of itself vicious." One of the controlling ideas of early modern liberalism was the notion that maximum liberty, with its terminological cognates "liberate" and "liberalize"—free speech, free press, free markets, free enterprise, free trade—was the best and surest way to liberate the downtrodden and exalt the "common man" everywhere. Early liberals tended to believe that the selfish upper classes used regulation by government as a means to protect their own privileged positions and to keep the lower classes "in their place."

So it stood to reason that the Democratic Party, as founded by Andrew Jackson and others in the 1830s to promote the well-being of the common man, adopted the following pithy slogans: "The world is too much governed" and "That government that governs best, governs least."

Small wonder in the aftermath of the Panic of 1837 that Jackson's successor, Martin Van Buren, was hampered by his own party's ideology from proposing any public works efforts that would stimulate the economy or create jobs.

In the aftermath of the Civil War, the rise of Social Darwinism propelled the creed of minimal government to the other end of the ideological spectrum: conservatives began to embrace it as a means of justifying economic and social inequality.

Conservative advocates of social stratification used the "natural law" of "survival of the fittest" to oppose governmental intervention to help the suffering, even in times of economic depression when millions of hapless and blameless individuals were caught in a vast economic chain reaction beyond their power to control. Blameless and hapless they might be, but according to proponents of Social Darwinism, they were also inherently . . . weak. Laissez-faire was increasingly invoked by the comfortable and powerful as a "natural law," the defiance of which was nothing less than . . . "unnatural." "If we do not like the survival of the fittest," wrote sociologist William Graham Sumner, "we have only one possible alternative, and that is survival of the unfittest."

As John Kenneth Galbraith noted sardonically years ago, it was all too characteristic of Gilded Age academic culture for economists and other "social scientists" to "find virtue in what the reputable and affluent applaud." But it also needs to be noted and emphasized that many wealthy individuals in America were philanthropic and did not subscribe to the orthodoxies of laissez-faire or "survival of the fittest." And a number of prominent economists continued to dissent from these doctrines as well. In 1886, economists Richard T. Ely and John R. Commons included the following statement in a draft prospectus for the new American Economic Association that they and others were founding: "While we recognize the necessity of individual initiative in industrial life, we hold that the doctrine of laissez-faire is unsafe in politics and unsound in morals."

By the 1890s, a widespread critique of Social Darwinism as a justification for laissez-faire began to spread in America and elsewhere. Scholars and social critics who were quite convinced that Darwinian biology had scientific validity nonetheless disputed the proposition that "rugged individualism" was the best and soundest application of evolutionary theory to society.

Sociologist Lester Frank Ward, for example, observed that natural selection in the biosphere often manifests itself in patterns of group *cooperation* rather than competition: packs of wolves and flocks of birds worked together to help the group survive. If government intervention is unnatural, he gibed, then perhaps the human arts of medicine and agriculture are also unnatural and ought to be dispensed with.

One of the most important and influential thinkers along these lines was none other than young Theodore Roosevelt, an ardent exponent of the "strenuous life" and individual fitness. But Roosevelt also insisted that *societies* that found themselves locked in international competition had to practice internal *teamwork*.

Perhaps most importantly of all, an important economist in Britain began to write books that advocated public works jobs as an antidote to economic depressions—books that prefigured the later work of John Maynard Keynes. Economist John A. Hobson argued that a shortage of purchasing power was the problem that kept depressions going. The following books by Hobson rolled from the presses decade by decade: *The Evolution of Modern Capitalism* (1894), *Work and Wealth* (1914), *The Economics of Unemployment* (1922), and *Confessions of an Economic Heretic* (1938).

THE CREATION OF THE FEDERAL RESERVE SYSTEM, 1907–1913

In 1907, a serious financial panic shook Wall Street and it triggered consequences in different parts of the United States. When an attempt to corner the stock of a major corporation failed—an attempt that used bank loans based on fractional reserve methods—the repercussions led to runs on some banks that had financed the scheme. The Knickerbocker Trust Company, one of New York's largest, went under, and the panic spread. This crisis was contained and alleviated by the sedulous action of investment banker J. P. Morgan, who directed fellow investors to do his bidding and place deposits in selected financial institutions in order to save them. Morgan even persuaded President Theodore Roosevelt to make some federal funds available for this purpose.

The crisis led to one of the most important interventions in the marketplace for the purpose of forestalling and preventing depressions: the establishment of the Federal Reserve System as a "lender of last resort," a federally chartered institution that would serve as a central bank, the sort of bank that America once possessed in the long-defunct first and second Banks of the United States.

In 1908, Congress passed the Aldrich-Vreeland Act, which created a National Monetary Commission to make recommendations. The act also established some National Currency Associations within the national bank system, associations set up to issue emergency currency with Treasury Department approval. The National Monetary Commission was chaired by Senator Nelson W. Aldrich, and its deliberations took several years.

Many leading bankers supported the creation of a unitary national bank. But in part for political reasons, not least of all due to congressional investigations into the influence of financial cartels that allegedly constituted, in the words of reformer and future Supreme Court Justice Louis Brandeis, a "money trust," the Aldrich Commission recommended the establishment of a National Reserve Association with regional branches.

This led to congressional creation of the Federal Reserve System in 1913 during the first year of Woodrow Wilson's presidency.

The legislation that created the system was sponsored by Senator Robert Latham Owen of Oklahoma and Representative Carter Glass of Virginia. The Owen-Glass bill was revised steadily because of disagreements as to the nature and structure of the system. Glass, for instance, favored a privately owned and decentralized system, whereas Treasury Secretary William Gibbs McAdoo wanted more centralization and federal control. The compromise bill included a presidentially appointed Federal Reserve Board whose powers were preliminarily weak and ill-defined.

The act created a system of twelve regional, federally chartered banks, and these banks would be owned by member banks within the district via capital stock purchases. Membership in the system by national banks was made compulsory, but state-chartered commercial banks could also join the system by purchasing stock in the regional bank. Each Federal Reserve bank was to be run by a board of nine directors, three of whom were to be designated by the Federal Reserve Board.

Building on the precedent of the first and second Banks of the United States, each Federal Reserve Bank received a charter that was only good for twenty years. In 1927, Congress extended these charters indefinitely. In the meantime, a power struggle shaped up between the Federal Reserve Board and the regional banks as to how much autonomy each bank ought to possess. The Federal Reserve Board struggled to assert control. But the preponderance of power and influence rested preliminarily with the Federal Reserve Bank of New York, with its proximity to and its intimate connections with Wall Street.

Building on the precedent set by the Civil War national banks, Congress made provisions for the treasury to print up bank notes—Federal Reserve Notes—that would be made available to Federal Reserve Banks when their customers desired cash. The notes would be treated as something of a loan: to get some bank notes, the regional bank would deposit assets (bonds and other investments) with the treasury as collateral. When the bank no longer needed to "carry as much cash," it could return some notes and get some assets in exchange.

These Federal Reserve Notes were given legal tender status. They could also be redeemed in solid coin. But the Federal Reserve Banks practiced fractional reserve money creation, making use of the same method as regular commercial banks: they established checking accounts. Bank note currency continued to dwindle as a feature of America's monetary system.

It remained to be seen if this experiment in central banking would serve to prevent the kinds of panics that could lead to depressions.

THE ISSUE OF A PLANNED DEMOBILIZATION
AND THE SHORT DEPRESSION OF 1919–1921

The outbreak of World War I caused fears of a new depression: the short-term disruption of overseas trade exerted a contractionary effect on the economy. Jacob Coxey led a second march of the unemployed, in part to commemorate the anniversary of the first march in 1894 and in part to spread the new alarm. But the problem reversed itself as massive orders for U.S. food supplies and war materiel began to pour in from the belligerent powers overseas. A wartime economic boom was under way by 1915.

But after U.S. entry into the war in 1917, some policymakers worried about the need for an intelligently planned demobilization to avert the threat of unemployment after the war. As early as 1917, Secretary of Labor William Bauchop Wilson established the U.S. Employment Service as an agency within the Labor Department. In 1918, Senator Robert Latham Owen warned President Woodrow Wilson that "the Government will be obliged . . . to make a gigantic effort to employ . . . men on living wages" in order to expedite a seemly and prosperous transition to a peacetime economy.

One of the people in the Wilson administration who was most concerned about the problem was Joseph Tumulty, Wilson's secretary and political adviser. Early in 1919, when Wilson took a short break from the Paris peace conference—he returned to Washington for several weeks in order to sign legislation—Tumulty cabled him as follows: "Business conditions are strange and . . . there are a great many idle men in places."

But when Wilson returned, he did nothing more than summon a governors conference, thus foisting on the states and localities the responsibility for maintaining employment as the wartime industries retooled. He essentially washed his hands of the matter.

The failure of Wilson to preempt the threat of unemployment can be cited as a principal cause of a severe economic downturn in 1919. And this downturn qualifies by the standards of some as a full-fledged depression.

The situation was worsened by the fact that wartime price controls were lifted. As industries retooled, civilian commodities, already scarce, rose steadily in price, and so inflation surged at the very same time that unemployment was on the rise. (Something comparable would occur later on in the 1970s during the Nixon era's "stagflation.") In order to counteract the inflation, the new Federal Reserve Banks began to hike up interest rates. This accelerated the economic contraction. A huge wave of strikes swept the country as layoffs and wage cuts spread.

The "short depression" of 1920–1921 (as some have called it) ran its course. Recent historical accounts of this event that have been written by authors with a penchant for free market theory have praised the new president who was elected in 1920—Warren G. Harding—for doing little or nothing to affect the situation. But even if Harding was inattentive, there were others in his administration who recommended action.

Commerce Secretary Herbert Hoover advocated the creation of a cabinet-level Department of Public Works, and he urged the president to put some money into construction projects to take up the economic slack. In 1921 he had urged President Harding to call a "President's Conference on Unemployment." And he advocated long-term planning of public works projects to even out the fluctuations of the business cycle and help the unemployed. It bears noting that Hoover had apparently read an important book published in 1913: *Business Cycles* by economist Wesley Clair Mitchell.

At this point in his career, Hoover was a moderate progressive who advocated both governmental regulation of industry and big-ticket public works projects including a St. Lawrence Seaway and a massive power-producing dam to be located in the Boulder Canyon of the Colorado River.

But Hoover was also pulled in different directions philosophically—a point that is essential to grasping the contradictory and even enigmatic nature of his behavior when the Great Depression unfolded later on.

Hoover was torn between visions of social coordination—he often emphasized "cooperation" and "service" as cardinal points in his political creed—and themes of sturdy individualism that would sometimes make him reluctant as president to support relief measures to alleviate poverty and hunger. But what was very peculiar (and even mysterious) about this reluctance was its contrast to his previous career as a humanitarian.

His work with the wartime Committee for the Relief of Belgium, for instance, his action to assist and relocate the homeless in the Mississippi River flood of 1927, and above all his work with the Red Cross has led many observers to wonder how Hoover—a man with what appeared to be an ideal resume for combatting the Great Depression—became so mastered by events. But we will get to that story by and by.

ATTEMPTS TO ALLEVIATE AND ANTICIPATE
ECONOMIC TROUBLES, 1923–1928

For a long time, historical controversies regarding the causes of America's Great Depression have probed the underlying economic conditions that prevailed in the 1920s. After the short depression of 1920–1921, the economic "boom" of the Roaring Twenties took off—but how genuine and well-grounded was this boom? What weaknesses prefigured the collapse of prosperity that followed?

One fact about the American economy during the 1920s is beyond dispute: the overall "farm problem" of the Gilded Age returned with a vengeance. Depression conditions were returning to rural America, and some of the remedies touted years earlier by Gilded Age reformers were advocated once again. Especially prominent was inflationism, which included a spate of new calls for a federal program of agricultural price supports.

American farmers had increased their output dramatically during World War I—not least of all for the purpose of exporting food to Europe—but when European agriculture recovered, American farmers were stuck with a "surplus" of productive capacity and the prices for farm commodities plummeted.

By the 1920s, the "farm bloc" was more powerful, and so reformers got results. In 1923, Harding's agriculture secretary, Henry Cantwell Wallace—not to be confused with his famous son, Henry Agard Wallace, who would serve Franklin D. Roosevelt as secretary of agriculture and later as vice president—threw his support behind an Agricultural Credits Act that extended low-interest loans to rural buying and selling cooperatives. Among the reformers working on the "farm problem," two in particular are worthy of note: George Peek and General Hugh Johnson, both of whom had worked for the War Industries Board (WIB) and both of whom collaborated on plans to assist the farmers in the 1920s. Both would play key administrative roles in the early New Deal under FDR.

An ambitious proposal to help the farmers was the McNary-Haugen Farm Relief bill of 1927, which would have established a federal corporation to boost farm prices by purchasing the so-called agricultural surplus and storing it or selling it abroad. President Calvin Coolidge vetoed this bill. But in 1929, newly elected president Herbert Hoover supported the Agricultural Marketing Act, which established a Federal Farm Board endowed with $500 million to lend to agricultural cooperatives.

Beyond the farm problem, some observers believed that the overall boom of the 1920s contained some larger structural weaknesses. Granted, the growth industries such as radio, automobile manufacturing, aviation, and real estate seemed robust (notwithstanding the spectacular collapse of a speculative Florida land boom in mid-decade). But labor unions were weaker in the 1920s, and some predicted that an economic slump might set in as paychecks failed to keep pace with productivity.

In 1927, former Harvard classmates William Trufant Foster (by then the former president of Reed College) and Waddill Catchings (an investor) published a book titled *Business Without A Buyer*. "We cannot sell the goods," these authors claimed, "because the people who would like to buy them do not have sufficient incomes." This was not at all a problem of "overproduction," they insisted. No, it was the other way around: it was a shortage of purchasing power and thus a problem of *underconsumption*.

In 1928, they published *The Road to Plenty*, a sequel that suggested the solution that so many others had proposed to cure America's depressions in the past: public works to alleviate unemployment while simultaneously expanding the customer base for free enterprise.

Several bills were introduced in Congress, one of them co-sponsored by Senator Wesley Jones of Washington and Senator Robert F. Wagner of New York, to create a federal policy of timing the construction of public works for the purpose of counteracting economic contractions. In 1928, Governor Ralph Owen Brewster of Maine—who announced that he was speaking in effect on behalf of Herbert Hoover—proposed at the National Governors Conference a federal-state-municipal "reserve" fund of $3 billion that might be used as a fiscal "balance wheel" for investment purposes in the event of an economic slump.

But few could foresee how precipitous a slump was just around the corner.

5

The Onset of the Great Depression

FOR A LONG TIME, many people believed that the Wall Street crash caused the chain of events that precipitated the Great Depression of the 1930s in America.

But that view is often challenged as an oversimplification. Some have argued that economic weaknesses predating the 1929 crash should be given equal or greater weight in explaining what happened; others have emphasized the international dimensions of the crisis. Some have claimed that there is insufficient evidence to link the crash with the damage to the macroeconomy, especially because the early events of the Depression played out over several years. In 1999, historian David Kennedy wrote that "most responsible students of the events of 1929 have been unable to demonstrate an appreciable cause-and-effect linkage between the Great Crash and the Depression."

The case can be made that a linkage existed, but the onset of this depression was indeed a complicated process.

WORLDWIDE ECONOMIC PROBLEMS

Global economic conditions were dire in the 1920s and the problems derived from the dislocations of World War I and the postwar settlement. British trade had been crippled and Britain found itself hugely in debt to the United States, as did France. Requests to the Wilson administration for debt relief or even a debt moratorium were ignored. Britain went off the gold standard during the war, and when Winston Churchill, in the course of his service as chancellor of the exchequer, reinstated the gold standard in 1925, he set the pound at a high exchange rate relative to other currencies.

This "strong" pound put Britain's foreign customers at a disadvantage. It took a lot of foreign currency to buy a single pound at the exchange rate set by Churchill, and so after the currency conversion British goods were in comparative terms more expensive than they had been. Declining exports caused British businessmen to cut their prices to stimulate sales. The price cuts led ineluctably to wage cuts, and dramatic strikes resulted.

Among the Germans the results were bad for opposite reasons. Germany was saddled with tremendous reparations payments, and some have associated this with a raging hyperinflation that wracked the German economy between 1921 and 1923. It appears that the prospect of higher taxes to bring in revenue to pay the reparations caused the rich to shift their wealth from money into nontaxable assets, thus establishing a downward trend in the value of money compared to other forms of wealth. When Germany defaulted on its reparations, the French sent troops into the Ruhr in 1923 to seize goods that could be sold to pay France's debts to America. This crippled the German economy. So a consortium of American bankers lent the Germans money via the Dawes and Young Plans. But when American banks ran into trouble, Germans found themselves in a massive credit contraction that sent unemployment soaring. Then the rise of Hitler was almost impossible to stop.

Transatlantic causality in the Great Depression was complex and the international patterns were often reciprocal. Of that there can be no doubt.

THE SLOWDOWN PREDATING THE CRASH

Months before the stock market crash, the American economy was entering recession. Many indicators of economic activity—sales, factory payrolls, freight traffic—started falling. Residential construction was declining, inventories were piling up, and consumer spending was down. There is reason to believe that the "overproduction/underconsumption" continuum was beginning to play out more or less along the lines of the worried predictions. All through the decade worker productivity had increased while salaries were more or less stagnant. Wealth distribution was grossly hierarchic; by 1929, roughly 5 percent of the American population accounted for a third of American income. Spending by the wealthy on capital goods drove an inordinate amount of economic activity, and it is perhaps an open question whether stock speculation, which diverted significant investment from the purchase of additional goods, led to the building up of excessive inventories, which led to resultant cutbacks in production and layoffs.

THE MECHANICS OF THE STOCK SPECULATION

But the 1929 stock market crash was fundamental, and the process by which the crash caused a financial chain reaction is relatively easy to fathom.

Reckless investments in stocks had been criticized in America as early as 1925, but the frenzy on Wall Street really began in the second half of the decade. The problem was that the great bull market that began in 1927 and 1928 was speculative, meaning that the hottest stocks on Wall Street did not necessarily represent ownership shares in corporations that were doing well financially. Stock dividends are fine, but the buy-and-flip strategy of stock speculation makes long-term dividend earnings an afterthought. During 1928, for instance, RCA stock surged from $77 a share to over $400 a share and the company was not paying dividends.

Wall Street was still unregulated in the 1920s; the creation of the Securities and Exchange Commission would constitute a major New Deal reform. Stockbrokers slipped easily into patterns of conflict of interest. "Investment trusts" proliferated—companies that purchased vast holdings of securities on behalf of their customers and used them at their own discretion. It was easy to manipulate values and engage in insider trading under these circumstances.

The self-dealing and chicanery were sometimes bold, blatant, and spectacular: investment trusts would use their stock holdings as the basis for issuing stock of their own, and in collusion with others—in return for reciprocal favors—they would arrange to have their own stock "boomed" in purchases that would double, triple, or quadruple its market value. Investment trusts would use such "leverage" to create spinoff trusts, which in turn would create more trusts. Stock values were increasingly detached from the real-life worth of the companies involved and the real well-being of the goods and services economy.

Wall Street was building up a "bubble" in the classic and centuries-old pattern of speculative frenzies. The lure was hard to resist. In 1928, an investor in radio stock could calculate a 500 percent appreciation in the value of his shares by the time he cashed in.

This dangerous and reckless gambling was connected to the larger financial sector: the speculative profits to be made were so vast that commercial banks lent prodigious amounts of money to abet the speculation. Many stock purchases were made via "margin" trading, through which the speculator would pay just a fraction of the purchase price (the "margin") while the rest of the purchase was bank financed—and the stock itself was the collateral. To be sure, if the value of the stock should fall, then the brokers would require more cash from the investors (they would increase the amount of the margin). If the cash were not paid, the stock would be sold, and this supposedly protected the banks.

By the end of 1928, the interest rate for these "brokers' loans" in the "call market"—so called because the banks could "call" these loans on demand—was up to 12 percent, which was a wonderful rate of return. New York banks could borrow money from the Federal Reserve Bank of New York at 5 percent and then relend it to the "call market" for 12 percent. The volume of these loans increased from roughly $2 billion in 1926 to $6 billion by the end of 1928.

But this was unsound banking at its worst, and one of the very worst things was that the bank loans derived from the fractional reserve methods of money creation, which put the banks in danger of default if (nay, when) the value of the loan collateral collapsed.

Perhaps worst of all, many corporations poured money into stock market loans—sometimes the profit to be made was even greater than the profits to be made in the course of their regular business—and when these corporate investments went sour, the companies would obviously have to adjust by contracting their normal operations. In 1934, a congressional investigation suggested that the volume of these nonbanking (that is, corporate) sources of funds for stock market speculation was equal to the volume of the bank loans used for that purpose in 1929. During 1929, Standard Oil of New Jersey invested $97.8 million in the call market and earned $4.9 million in interest. By the time of the crash, corporations were even more grievously entangled than banks.

The situation was inherently catastrophic: the values of these stocks were inflated so grotesquely that collapse was a matter of time—a matter of the time before investors decided it was time to cash in. And once the selling began, it would continue.

Of course, some short-term calculations would occur, and this complicated the pattern: as stock prices dropped, there would be action by the usual cohort of clever buyers who would try to pick up bargains and reap the benefits later. "Short selling" was, as always, a classic ploy on Wall Street in 1929. But what if the value of stocks, whatever short-term rallies might occur, should continue to plunge?

And a huge amount of borrowed money was involved. This put the banks at great potential risk. How could this money—newly created money, which emerged through the hocus pocus of fractional reserve commercial banking—be repaid by the sale of worthless collateral? And if the loans could not be repaid, if the borrowers defaulted, then the banks would begin to default.

At least one banker was honest and courageous enough to predict what would happen. In March 1929, Paul M. Warburg of the International Acceptance Bank wrote that the "unrestrained speculation" that was taking place on Wall Street would "bring about a general depression involving the entire country."

THE CRASH

In March 1929, a market downturn began on Wall Street. The Federal Reserve had issued a warning against the misuse of its loans for speculation. When the board went into closed meetings for several days, banks began to raise the interest rates on call loans and cut back their volume. But when Charles E. Mitchell, the president of National City Bank, expressed confidence in the stock market along with a willingness to keep the credit flowing for speculators—to the tune of $25 million— Wall Street recovered; indeed, the boom climbed to ever-giddier heights during the summer of 1929.

In September, however, things changed. A financial consultant named Roger Babson predicted that a plunge in stock values might be coming; "factories will shut down," he said, "men will be thrown out of work . . . the vicious circle will get in full swing and the result will be a serious business depression." Investor confidence was shaken and the prices of stocks began to decline on September 18. Two days later the London stock market crashed when a prominent investor named Clarence Hatry and several of his associates were imprisoned for fraud.

The catastrophe began in October, though the crash was extended over weeks and months: the market lurched up and down as some rallies occurred between the spasms of selling. But each stock market rally was a temporary respite: the market shuddered downward again in yet another great lurch of despair and fear.

On Saturday, October 19, the market declined in no uncertain terms; the values of blue chip stocks were down and the speculative shares plummeted. The next day, on Sunday, brokers began to increase their margin calls in order to protect the banks from the decline in the value of their collateral. On Monday, October 21, the volume in stock sales was the third largest in the history of the New York Stock Exchange; indeed, it was so great that it was hard to keep up with what was happening.

October 24 was "Black Thursday," a day when sales were so immense that the tickertape reports in brokerage offices were hours behind the events.

At this point a group of prominent bankers decided that an intervention was needed, an intervention like the one that J. P. Morgan had engineered to stop the Panic of 1907. Charles Mitchell of National City, Albert Wiggin of Chase National, and Thomas W. Lamont of Morgan approached Richard Whitney, the vice president of the Stock Exchange, to bid on large blocks of blue chip stocks above the current price on their behalf. (It bears noting that several of these illustrious figures would be prosecuted for larceny during the 1930s.)

The market rallied, but only temporarily.

On October 28 ("Black Monday"), the crash resumed, and on the next day, "Black Tuesday," the selling encompassed a volume of sixteen million shares. Almost $30 billion in stock values had been vaporized in these two days alone.

Except for a few brief rallies, the market continued to decline in November, reaching a temporary low point by mid-month. A modest rally took place in the early months of 1930, but then the downward trend resumed, albeit at a slower rate of decline.

ECONOMIC CONTRACTION, 1930

It is often observed by some that the Wall Street crash could not have "caused" the Great Depression because it took another three years for the full magnitude of the contraction to occur. And yet, whatever the abundant evidence that a recession was starting in the summer months of 1929, well before the crash, there can be little doubt that the crash accelerated and worsened this contraction.

John Kenneth Galbraith argued years ago that the precrash recession was not severe enough to account for the events that followed: "Only after the market crash," he wrote, "were there plausible grounds to suppose that things might now for a long while get a lot worse." It seems reasonable to suppose that the involvement—the extremely heavy involvement—of banks and corporations in the market speculation yanked immense amounts of money from those sectors when the stock values collapsed and that the resulting chain reaction did enormous damage. And the market losses of the wealthy cut back their luxury purchases, which had been such a driving force in the 1920s economy. Result: more cutbacks and layoffs.

The accelerated slump in such key indicators as prices, the index of industrial production, consumer spending, and the output of fuel continued in early 1930. Most important of all, however, were the figures for unemployment, which doubled from the crash to the spring of 1930: from roughly 1.5 million in October 1929, the total number of unemployed workers in the United States climbed to 3.2 million by March 1930. By the end of the year, that figure had surged again—to 4.3 million, more than 8.5 percent of the workforce. Parallel results were occurring in Britain: unemployment climbed from roughly 1 million to 2.5 million in 1930. At least Britain had unemployment compensation.

But the response of the British Labour government (headed by the socialist Ramsey MacDonald) was austerity, and the policy of Germany under the leadership of Chancellor Heinrich Brüning was the same. President Hoover was also committed to the policies of fiscal orthodoxy.

At first he acknowledged that America's economic contraction required counter-measures: he advocated increased public works spending. But as America's national income fell, the tax receipts of the federal government (as well as the state governments) plummeted. According to the standard financial methods, only deficit spending could maintain a public works agenda under such conditions, and Hoover drew the line at unbalancing the budget. Over time, this principle became something very close to an obsession for Hoover and it warped his other instincts accordingly. He retreated from confronting the Depression and issued a steady flow of unconvincing statements that the worst was over and recovery was well under way.

Millions of Americans knew from their everyday experience that Hoover's statements were nonsensical.

An outbreak of human misery in the United States that resulted from a meteorological and ecological disaster revealed the great change that was occurring in the outlook of President Hoover. In 1930 and 1931, a drought in the Mississippi valley offered a prelude of what the larger "Dust Bowl" would bring within a few short years. Farmers and sharecroppers in several states were unable to raise any crops, and the situation in Arkansas threatened mass starvation. Private charities such as the Red Cross were overwhelmed and calls for direct federal relief were heard in Washington. Threats of violence were beginning to circulate: farmers would rather seize food through the use of force than see their children go hungry.

When President Hoover addressed the situation, he denied that there was credible evidence that hunger or malnutrition existed in Arkansas. He also opposed direct federal relief, except for some seeds to plant crops in parched soil. And this was the man who won international fame during World War I and afterward for feeding the hungry. Herbert Hoover was internationally renowned as a great humanitarian and streets had been named in his honor.

Something changed Herbert Hoover—the erstwhile humanitarian hero and advocate of contra-cyclical public works—into a stubborn and rigid defender of orthodoxy, a pessimist who uttered optimistic nonsense that was clearly at odds with the observable facts, an angry dogmatist who exalted balanced budgets over any other consideration of public policy.

In truth, he had been torn between opposite proclivities for a long time. In 1922, he had authored a book titled *American Individualism*. More and more, Hoover seemed to have convinced himself as the Depression deepened that charity—the best of all forms of humanitarianism in his view because it flowed from spontaneous sharing—was infinitely preferable to other kinds of help. He said he wanted to prevent bureaucracy from "usurping" the spirit of community and initiative. To be sure, he promised that if other methods failed to bring sufficient relief, he would "ask the aid of every resource of the federal government." He stated this explicitly on February 3, 1931.

But Hoover never acknowledged that the time for such action was at hand. The moment never arrived when he was finally willing to provide direct federal relief.

So the question must be asked: Was Herbert Hoover in denial? Was he reluctant to probe more deeply into the extent of human suffering for fear that his previous statements might show him up as a man who didn't know what he was talking about? Consider these predictions from Hoover that were proven false by events. In August 1928 he had said that "we shall soon with the help of God be in sight of the day when poverty will be banished from this nation." In March 1930, Hoover said that the worst effects of the crash on unemployment would be over in sixty days. In May he said that "we have now passed the worst and with continued unity of effort shall rapidly recover." Was it therefore surprising that a man in this state of mind would shrink from a vigorous inquiry into the facts?

Stubbornness feeds on itself, and perhaps Mr. Hoover was averting his eyes from what he did not wish to believe could be true because he had *doubted* that it could be true and had predicted otherwise. Perhaps this is the time to observe that he was not a politician by nature—the presidency was the first public office into which he had been elected rather than appointed—and he prided himself on his expertise, his engineer's rationality—"when you know me better," he had once told General Peyton C. March, "you will find that when I say a thing is a fact it is a fact"—and his stern efficiency.

Somehow, this juxtaposition of traits made him reluctant to roll up his sleeves and confront the crisis in a manner consistent with his prepresidential reputation as an activist "whiz kid." One other point may be relevant: there are many signs that Hoover might have been suffering from psychological depression as the economic crisis played out.

By the end of his presidency he was claiming that the international dimensions of the crisis made it impossible for any nation on its own to fight its way back to prosperity single-handedly.

In November and December 1930, a major crisis in the banking sector started. The collapse of Caldwell and Company, a large financial holding company in the South, was followed by the failure of New York's Bank of the United States (a commercial bank founded in 1913). A total of 1,352 banks failed in 1930, and another 2,294 failed in 1931. Thus began a steady contraction of banking operations that culminated early in 1933 with a wave of bank failures so vast that it threatened to strangle American capitalism at its very source.

One of the most sinister and little understood facts about this banking contraction was the fact that it cut America's money supply by almost a third. In 1929, America's supply of bank-created money (created by the banks right out of thin air and then lent into use via checking accounts) amounted to $23 billion, according to the contemporaneous calculations of economist Irving Fisher. But only $4 billion in cash backed up these checking "deposits." Once bank panics started, the banks would quickly go into default and then the checks presented to be "cleared" would have no value. When this happened, a part of the money supply got destroyed. In this manner, the amount of circulating "check book money" shrank from $23 billion in 1929 to some $15 billion by 1933. (Please note that other financial calculations such as the size of "national income" and gross national product result in figures well above the numerical value of the nation's total money supply. The reason for this is that money changes hands many times in the course of any business day and facilitates multiple purchases; economists call the rate of this recirculation "velocity.")

"An essential part of this depression," wrote Fisher, "has been the wiping out of 8 billions of dollars of the nation's chief circulating medium. . . . This loss, or destruction, of 8 billions in check book money has been realized by few and seldom mentioned."

Unfortunately, the Federal Reserve did not act in this financial crisis as the "lender of last resort" as its founders had intended. One of the problems was the fact that many banks were not members of the Federal Reserve system.

HOOVER'S—AND AMERICA'S—CATASTROPHE

All through 1931, the economic contraction got worse: it fed on itself as the bank failures and factory layoffs continued. By the end of the year, the rate of unemployment had doubled once again; more than eight million people were out of work. This was approximately 15 percent of the workforce.

At the beginning of the election year 1932, this depression was the worst in American history and things began to turn violent. In March, three thousand furloughed workers of the Ford Motor Company marched on the plant, which was closed for retooling. Company guards and police fired into the crowd, killing four people and injuring many others. The rate of unemployment in greater Detroit was almost 50 percent and thousands had been evicted from their homes in a particularly harsh winter. The situation was just as bad in other cities; the rate of unemployment in Chicago was 40 percent.

Farmers wielding pitchforks and swinging nooses threatened lawyers at farm foreclosures in rural America. Miners in West Virginia smashed the windows of a local company store and seized food. A widespread feeling began to develop that the crisis might lead to conditions of outright revolution—a violent revolution that could overturn democracy itself. People can only be pushed so far before they get desperate.

An undated photograph by Brown Brothers depicting an American breadline early in the Great Depression of the 1930s.
Source: Courtesy of the Library of Congress.

But many people in America simply suffered during 1932 in silent agony. They were totally defeated, and they knew it.

All over the country, once prosperous middle-class families were being hurled into sudden poverty. They lost everything, including their homes. Many withdrew to the city dump, where they built crude shacks made of half-rotted lumber, corrugated metal, even cardboard. Many called these communities of shared misery "Hoovervilles."

As for food, they would scour the dumps for whatever the garbage trucks left. In Chicago, fifty men fought over a barrel of garbage in an alley behind a restaurant. In the countryside, families tried to subsist for months on dandelions and other weeds. Children were dying of starvation and malnutrition. Infant mortality in many parts of the country reached appalling levels. Many fathers, previously breadwinners, abandoned their families in shame and rode the rails as hoboes.

Some committed suicide.

Localities found ways sometimes to help the homeless and starving: police stations opened up their basements and allowed the homeless to wander in and get out of the cold. "Bread lines" and "soup kitchens" were created in some of the larger American cities; in New York by the end of 1931, an estimated 85,000 cheap meals were served every day in the eighty-two bread lines set up throughout the city.

There was finally some action in Washington: Eugene Meyer, chairman of the Federal Reserve Board, convinced Hoover that a federal corporation ought to be set up to make loans in a manner that would compensate for the limitations of the Federal Reserve System. And so with Hoover's support, Congress created this new entity, the Reconstruction Finance Corporation (or RFC), to lend money to smaller banks and other financial institutions. RFC sold bonds to the treasury, which in turn sold bonds to the public, to finance this operation.

But RFC loans did not succeed in containing the banking crisis, which continued to unfold. Some members of Congress tried to get the RFC to make loans beyond the banking sector, but Hoover disapproved. In fact, under orders from Hoover, all RFC loans were kept secret. In truth there were very few corporate takers for loans of any kind in many parts of the country, and for good reason: the business climate. Why borrow money, hire workers, and produce goods when the sales expectations were terrible? Where were the customers going to come from—where was the purchasing power to come from—with rates of unemployment in some parts of the country reaching 50 percent or more?

The Depression worsened and Hoover finally consented to an extremely limited relief measure: the creation of the Emergency Relief Administration (ERA), set up to make loans to states and localities to help them develop relief programs. But the scope and conception of this program fell woefully short of what was needed. ERA would be reorganized into FERA during the first year of FDR's New Deal and instead of loans to the states it would supply outright federal grants.

Businessmen were beginning to break ranks in regard to the Depression's severity. On the one hand, some, like the president of the National Association of Manufacturers, argued that the "business cycle" was a regular phenomenon that would run its course: "We have had at least seventeen of these cycles of depressions in the last 120 years," he wrote. Richard Whitney of the Stock Exchange promoted optimistic laissez-faire; he asserted that "the fact that we have let nature take its course may augur well for the ultimate prosperity of the country." But other business leaders decided it was time for a planned economy.

In 1931, Gerard Swope, the president of General Electric, advocated industry-wide trade associations that would force cooperation and planning and also institute unemployment compensation. His proposal hinted at the sort of program that the New Deal would institute with the National Recovery Administration (NRA). Henry L. Harriman, a utility executive who was elected president of the U.S. Chamber of Commerce in 1932, concluded that "we have left the period of extreme individualism. . . . Business prosperity and employment will be best maintained by an intelligently planned business structure."

Others in Washington had differing ideas in 1932. Congressman Wright Patman of Texas had introduced legislation to pay a retirement bonus to World War I veterans years before it was due. In 1932, Patman pushed this bill, and a veteran in Oregon named Walter Waters proposed a march of unemployed veterans on Washington to lobby Congress. Thus began the march of the so-called Bonus Expeditionary Force, or Bonus Army, which reached the outskirts of the nation's capital within several weeks. Along the way, they marched down the main streets of American towns holding out a large flag into which onlookers were invited to throw nickels and dimes to help the marchers buy gasoline and food.

The marchers camped out in some vacant buildings on Capitol Hill as well as on "Anacostia Flats" on the other side of the Anacostia River. Hoover was opposed to the bonus bill for a very simple reason: it would unbalance the budget. But his humanitarian side came to life when (according to some accounts) he directed the army to provide the marchers with surplus tents, blankets, and other supplies.

If these accounts are correct, Hoover took no public credit for this action.

The House passed the Patman bill on June 15, but the Senate, following Hoover's advice, defeated it. Then Congress adjourned.

The bonus marchers were stunned—completely at a loss. And so they shuffled back and forth in front of the U.S. Capitol for days on end in a protest gesture that they called the "death march." But then some of them began stoning the cars of senators. The District of Columbia police were called out and they clashed with the bonus marchers. Hoover, worried that disorder might spread throughout the federal enclave, ordered the army to move the marchers back to their camp in Anacostia Flats.

General Douglas MacArthur, the U.S. Army chief of staff, showed up in person with mounted troops—sabre-bearing cavalry—and light "Whippet" tanks. Promptly exceeding Hoover's orders, the general used tear gas to propel the marchers over the Anacostia bridge and ordered his troops to burn their camp. Newsreel photographers recorded this event, and their films were shown in movie theaters all over America. Newsreels were routinely shown as featurettes before the main attraction at the cinema.

Hoover, sunk deeply in gloom, never told the public that MacArthur exceeded his orders. And so millions of Americans blamed their incumbent president for treating the veterans who had served their country on the front in the Great War like bums when they were simply down and out—unable to feed their own families.

In the presidential election of 1932, Herbert Hoover was defeated in a landslide.

6

The Early New Deal and the Depression

THE GREAT DEPRESSION OF THE 1930S is the standard by which all other episodes of hard times in American history are usually judged: it is the standard of measurement in terms of severity, magnitude, suffering, and duration. It is in a class by itself as the worst depression in American history.

Likewise, the response to this depression in the New Deal of Franklin D. Roosevelt is (and will probably remain) a standard issue in disputes about economics, not only arguments about what ought to be done or not done about depressions but also disputes about fiscal and monetary policy in general. It is a touchstone for left versus right disagreements on the role of government. And it occupied a central place in generational memory for millions of Americans who lived through the Depression and were touched by the leadership of a man who was elected to the presidency four times in a row.

The key economic and ideological questions boil down to the following: (1) Did the New Deal in general make the American economic situation better or worse? (2) Did the New Deal hasten or retard recovery? and (3) What finally ended the Great Depression of the 1930s?

One of the problems in assessing the New Deal is the fact that it contained internal contradictions. It also changed and evolved, not least of all because of politics.

Overlapping these questions is the issue of Keynesian theory, which rose to a position of great influence in economic thinking by the 1950s only to be challenged and to some extent toppled by the 1970s.

APOCALYPTIC MOODS

By the time that Franklin Roosevelt assumed the presidency in March 1933, the Great Depression was seen by many as the worst national emergency since the Civil War. Gross national product was down by a third. The steel industry was operating at less than 12 percent of capacity. The unemployment level was approximately 23 to 24 percent, which meant that a fourth of the workforce was unemployed and almost thirteen million Americans and their families had no source of income at all. Over the winter of 1932–1933, the banking crisis had worsened to the point where the complete collapse of banking appeared to be possible.

In January 1933, the Senate Banking and Currency Committee held hearings on the commercial banking practices that were related to the Wall Street crash. Committee Counsel Ferdinand Pecora grilled bankers for days on end, exposing all sorts of sleazy, unethical, or downright ille-

"Depression."
Unemployed men on a park bench in Haddon Heights, New Jersey, in 1934. Photograph by Mark Benedict Barry.
Source: Courtesy of the Library of Congress.

gal behavior, such as the tricks that they used to avoid paying any income tax and the way they lent the bank's own capital to bank officers to use in Wall Street speculation. Charles Mitchell of National City Bank was reduced to a veritable wreck on the witness stand. And newspapers all over the country featured front-page coverage of the hearings.

Perhaps this was one of the key triggers to the massive wave of bank panics that began in February. Banks all over the country were closing their doors, the life savings of millions were disappearing, and the source of even normal investment funds was vanishing. One governor after another proclaimed a bank holiday, closing all the banks in the state. It began in Michigan. Just before FDR's inauguration, all the banks in New York and Illinois had closed their doors.

In light of the rise of European totalitarianism, some thought that American democracy itself might soon be toppled by a revolution or the rise of a dictatorship—or both. A friend reportedly told FDR that he would go down in history as the greatest American president if he succeeded. FDR is supposed to have replied that if he failed, he would be remembered as the last American president.

Some welcomed the idea of dictatorship because many college-educated people who read the Latin classics understood the term in the context of the ancient Roman republic, where in times of grave peril the elected leaders would lay down their powers and appoint one Roman who was universally respected for his wisdom, courage, and decency to save the state. Such was the dictator hero Lucius Quintus Cincinnatus, at least according to the account of the Roman historian Titus Livy. Alfred Landon, whom the Republicans would nominate to challenge FDR in 1936, said in 1933 that "even the iron hand of a national dictator is in preference to a paralytic stroke." Early in 1933, the film *Gabriel Over the White House* portrayed the religiously inspired heroism of a president (played by Walter Huston) who turns himself into a benevolent dictator and saves the country.

These moods account for the fact that in the first "hundred days" of FDR's first term, legislation was shouted through Congress with Republican leaders not only providing full support but actually calling for all debates to cease. One Republican congressman had this to say: "The majority leaders have brought us a bill on which I myself am unable to advise my colleagues, except to say that this is a case where judgment must be waived, where argument must be silenced."

DRASTIC—AND OPPOSITE—SOLUTIONS

Over the winter of 1932–1933, the Depression elicited far-reaching visions from theorists and oracles who saw the crisis as a grim (or providential) occasion for some drastic long-term changes in the American way of life.

Some of these visions amounted to a doctrine of permanent limitations. Many argued that the Depression was a sign that the economy, or even the industrial and urban process, had reached its final limits, that America had reached a permanent plateau beyond which further upward progress and outward expansion were impossible. For this reason, the popular culture of the 1930s was rife with visions of a "back to the land" movement, and various New Deal policymakers flirted with this idea to a greater or lesser extent. A writer named Ralph Borsodi laid out a vision of self-sufficient farmsteads, arguing that the eighteenth-century agrarian visions of Jefferson provided the only answer to the challenge of the Depression. In 1933, he wrote a book titled *Flight from the City*. In 1934, the film *Our Daily Bread*, produced and directed independently by King Vidor (hitherto a major director at MGM), portrayed a cooperative farm in which nearly everything is owned in common and simple pleasures make life direct, honest—"natural."

FDR himself was interested in subsistence homestead projects, and his wife, First Lady Eleanor Roosevelt, took charge of an experimental subsistence community created in Arthurdale, West Virginia, making it a pet project.

Whatever the optimistic or even utopian associations of these ideas—and the euphoric happy ending of *Our Daily Bread* is a must-see item for students of Depression-era cinema—there was a profoundly pessimistic side to this outlook, a sense that Americans had to live within a new and permanent set of reduced expectations. Even Harry Hopkins, a busy, fervent, and activist social worker who played a key role both as an adviser to FDR and as a New Deal administrator, sounded a defeatist note in 1937 when he wrote that it might be "reasonable to expect a possible minimum of 4,000,000 to 5,000,000 unemployed men even in future prosperity periods."

At the other extreme was the optimistic and expansionist view of John Maynard Keynes, who argued that austerity policies were nonsense and that only vigorous and unlimited efforts to create new super-abundance would end the depression.

"The voices which . . . tell us that the path of escape is to be found in strict economy and in refraining . . . from utilizing the world's potential production, are the voices of fools and madmen," Keynes wrote in 1932. "There will be no escape," he continued, "from prolonged and perhaps interminable depression except by direct state intervention to promote and subsidize new investment," adding that the scope of intervention had to be nothing less than what a nation would spend on total war: "In the past . . . we have not infrequently had to wait for a war to terminate a depression. I hope that in the future we shall . . . be ready to spend on the enterprises of peace what the financial maxims of the past would only allow us to spend on the devastations of war." In any case, he predicted "with assured confidence that the only way out is for us to discover some object which is admitted even by the deadheads to be a legitimate excuse for largely increasing the expenditure of someone on something."

William Trufont Foster, who had advocated similar ideas in America, reiterated his longstanding view that only massive federal spending on public works would replace lost purchasing power and end the Depression. "The only sound way speedily to stop the depression," he wrote, "is to increase total pay-rolls." Like Keynes, he made the comparison to wartime spending: "If anyone still doubts that our economic troubles are mainly mental, let him consider what would happen if the United States declare war today. . . . Some day we shall realize that if money is available for a blood-and-bullets war, just as much money is available for a food-and-famine war."

There were some within the leadership echelons of the New Deal who agreed—especially Marriner Eccles, a Utah banker who had read and considered the arguments of Foster carefully. FDR appointed Eccles chairman of the Federal Reserve Board in 1934. Moreover, Thomas Corcoran and Benjamin Cohen, attorneys who were to serve as advisers to a number of New Deal agencies, agreed that only vigorous and lavish federal spending to achieve full employment would end the Depression. But others, including FDR himself, were almost as committed to the principle of balancing the budget as Herbert Hoover had been. FDR was extremely reluctant to engage in deficit spending.

An alternative to deficit spending (Keynes's preferred fiscal method) could be found in the Greenback tradition, and the Great Depression of the 1930s provided an important occasion for espousing the issuance of legal tender/fiat currency. In 1934, economist John R. Commons wrote that "in order to create the *consumer demand*, on which business depends for sales, the government itself must create . . . new money and go completely over the head of the entire banking system by paying it out directly to the unemployed, either for relief or for construction of public works." This was essentially Jacob Coxey's proposal of 1894. But FDR was orthodox on monetary matters and he ignored such proposals.

The Keynesian method advocated massive and energetic action to create a new abundance. But to many New Dealers, such ideas seemed reckless and even appeared to smack of the behavior that had caused the Depression in the first place during the heedless Roaring Twenties, when money was hurled in every direction, scattered to the winds. A new stability—a new order and discipline—was what some New Deal policymakers recommended, a planned and prudently managed economy. Brain trust member Raymond Moley supported this approach. Some used the precedent of the World War I mobilization as the model for federal policies not only to guide the nation through a new emergency with policies of thrift and careful allocation but also to guarantee that things would never again get out of control—that Americans would never again have to suffer through a Great Depression because the people's elected leaders would keep things sane and sensible.

In 1932, a Greenwich Village oracle named Howard Scott touted a program he called "Technocracy" through which a scientific elite of expert planners would calibrate and adjust the industrial process to establish a new and permanent equilibrium. The economy, he argued, was akin to a vast machine, and it should hum along in steady patterns. Scott was a disciple of the economist Thorstein Veblen, who argued that industry, if freed from business control, would run perfectly under the guidance of expert engineers.

A related vision of sanity and equilibrium was the proposal of a bevy of economists in 1933 for the abolition of fractional reserve banking. The so-called Chicago Plan of 1933 was the brainchild of several economists from the University of Chicago, principally Henry C. Simons and Paul Douglas. They were quickly joined by the illustrious Irving Fisher, whose 1935 book *100% Money* argued that only government should have the sovereign power to create new money, that the government should buy up the securities of commercial banks with new United States Notes in order to bring their checking reserves to 100 percent, and that loans should originate only from the proceeds of savings and never from thin air. In 1934, Senator Bronson Cutting and Representative Wright Patman introduced legislation to create such a monetary regime.

THE ADVENT OF THE NEW DEAL

Franklin Delano Roosevelt, who threw Herbert Hoover out of office, had a blithe and easygoing personality, a droll and often mischievous sense of humor, and the power to charm people out of their senses. He could also inspire many millions with his stately and elegant oratory. These points are important because the FDR charisma, displayed right away in his legendary first inaugural address—which was broadcast live on the radio to a nation-wide audience—led to further radio performances, namely his folksy and intimate "fireside chats," that became a regular feature of American popular culture. Moreover, his breezy and whimsical give and take with the Washington press corps could be seen as well as heard by the public via newsreels at the movies.

His easygoing charm had a very significant intellectual corollary: he was as flexible on policy matters as Herbert Hoover had been rigid. Though the following conjecture is admittedly guesswork, it seems as if Hoover found it hard to reverse a policy decision because the act of publicly changing his mind would reveal that a previous decision of his had been wrong, and to Herbert Hoover this was nothing short of humiliating. He could not admit he had been wrong: this was somehow (for him) a matter of maintaining his self-esteem, a way of staving off a sense of shame. But for FDR, it was completely different: the act of changing his mind, changing policy, admitting that he had been mistaken—even joking light-heartedly about these facts—came easily and naturally, and such behavior not only endeared him to millions, it also facilitated the politics of changing course when necessary.

But FDR's flexibility had a more unfortunate side: he was deeply uncertain about economics, uncertain about what policies to choose, and so he gathered around him a bevy of advisers (some of them professors from Columbia University and elsewhere who became known as his "Brain Trust") who argued relentlessly about policies and urged courses of action that were totally at odds with each other. Their names became familiar to millions of Americans before very long: Raymond Moley, Rexford Guy Tugwell, Frances Perkins, Harry Hopkins, Harold Ickes, and Henry Wallace. Some were cabinet members, while others were aides and advisers. Perkins and Hopkins were social workers who had served FDR when he was governor of New York. And thousands of idealists—some of them law students and law clerks—flocked to Washington during the spring of 1933 to volunteer their ideas and get in on the excitement of the new mobilization. Washington's boardinghouses were jammed to overflowing.

FDR's technique was to generate a program that was—how to put it charitably?—eclectic. A less charitable way in which his critics would describe his method was to call it a self-contradictory mess, a concoction of half-measures that, though constituting an immense improvement over Hoover's methods, proved inadequate to the economic needs of the nation.

The point must be confronted squarely and definitively: the New Deal did not end the Great Depression, though it certainly contained its most destructive forces, an achievement of no small significance. It prevented things from getting even worse. Nonetheless, by the end of FDR's second term in 1939, the unemployment figures were almost as bad as they had been back in 1933. This does not necessarily justify a widespread conservative complaint—a commonplace claim among conservatives as early as 1935 and now a staple of conservative doctrine among many writers who partake of the *Wall Street Journal* sensibility—that the New Deal delayed an economic recovery that surely would have come much faster had it not been for FDR's bureaucratic "meddling."

This is not a convincing argument, and for a very simple reason: underlying business conditions bespoke a truly crippled private sector throughout the 1930s. The policies of the Federal Reserve under Marriner Eccles were to cut the prime interest rate to the vanishing point and create substantial amounts of new "credit" that were made abundantly available as venture capital for entrepreneurs. And year after year this new credit just sat there deep within the banking system, inert, unused because the sales prospects were dismal in many parts of the country.

The mood in the spring and early summer of 1933 was to rally around the buoyant leadership of the new president and give him almost everything he asked for. FDR encouraged this mood by positioning himself as a leader who would operate far above party or class. The bipartisanship of the early New Deal was to a large extent based on the fact that both parties were internally divided on matters of ideology, and "Progressive" Republicans, those who had supported FDR's illustrious relative and presidential forebear Theodore Roosevelt, were eager to support a "New Deal" that would extend the "Square Deal" that Teddy Roosevelt had promised in 1904.

Many Republicans were glad to cooperate with and even serve in the administration of FDR, Republicans such Harold Ickes, who was secretary of the interior, and Senator George Norris of Nebraska. The Republican roots of the New Deal went deep because even First Lady Eleanor Roosevelt—an activist figure in her own right who published a syndicated column, "My Day," throughout the 1930s—had been brought up as a Republican when, as a young lady and debutante, she was frequently known as Theodore Roosevelt's niece. It is true that in the 1920s she became a Democratic Party activist. But in general terms she remained a "Lincoln Republican," especially in her advocacy of black civil rights throughout the 1930s. In doing this, she helped to change the Democratic Party, and so did Republican Harold Ickes, a member of the Chicago chapter of the NAACP.

THE FIRST HUNDRED DAYS: BANKING LEGISLATION

In the spring and early summer of 1933, the New Deal emerged as an exuberant and almost joyous outburst of new legislation, new agencies, new policies, and new initiatives. It was a thrilling time for many, an interlude of passion and hope. But the first priority was rescuing the banks.

After FDR called Congress into an immediate special session, he declared a national "bank holiday." Then he and his advisers, together with some key members of Congress, threw together the Emergency Banking Act of 1933, which provided for reorganizing and reopening banks via a multistage process through which the comptroller of the currency (an officer of the Treasury Department) and his staff would

(1) examine and analyze the affairs of troubled banks and then develop arrangements to reestablish their solvency in return for changes in their operating methods, (2) extend credit to deserving banks by having the Reconstruction Finance Corporation (RFC) purchase shares of their stock, and (3) direct the Federal Reserve to extend more credit and furnish an expanded issue of Federal Reserve Notes to member banks. FDR explained these actions to the public in a calm and reassuring "fireside" chat on the radio.

The RFC, now under the leadership of Texas banker Jesse Jones, bought bank stock to save troubled banks instead of lending them money. By improving their capital position (instead of increasing their debt liabilities via loans), Jones gave the federal government a say in how the banks would function. Indeed Jones, himself a banker, made RFC in essence a public bank because he was also willing to advance credit to nonfinancial institutions.

Additional early action required citizens and banks to turn over gold to the federal government to shore up the treasury's gold reserve and reduce hoarding. The gold, to be remitted via banks to the Federal Reserve, would be exchanged for currency. Then the Federal Reserve would give the gold to the treasury in exchange for gold certificates. This was the first step in a multiyear process that, for reasons soon to be explained, would put an end to gold coinage and create the great federal gold depository at Fort Knox.

A second and more definitive Banking Act of 1933 (the Glass-Steagall Act) forced the separation of commercial and investment banking, thus establishing a firewall to prevent the destruction of money (when the fractional reserve process of money creation reversed itself) if the investment arms of banks engaged in bad practices that might threaten the savings and checking deposits of regular customers.

Most importantly, Glass-Steagall created on a short-term experimental basis the Federal Deposit Insurance Corporation (FDIC), which would insure not only savings accounts in commercial banks but also checking accounts through a process by which the banks would build up a cumulative insurance fund (to be administered by FDIC) and submit to the following *quid pro quo*: in exchange for this new federal protection, participating banks would agree to federal inspection to ensure sound banking practices. Significantly, FDR initially opposed the creation of FDIC, but then he changed his mind and thus established one of the long-term policy achievements of the New Deal.

In addition to these measures to prop up the financial sector and create future safeguards to protect it, Congress and the administration took significant action to relieve unemployment through job-creating projects—but always within the constraints of fiscal discipline. Lewis Douglas, FDR's budget director, was a militant defender of balanced budgets.

THE FIRST HUNDRED DAYS: JOB-CREATING PUBLIC WORKS

The most modest but captivating program to create new jobs in the early New Deal was a joint operation conducted by the War and Interior Departments, the Civilian Conservation Corps, or CCC, which put hundreds of thousands of young men to work doing reforestation and construction in America's national parks under military discipline. The maximum enrollment permitted by funding was 300,000, so the impact of the program on the unemployment problem as a whole was slight. The director, Robert Fechner, was a former labor union official.

More significant in scope was the Public Works Administration, or PWA, headed by Interior Secretary Harold Ickes. Originally called the Federal Emergency Administration of Public Works, PWA was funded in 1933 at $3.3 billion and it made both loans and grants to other federal agencies as well as to state and local governments. PWA funds were dedicated to construction of capital projects. Among the projects funded by PWA were public buildings, dams, schools, airports, hospitals, and even ships for the U.S. Navy. All work was contracted out to private sector companies.

Then there was the Tennessee Valley Authority, or TVA, a federally chartered corporation set up to build a multistate network of dams that would provide both flood control and hydroelectric power. TVA jurisdiction covered the following states through which the Tennessee River flows: Tennessee, Kentucky, Mississippi, Alabama, Georgia, North Carolina, and Virginia. TVA was initially administered by a board headed by Arthur E. Morgan (a visionary engineer), Harcourt Morgan (an agricultural scientist), and David Lilienthal (a protégé of Felix Frankfurter and an advocate of public power). The project was in some respects the brainchild of a progressive Republican, Senator George Norris of

Nebraska, and in conceptual terms it built directly on the precedent of Hoover Dam, which was still under construction at the time. The major difference was that the Hoover Dam built up an artificial lake—it captured the waters of the Colorado River—to provide irrigation to parched regions, whereas the TVA dams were intended to keep water out of a floodplain. But all of these dams produced hydroelectric power.

Most importantly, the more sweeping and in some respects radical features of TVA flowed directly from the longstanding interests of FDR himself, and especially his passion for conservation and land stewardship, a priority that he shared with his older cousin Theodore and that he demonstrated in the care that he lavished on his own Hyde Park estate.

It should also be mentioned that Hoover's Emergency Relief Administration (ERA) was transformed under New Deal auspices into the Federal Emergency Relief Administration (FERA), and instead of making loans to states and localities it gave direct grants to be used for the creation of jobs for unskilled workers as well as for direct relief. The agency was run by social worker Harry Hopkins.

All of these programs initiated in 1933 were designed to create tangible benefits—brick and mortar assets, reforestation, flood control, provision of inexpensive electricity to rural areas that were not served by private utilities, and the direct relief of hunger and misery. But most of all they were put in place to create new jobs and generate an economic stimulus.

THE FIRST HUNDRED DAYS: A PLANNED ECONOMY

But other signature New Deal programs created in 1933—even those that were dedicated if only in name to the goal of economic recovery— were founded according to very different premises. And the dynamics of these programs flowed at times in the opposite direction from the ones that were designed to stimulate economic expansion.

The most famous of these was the National Recovery Administration, or NRA, run at first by a retired general named Hugh Johnson. NRA was created to stabilize the economy, to promote "fair" competition instead of "destructive" competition, and to initiate industry-wide codes that would "stabilize" wages and prices.

Price "stabilization" was one of the supreme objectives of NRA, the presumption being that deflation and competitive price cutting were weakening the efforts of the private sector, thus stultifying recovery. For labor, section 7(a) of the National Industrial Recovery Act promised unions the right to collective bargaining in order to maintain decent levels of wages.

The idea was a planned economy. On June 16, 1933, FDR proclaimed that "if all employers in each trade now band themselves faithfully in these modern guilds—without exception—and agree to act together and at once, none will be hurt and millions of workers, so long deprived of the right to earn their bread in the sweat of their labor, can raise their heads again. The challenge of this law is whether we can sink selfish interest and present a solid front against a common peril."

The act that created NRA (the National Industrial Recovery Act, or NIRA) also created the PWA, and General Johnson, to his credit, presumed that a public works component would give the NRA program economic dynamism. But FDR (unfortunately) believed that running both NRA and PWA was beyond the capabilities of any single administration, so the programs were separated.

The NRA program caught the public's imagination for a while: its logo, a silhouetted blue eagle clutching thunderbolts, was displayed on flags and window posters, in the credit sequences of Hollywood movies, in newspaper mastheads, and along with the blue eagle logo was the slogan "We Do Our Part." NRA parades were held around the country in order to drum up support, and in New York City, no fewer than 250,000 people turned out to march down Fifth Avenue under blue eagle banners.

Though NIRA made participation compulsory for businesses participating in interstate commerce, Johnson, believing that the act itself might be unconstitutional, insisted on enticing compliance on a voluntary basis.

The program proved difficult to administer, cumbersome, and was tangled up in details. Its industry-wide codes were complicated and hard to enforce, and a great many small business owners complained bitterly about the program's effects on them. Industrialist Henry Ford refused to participate. Within a year, labor leaders were complaining from direct experience that the collective bargaining guarantees—in section 7(a) of the legislation—were meaningless. Over time, NRA became controversial, a flashpoint for conservative attacks on the overall "bureaucracy" of the New Deal. Perhaps most tellingly of all, there was little convincing evidence that NRA was contributing in any meaningful way to its nominal objective: recovery.

Equally controversial and problematical was the Agricultural Adjustment Administration, or AAA, an agency established within the Agriculture Department and run preliminarily by George Peek. As previously noted, Peek had worked with the War Industries Board during World War I and both he and his friend Hugh Johnson were tapped for their New Deal positions in part because of their experience in planning and allocation.

AAA was grounded in the decades-old demand for price supports by farmers. It sought to raise prices for farm commodities, thus constituting a direct extension of a Gilded Age agrarian agenda.

AAA instituted a processing tax on food, and the proceeds from this tax were channeled into a fund that would be used to pay farmers to cut back on production (though Peek initially favored sending the "surplus" abroad). In any case, the idea was to create an artificial shortage of farm commodities, thus, through supply and demand, raising prices. Critics of this program were vehement, sarcastic, and angry—very angry. They complained that AAA would do away with the problem of hunger in the midst of plenty by abolishing the plenty. AAA also worsened the unemployment situation: with planting cut back, fewer farm hands would be needed, so farm workers and tenant farmers were promptly thrown out of work and off the land.

The Agricultural Adjustment Act of 1933 was the result of decades' worth of agitation by agrarian reformers, some of whom could remember the National Farmers Alliance and Industrial Union, the crusades of the Populist Party, and the 1896 "free silver" candidacy of William Jennings Bryan. Many had lobbied very hard for the McNary-Haugen bill of 1927.

Significantly, the legislation that created AAA went far beyond the goal of raising farm prices: it sought to "devalue the dollar." The reasoning behind such efforts, which originated in the 1870s, was described in a previous chapter of this book. The result in 1933 was a far-reaching campaign by FDR—counterintuitive to the point of incomprehensibility by today's standards—to seek inflation as a national goal.

To be sure, FDR acknowledged the concerns of some advisers (such as Rexford Guy Tugwell) who worried about the stultifying effect on recovery if higher prices should diminish aggregate purchasing power. Tugwell was especially worried about the NRA codes. And yet FDR took an openly inflationist line when it came to AAA policies and to monetary policy in general. To the consternation (and alarm) of some financial conservatives, FDR forthrightly embraced the goal of devaluing the dollar in April 1933 and he stated that he might be in favor of taking the United States off the gold standard. Budget Director Lewis Douglas, a militant advocate of strictly balanced budgets, retrenchment, austerity, and financial orthodoxy in general, predicted nothing less than the fall of Western civilization if FDR carried out his intentions. Douglas's days in the administration were numbered. A former congressman, he resigned late in 1934.

The Agricultural Adjustment Act gave the president all sorts of authority to tinker with the monetary base through adjustments to the coinage and also through the issuance of legal tender currency. Though FDR demurred in the creation of Greenbacks, he responded to the coinage provisions of the AAA bill with gusto. Most of these provisions were included in the "Thomas Amendment" to the Agricultural Adjustment Act, an amendment introduced by Senator Elmer Thomas of Oklahoma.

The program began in 1933 with some federal gold purchases and it continued in the following year with both a new silver purchase act and with the far more consequential Gold Reserve Act of 1934.

The gold-buying scheme—arguably one of the most quixotic of the New Deal's efforts—was espoused by economists George Warren and Frank Pearson, who were almost universally known at the time as the "gold dust twins." The idea was to have the federal government purchase gold above the world price, thus theoretically devaluing the dollar relative to gold, which would supposedly weaken the purchasing power of the dollar. But the desired inflationary effect did not result by the autumn of 1933.

Therefore, a more comprehensive policy was approved by Congress in 1934, with heavy support from the congressional delegations of the farm states. In the Gold Reserve Act of 1934, gold coinage was terminated. Per the policy already initiated in 1933, all gold in private possession (with a few exceptions for coin collectors and others) was exchanged for currency (via banks) and then (via Federal Reserve Banks and the Treasury Department) sent into permanent storage in the new gold depository to be built at Fort Knox. With the nation's gold supply now largely melted into bullion and sequestered in federal possession, the president was given authority to set a new "gold weight" for the dollar, which would thenceforth be valued at no more than 60 percent of its previous value in the ounces of gold that had previously constituted a minted gold dollar.

The dollar was "devalued."

These schemes were anathema to everyone for whom higher prices were bad news. The departure from the gold standard prompted some reactions among the wealthy that approached hysteria. Moreover, the logic behind these policies was hard for average citizens to understand. In the long run, however, the cessation of gold mintage—when combined later on with the cessation of silver purchases by the 1960s—abolished the precious metal basis for the U.S. money supply, a shift with major implications, some of them positive, because the long-term result was to place no effective limit on the scope of money creation in America. Even today, however, the implications of these facts are understood by very few Americans.

One more price support agency was created in the autumn of 1933: the Commodity Credit Corporation (the "other" CCC, which should not be confused with the Civilian Conservation Corps). The Commodity Credit Corporation, a stand-alone entity at first—another creation of RFC under the brilliant leadership of Jesse Jones—was later transferred to the Agriculture Department. It was one more direct application of an idea that was first proposed in the Gilded Age. In this case it flowed directly from the program of the National Farmers Alliance in the 1880s: in return for crop collateral, which would be pulled off market and stored, the corporation would extend long-term and low-interest loans to rural buying and selling cooperatives.

As previously noted, this policy was instituted on a very small scale in some earlier programs that Republicans had created in 1923 and 1929. Indeed, the first of the federal farm loan acts had been passed under Woodrow Wilson in 1916. By the 1950s, the work of the Commodity Credit Corporation was a mammoth undertaking, and agricultural price supports had long since become a staple of American political life by the Eisenhower era.

All of these New Deal measures were in simultaneous operation by the autumn of 1933. While some of them had prevented the Depression from getting worse, a full-fledged recovery was not taking place. The job-creating programs of CCC and FERA were very limited in scope, the TVA was merely regional in its impact, and PWA was being administered so slowly and cautiously by Harold Ickes—not least of all to insulate himself and his agency from charges of wasteful spending and financial boondoggles—that unemployment remained quite high.

With another harsh winter impending, Harry Hopkins convinced FDR that a major new job-creation program was in order. So in November 1933, the CWA—the Civil Works Administration—was launched.

By January 1934, CWA had created over four million new jobs, which, when added to the slowly expanding work of PWA, had a major economic impact. Working directly under federal auspices but in close cooperation with states and localities, CWA constructed or repaired 500,000 miles of roads, built 40,000 schools and over 3,000 playgrounds and athletic fields, and over 1,000 airports.

But CWA unbalanced the budget, which made FDR very nervous. Both Budget Director Lewis Douglas and Treasury Secretary Henry Morgenthau Jr. (a close personal friend of FDR's) pushed incessantly for balanced budgets. So the president sought to wind the program down as quickly as possible; by March 1934, CWA was defunct. "Nobody," said FDR, "is going to starve during the warm weather," and he warned that such projects should not "become a habit with the country."

We will never know whether large-scale economic recovery might have happened in 1934 if FDR had been willing to consider keeping CWA in operation for the better part of the year. But when the program shut down and its workers were shoved right back into unemployment, the politics of national unity that had characterized the early New Deal became a thing of the past and a new and turbulent phase of both the New Deal and the Great Depression set in.

The New Deal would continue to evolve, but now in a national atmosphere of anger and turbulence, as clashes of left versus right destroyed the previous year's consensus. In 1934, as FDR and his team began working on new legislation to create the Securities and Exchange Commission (SEC) and the Federal Housing Administration (FHA), both of which were to have some profound effects on American life in the long term, labor violence broke out around the country, radical reformers emerged who would challenge FDR for leadership—one of them intended to do nothing less than challenge him for renomination by the Democratic Party in 1936—and extreme surges of hope, anger, and (in some cases) terror swept over American life.

7

1934—A Year of Fear and Rage in America

AS PREVIOUSLY STATED, we will never know what might have happened if FDR had been willing to keep his new Civil Works Administration (CWA) in operation. But a tragic comparison suggests what might have happened.

Adolf Hitler took over in Germany in 1933, and among his first acts was a massive and sustained attack on unemployment, abetted by unlimited money creation by the Reichsbank. By the end of 1935, unemployment in Germany had shrunk to the vanishing point and without significant inflation. Hitler did it through extravagant spending on public works, most famously the Autobahn system. The Great Depression was over in Germany by 1936.

John Maynard Keynes corresponded with FDR in 1934, but the Keynesian fiscal method, deficit spending, was as hateful to Franklin Roosevelt as it was to many millions of other supporters of the balanced budget principle. But a very different method existed, the method that economist John R. Commons suggested in 1934, the direct creation of debt-free legal tender money, Greenbacks—to be spent "off budget" because the money after all would not constitute "revenue" that would have to be balanced against expenditure in technical accountancy—to fund federal spending without costing anybody anything.

Does this seem like a fanciful suggestion? Support for Greenback issuance existed in Congress as proven by the legislative record: the Thomas amendment to the Agricultural Adjustment Act of 1933 had authorized FDR to create and then spend $3 billion worth of United States Notes, albeit to buy back federal bonds, thus reducing national debt while expanding the money supply. FDR ignored this particular provision of the Thomas amendment. But the principle held good for time-tested reasons, not least of all in response to a national emergency, the very reason why Congress had passed the first Legal Tender Act in 1862: to save the Union.

Moreover, by 1934, after Congress had passed the Gold Reserve Act, there would be no question of redeeming new United States Notes in gold coin, for gold coinage was being abolished. The new Greenbacks would simply continue to circulate as legal tender currency—"fiat currency"—whose value might fluctuate up and down but whose legitimacy was firmly grounded in case law. The constitutionality of the Legal Tender Act had been upheld by the Supreme Court in the 1871 case of *Knox v. Lee*. The majority opinion, which was written by Justice William Strong, affirmed that "if Congress may issue a currency as an appropriate means to lawful ends, it may, in its discretion, give to that currency few, many, or all of the faculties of money. The main objection to this mode of reasoning is that it goes very far. So it does."

A macroeconomic fact that was previously noted is germane and bears repetition: because the U.S. money supply had contracted by approximately 40 percent since 1929 (at least according to the calculations of Irving Fisher), there was ample justification in 1934 for doubling the money supply by direct federal action.

And this, by the way, would be the method by which the United States would pay its way to victory in World War II a decade later: the monetary base would be doubled by 1945—thus providing the basis for war bond purchases by banks as well as by the public—but it was done in the orthodox manner of fractional reserve banking, through which it was the Federal Reserve, and not Congress, that created new money, a fact that most Americans failed to understand at the time because economists seldom explained it, at least in terms that lay readers could follow.

It appears from the evidence that FDR was among the many millions who never fully grasped the fundamentals of money and banking, as a wartime interview suggests.

During World War II, as the money supply of the nation was doubled through the deeply hidden methods of "the Fed," FDR discoursed with a group of reporters on the subjects of war finance, economics, and the nature of money in general. The interview was filmed. In his charming manner, the president joked with the reporters as follows, alluding to some arguments from a mysterious and unnamed textbook: "Cost of production—the stock argument of the stars. A control of prices by that means is inarguable, and with scientific money and the prevention of combines and monopolies, practically impossible. Another great thought." Reporter: "What book is that?" Roosevelt, laughing: "I don't know!" Then he continued: "The possessor of money is entitled to a certain amount of worth as divided by money. Now don't forget that, divided by money."

THE DUST BOWL

Economic recovery did not occur during 1934, and so the political unity that had characterized the creation of the New Deal in 1933 collapsed. Instead of an atmosphere of patriotic teamwork, American politics dissolved into a bitter struggle of left versus right, and the old theme of class warfare emerged more powerfully than at any time since the 1890s. FDR was challenged and vilified by attacks from both left and right, and several of his challengers were demagogues whose politics could shift back and forth between left and right as opportunities permitted. Labor violence broke out in different parts of the country, and behind the struggles that were based in vested interests was a natural disaster of almost apocalyptic qualities—the Dust Bowl.

Collectively, these developments suggested a nation in decline, and some conjured with the notion that America was suffering a providential punishment along Old Testament lines.

The drought that struck Arkansas and adjacent states in 1930 recurred in late 1933 and then intensified in 1934. During the 1920s, the mass production of gasoline-powered tractors (such as the Ford Motor Company's "Fordson") prompted many farmers in the Great Plains to plow up prairie grasslands, hoping to convert them to cultivated acreage. A massive displacement of indigenous deep-rooted grasses occurred, and so in drought years nothing much was left to anchor dry soil during windstorms. On November 11, 1933, a huge dust storm devastated the Dakotas. Then on May 9, 1934, an immense two-day dust storm spread across the Great Plains, and literally millions of tons of soil became airborne in particle form. The term "dust storm" is completely inadequate as a descriptive usage: these storms brought blackness at noon and the airborne filth could smother people to death, for which reason gas masks

Penniless dust bowl refugees near Bakersfield, California, in 1935.
Photograph by Dorothea Lange.
Source: Courtesy of the Library of Congress.

that were left over from World War I were distributed while supplies lasted. These storms reached all the way to the East Coast and beyond so that "red rain" fell on ships in the Atlantic Ocean.

By 1935, roughly half a million people in Texas, Oklahoma, and adjacent states were left homeless after dust storms literally buried their homes or made them totally uninhabitable. In any case, the drought made farming impossible in much of the affected area. And thus began the great migration of thousands of "Okies" who took to the road in obsolete and rundown automobiles piled high with people and possessions. They headed west to seek jobs and employment on the West Coast, where many of them would be greeted with immense hostility because their presence swelled the ranks of the unemployed. Others were reduced to the kind of peonage on southern California fruit ranches that was comparable to some of the worst conditions of sharecroppers in the South.

The spectacle of America—the land of "spacious skies and amber waves of grain"—being scourged in this manner brought a feeling of sickening anxiety that added to an overall mood of desperation and despair well outside of the prairie states.

STRIKES

As in the depression of the 1890s, the Great Depression of the 1930s elicited widespread labor management conflicts that led to some violence. The labor unrest during 1934 was symptomatic of a growing discontent on the left with the early limitations of the New Deal.

For a long time, the labor movement in the United States had been divided between the American Federation of Labor (AFL) and other unions whose leaders believed that more radical and determined methods were required to improve the lot of industrial labor. An extremely radical union, the Industrial Workers of the World (IWW), had arisen in the early 1900s, but its power was largely broken by the 1920s due to federal and state prosecutions of its leaders, especially during World War I, as well as by vigilantism, some of it murderous.

Less radical than the openly Marxist IWW were unions that rejected the AFL's craft guild approach in favor of industry-wide unions that included both skilled and unskilled workers. Such had been the case of the American Railway Union (ARU), founded by Eugene Victor Debs in the 1890s. Debs, of course, became more radical after the Pullman Strike was crushed and he had led the way in founding the American Socialist Party. And notwithstanding the decline of the IWW, some labor leaders in the early 1930s were Marxist and some of them even worked with the Communist Party USA. But other union leaders sought to distance themselves from any communist links.

By the end of 1933, labor leaders and rank-and-file industrial workers were concluding that the NRA's section 7(a), which supposedly protected their right to engage in "collective bargaining," was meaningless. When push came to shove, NRA provided little or no protection. On October 5, 1933, for example, a strike that was led by the Steel and Metal Workers Industrial Union in Ambridge, Pennsylvania, was broken up violently as police and vigilantes attacked union members. This attack on the union members was filmed, so there is little doubt about what happened.

In 1934 a number of militant leaders and organizations began to arise within the labor movement and the result was a new series of strikes as well as an organizational schism within the AFL that would lead to dramatic consequences within a year. One of the militant leaders was John L. Lewis, president of the United Mine Workers, who led seventy thousand Pennsylvania coal miners out on strike in the summer of 1934 and encouraged confrontations with employers in other industries that were notoriously "anti-labor," such as the steel industry.

Labor organizing was taking place in rural America as well.

Under the Agricultural Adjustment Act (AAA), the federal government paid a subsidy to farmers who agreed to cut back production. In the case of southern plantations, the owners were supposed to share this subsidy with tenant farmers and sharecroppers, but most, predictably, did not. In 1934, under prompting from Socialist Party president Norman Thomas, Arkansas labor organizers Harry Leland Mitchell and Clay East created the Southern Tenant Farmers Union (STFU), whose activities, while centered in Arkansas, spread to nearby states such as Oklahoma, Missouri, and Texas. A local businessman, H. K. Mitchell, supported the group. One of the notable features of the STFU was its racial inclusiveness; like the southern Populists during the 1890s, the leaders of the STFU reached out to both white and black sharecroppers and tenants. Their objectives: to force planters to share the AAA subsidies and reduce the evictions of tenant farmers.

The immediate result was a shocking wave of terrorism as planters used tactics reminiscent of the Ku Klux Klan to suppress the STFU: murders and floggings by nightriders spread across Arkansas, and labor leaders were the targets. One Arkansas sharecropper described the campaign of intimidation as follows: "We Garded our House and been on the Scout until we are Ware out, and Havent any Law to looks to, thay and the Land Lords hast all turned to nite Riding . . . thay shat up some Houses and have Threten our Union."

STFU leaders persisted in their efforts throughout the 1930s, sending representatives to meet with Agriculture Secretary Henry Wallace and engaging in sporadic strikes and protests. They achieved some victories, but almost all of them were quickly rolled back by new waves of terrorism, night riding, and threats of lynchings. A powerful member of the U.S. Senate from Arkansas, Joseph Robinson—otherwise a big supporter of the New Deal—interceded to thwart federal actions to protect the leaders of the STFU. The union's supporters within the AAA were shoved to the sidelines, even fired. FDR, for political reasons, was reluctant to challenge Robinson.

On the West Coast, a very different sort of labor management conflict broke out during the summer of 1934: a longshoremen's strike that threatened to shut down every port in California as well as a general strike in San Francisco that lasted for several days.

In March 1934, the East Coast leadership of the International Longshoremen's Association (ILA) was challenged by a radical union insurgency in California. On May 9, the radicals organized a strike in every West Coast port. Employers brought in strikebreakers, and pitched battles ensued in San Pedro, San Francisco, Oakland, and Seattle. Several strikers died in the course of these battles: they were shot down by company guards.

On July 5, fighting broke out between strikers and police in San Francisco. Strikers overturned police cars and police fired into crowds. Two men were killed, and California governor Frank Merriam called in the National Guard.

On July 14, the San Francisco Labor Council called for a general strike at the behest of several dozen unions whose members had voted to shut down commerce in the city—with the exception of food deliveries—in reprisal for the suppression of the dock strike. This general strike lasted for four days. It was broken in part by several vigilante raids on union halls; some of the vigilantes were protected by police and National Guardsmen who prevented interference. NRA director Hugh Johnson urged responsible union leaders to cleanse their movement and "run these subversive influences out from its ranks like rats."

But another reason why the strike subsided was the offer of federal mediation, which won a number of concessions for the strikers.

These battles on the part of organized labor in 1934 increased the militance and determination of radicals within the labor movement.

In October, the American Federation of Labor held its annual convention in San Francisco. John L. Lewis began an agitation that would lead to the creation of a tough new "Committee for Industrial Organization" to push the formation of industry-wide unions.

This committee would eventually evolve into a separate organization, the Congress of Industrial Organizations—the CIO—by 1938. Very soon, both Lewis and his followers would be powerful enough to influence congressional legislation and carry the labor movement to one of the greatest milestones in its development.

UPTON SINCLAIR AND "EPIC"

In September 1933, Upton Sinclair, the famous American novelist— famous as a "muckraker" who sought in the manner of Victor Hugo and Émile Zola to influence public opinion on behalf of good causes— made a startling announcement that would change the political climate more directly.

In 1933, this author changed his party allegiance. Sinclair for years had been a Socialist, a follower of Eugene Victor Debs. But in 1933 he registered as a Democrat and announced that he would run for the governorship of California the following year.

He released a booklet setting forth his program, a booklet with a captivating title: *I, Governor of California, and How I Ended Poverty: A True Story of the Future*. His slogan, "End Poverty in California," produced an equally captivating acronym: EPIC.

The "EPIC Plan" called on the state government to seize idle factories and farms if the owners fell behind in their payment of taxes. The state would then allow the unemployed to make use of these factories and farms, to turn them into cooperative communities dedicated to "production for use" instead of production for profit. Goods and services would be exchanged directly in most cases. But when a circulating medium was needed as an intermediary means of exchange, a new state agency, the California Authority for Money (CAM), would issue a "scrip" currency to facilitate transactions. No doubt this provision of the plan would have faced legal challenges because the federal Constitution forbids the states to issue money. But the Constitution of course can be amended. Two other new state agencies would be created: the California Authority for Land (CAL) and the California Authority for Production (CAP).

A less radical version of "production for use" had been launched in Ohio. Under this plan, the state *leased* idle factories for use by the unemployed, who would manufacture goods for barter or sale.

Sinclair's candidacy became a sensation with an influence far beyond California. He developed a massive support base and captured the Democratic gubernatorial nomination easily in August 1934. It bears noting that the San Francisco general strike had taken place just the month before.

Well before then, however, the grassroots Sinclair movement had a powerful momentum. Over eight hundred EPIC clubs had been formed throughout the state, and the campaign had produced an appealing iconography that exemplified the Fabian Socialist ideals of moderation, gradualism, and sweet reason. The EPIC emblem had a busy bee as its symbol and the EPIC campaign song was composed to be sung to a simple piano accompaniment. Gentle and powerful would be an apt description of Sinclair's charisma: a bookish-looking man in his fifties, he projected a confident intellectuality that prompted many people to look up to him as a teacher. Will Rogers called Sinclair a "darn nice fellow, and just plum smart."

Sinclair had some admirers in Washington too: Harry Hopkins, FDR's adviser and the administrator both of the FERA relief program and the short-lived CWA public works program, gave hints that he might be able to secure FDR's endorsement of Sinclair's candidacy.

But conservative leaders in California launched an opulently funded campaign to defeat Sinclair. Press barons William Randolph Hearst and Harry Chandler supported the incumbent governor, Frank Merriam, and, in addition to scathing editorials denouncing Sinclair, their papers perverted front-page coverage into editorializing as well. The *Los Angeles Times* ran a series of front-page articles quoting characters from Sinclair's novels out of context. These quotations appeared to portray the author as an enemy of religion, traditional family life, and common decency. Cartoons appeared with these articles and some of them labeled the "scrip" currency that Sinclair proposed "Sinc-liar" dollars. Editorials warned that if Sinclair won, tramps and vagrants would flock to California from all over the country, swelling the ranks of the unemployed and adding to the misery of the Depression on the West Coast.

Louis B. Mayer of MGM commissioned a series of nominally journalistic newsreels that were shown in movie theaters throughout the state. These newsreels featured interviews with California voters, interviews that were conducted by a nameless "impartial cameraman." These interviews used subtle (or not so subtle) tricks to portray Sinclair's supporters as gullible or simple minded.

Moreover, there were still enough traditional Democrats in California—Democrats disturbed to find their party dragooned into a socialistic campaign—to provide the basis for a third-party bid by Raymond Haight, who presented himself as a moderate alternative to the conservative Merriam and the radical Sinclair.

Despite fervent entreaties to FDR, including a face-to-face meeting at Hyde Park (FDR turned on the charm as usual, while committing himself to nothing), Sinclair never gained the president's endorsement. In the general election, Haight took enough votes away from Sinclair to throw the election to Merriam.

Despite Sinclair's defeat, the EPIC movement gained significant strength in the California legislature. But the defeat of Upton Sinclair, coming on the heels of the San Francisco general strike, underscored for many on the left the necessity of power-punching candidates who would take on the enemies of social uplift and defeat them on their own terms—through the use of raw power. And such a candidate had been emerging in the state of Louisiana, a candidate who meant to throw FDR out of office and occupy the White House himself.

HUEY LONG

Early in their marriages, Franklin D. Roosevelt, a law clerk born to a patrician Hudson Valley family and a cousin of the president of the United States, and Huey P. Long, a traveling salesman born to a moderately well-to-do farmer in north Louisiana, revealed their career plans to their wives.

Roosevelt told Eleanor that he would become president of the United States. He would replicate the career milestones of his famous older fifth-cousin Theodore: service in the New York legislature, appointment as assistant secretary of the navy, election as governor of New York, vice president of the United States, and then the presidency. With a few minor deviations from the sequence of this plan (he ran as a vice presidential candidate in 1920 before his election to the governorship), FDR made most of it come true.

Long told his wife that he would be elected to a secondary state office, win a reputation as the champion of the weak and powerless, run for the governorship of Louisiana, lose the first time but make a name for himself, win the governorship by a landslide the second time around, use the power of the state to elevate the weak and the downtrodden, build a national power base after winning a seat in the U.S. Senate, and then become president.

It all came true, just as Huey Long had foretold—until he was shot dead by an assassin in September 1935. If Long had lived, the history of the Great Depression, World War II, and the twentieth century in general might have been very different.

He was always controversial—to put it mildly. Though his "countrified" humor and his clowning around like a hillbilly—humor that endeared him to vast numbers of working class followers—made some dismiss him, there were others who regarded him as a genius. He was clearly a man of supreme audacity, an orchestrator of power. According to the different standards of reckoning victory in different sorts of fights, some might say that Huey Long never lost a fight, just as Julius Caesar never lost a single battle. Except that both lost a final battle when assassins cut them down.

Elected governor of Louisiana in 1928 (the same year that FDR was elected governor of New York), Huey Long built a mighty political machine, and through bribery he rammed many bills through the legislature, bills creating a massive program of road paving, bridge building, and other public works. He constructed a new campus for Louisiana State University, built a soaring skyscraper capitol building in Baton Rouge, and commissioned an ultra-modern airport for New Orleans. He opened hospitals for the poor and gave free textbooks to school children. And he forced the big corporations and the wealthy to pay for it. "Every Man a King" was his motto, and he called himself the "Kingfish."

Critics immediately called him a corrupt power monger and the point cannot be denied: his tactics were ruthless. Defenders, however, said that Long was just fighting fire with fire, combatting the existing political machine (an alliance of oil corporations and a hugely corrupt New Orleans–based network of political cronies, the "Old Regulars" or "Choctaws") and forcing on them a simple choice: join forces with his new and more powerful machine or be wiped out of existence, at least politically.

He deducted money from the salaries of people whom he rewarded with state jobs and then he used this slush fund for various purposes, sometimes to influence members of the legislature to do his bidding. All transactions were for cash and all decisions were made face to face, with nothing in writing.

Critics called him a dictator and a Southern demagogue to boot. He was certainly a rabble-rouser—he projected a powerful down home charisma—but unlike other Southern demagogues he seemed to have no discernable prejudices; he did not engage in race baiting, he eschewed any references to the Confederate cause, he made advisers of Jews and Catholics, and he almost ran the Ku Klux Klan out of his state. "Don't liken me to that son of a bitch," he once remarked to those who tried to compare him to Adolf Hitler. He compared himself to Frederick the Great.

Some believed that he was trying to revive the cause of Southern populism.

In 1930, he got himself elected to the Senate, and he ran his state by remote control from Washington, D.C., because the new governor was an obedient and worshipful henchman.

Though he swung his support to FDR in the election of 1932, he began to criticize the New Deal immediately. He announced a proposal to end the Depression: a massive redistribution of wealth, essentially a cap on fortunes to be enforced through a steep escalation of the income tax, and the creation of a welfare state through which no one would ever live in poverty again. He took to the radio like FDR, but his persona was completely different from the president's genial manner: Long was on the attack and he went after bloated plutocrats whose greed had been ruining the country. He encouraged the formation of "Share Our Wealth" clubs, and by 1934 there were hundreds of them.

Let a brief sample of his oratory suffice for connoisseurs of the art, a sample that shows his combination of humor, denunciation, and prophecy.

In December 1934, he addressed some young Senate staffers at the National Press Club. The presentation was filmed. He said that God had blessed the Americans with abundance, only to have the rich grab most of it away. He invoked the voice of the Lord: "'Come to my feast,' he said to 125 million American people! But Morgan—and Mellon—and Baruch—and Rockefeller—have walked up and took 85 percent of the victuals off the table. . . . Now what's Morgan and Baruch and Rockefeller and Mellon going to do with all that grub? They can't eat it. They can't wear the clothes, they can't live in the houses."

His voice rising and his arm extended with finger pointed, he began with some exclamations that broadened into a rolling incantation: "Give 'em a yacht! Give 'em a palace! Send 'em to Reno and give 'em a new wife when they want it, if that's what they want. But when they've got everything on God's loving earth that they can eat and they can wear and they can live in—and all that their children can live in and wear and eat, and all that their children's children can use . . ." His tone softened: it was time to take back enough "grub" to "feed the balance of the people."

Huey made it clear that he would challenge FDR for the Democratic nomination in 1936. His strategy appeared to be based on the way in which Theodore Roosevelt had ruined things for William Howard Taft back in 1912: Huey would challenge FDR, lose at the convention, but then form a third party that would rob FDR of sufficient votes to throw the election to some sort of hapless Republican. As the depression lingered, Huey would transform Louisiana into an economic utopia. Then in 1940 he would offer his state as a model for all America—and take over.

Just after his death, Huey's book *My First Days in the White House* rolled off the press. Adorned with extremely droll cartoons by an artist who signed her work "Cléathe," the book painted a comic scenario through which Huey's messianic urge would energize all except a recalcitrant few. He would bring Hoover, FDR, Al Smith, and others into his cabinet. He would give the job of redistributing the wealth to wealthy philanthropists, who would then convince their fellow plutocrats that money was a paltry form of glory compared to the true "sport of kings," the splendid work of healing the body and soul of a nation. At the end of the book, Huey takes a trip across America by train, and at every single stop throngs of adoring Americans greet him with choruses of thanks.

A very different book was published almost simultaneously: a novel by Sinclair Lewis titled *It Can't Happen Here*. In this nightmare yarn, a politician clearly modeled on Long is elected president. Then the sheep's clothing (such as it was) is tossed aside, and the totalitarian monster is revealed. Overnight, America is transformed into a fascist state, complete with concentration camps, barbed wire, whips, and a semi-official army of "M.M.s" ("Minute Men") who correspond to Hitler's "S.S."

In 1935, after the Supreme Court began to topple New Deal agencies, a reporter asked Long what he would do if the Supreme Court toppled a "Share Our Wealth" law. That's simple, Huey Long replied: "We'll just get a bill passed adding the whole membership of Congress to the Supreme Court and try the case again."

As early as the autumn of 1934, Huey's strategy was clear. He might have pulled it off, and we will never know what would have happened if he had lived. FDR was frightened of Long, and a political war between them was brewing by the end of 1934.

FATHER COUGHLIN, FRANCIS TOWNSEND, THE MIDTERM ELECTIONS, AND THE LEFTWARD TILT IN THE OFFING

Other political leaders with a public following began to challenge FDR in 1934. One of them, a Catholic priest named Charles Edward Coughlin, had at first been an FDR supporter.

"Father Coughlin," a Canadian-born priest who settled in Detroit in the 1920s, was transferred several times within the archdiocese. In 1926 he was assigned to the new Shrine of the Little Flower in Royal Oak, Michigan. He began to broadcast a radio show after some cross burnings by the Ku Klux Klan at his church, and the broadcasts were picked up nationally. In 1930, his broadcasts became more political and very angry. He attacked both the greed of Wall Street and the tyranny of Communism, adopting a populistic advocacy of the common man's economic needs.

An early supporter of FDR, he declared that "the New Deal is Christ's deal." But in 1934, he began to attack FDR as the stooge of Wall Street and he attacked "money changers," bankers, usurers, and profiteers. He founded a new organization, the National League for Social Justice, and, as his radio following increased, he began to flirt with Huey Long.

Coughlin was one of those ideological figures whose loyalties can migrate from left to right, and, whatever the leftist elements in his initial worldview, he turned toward Fascism and anti-Semitism as the decade played out. By 1934, his rhetoric was already wildly erratic and inconsistent.

FDR took note of Coughlin's popularity, and the possible development of a Long-Coughlin axis troubled him. Using intermediaries such as Joseph Kennedy, he tried to pacify Coughlin if he could.

Yet another freelancing advocate became a force to be reckoned with by 1934: Francis Townsend. An elderly physician, he developed a proposal to end the Depression by having the federal government establish an old-age pension system that would act to revive the economy by requiring elderly recipients to spend their payments right away. The introduction of this idea was modest enough: Townsend simply wrote it up in 1933 as a letter to the editor of a local California newspaper. By 1934, however, the proposal, known simply as "the Townsend Plan," began to spread like wildfire. A friend of Townsend's, a California real estate agent named Robert Earle Clements, used effective promotional techniques to push the Townsend Plan in other states. By 1935, the Townsend movement was formidable.

Of all those exerting pressure on FDR, perhaps Townsend was the most influential, though his program struck some New Dealers as dogmatic and its finance methods seemed to many unrealistic. Still, Roosevelt had concluded that a second wave of New Deal legislation was needed to preempt the menace of Huey Long in 1936. The Townsend Plan dovetailed in some respects with a principle that was dear to Roosevelt's heart because his presidential cousin Theodore Roosevelt had advocated it in 1912: social security. The idea of old-age pensions supported and provided by the state had been pioneered in Otto von Bismarck's Germany during the 1880s, then adopted in Great Britain between 1910 and 1911 through a liberal-conservative coalition in which both David Lloyd George and young Winston Churchill played prominent roles.

In June 1934, FDR convened a new "President's Committee on Economic Security" to study alternatives for such a system. The committee was chaired by Secretary of Labor Frances Perkins.

The churning events of 1934 produced results in the midterm elections that laid the groundwork for bold action in 1935: the voters were impatient with the pace of recovery and so the new Congress they elected would be ready to push through a series of measures the following year that might never have been adopted in any other period. The party in power often suffers in midterm elections. Not this time: Democrats won control of the Senate by more than two-thirds, and in the House they would dominate the Republicans by 322 to 103.

But this was just the beginning of the leftward tilt in the politics of FDR's New Deal. "Boys," said Harry Hopkins to his fellow liberals in the administration, "this is our hour. We've got to get everything we want—a works program, social security, wages and hours, everything—now or never."

A NEW FURY ON THE RIGHT

Notwithstanding the impatience with FDR's leadership by people on the left—discontent with his failure to make the NRA enforce promises about "collective bargaining," his failure to make the AAA keep its promises to sharecroppers, his failure to give any meaningful help to Upton Sinclair, his failure to sustain the public works spending long enough (by the standards of people like Harry Hopkins)—a growing discontent on the right was becoming apparent by late summer 1934, when the Liberty League was founded.

A bipartisan conservative organization, the Liberty League was heavily funded by several wealthy families, notably the DuPonts. Its complaint was that the New Deal was retarding economic recovery through bureaucracy, abridging the rights of private property in a manner that was unconstitutional, taking the United States down the path to collectivism, Communist style. Press baron William Randolph Hearst, after receiving a private audience with Adolf Hitler in 1934, praised the Nazis for staving off Communism. By 1935, Hearst was busily trying to foment a "red scare" in America.

It seemed to make no difference to many conservatives that the Communist Party USA had denounced FDR from the beginning as a capitalist stooge and that the New Deal's first priority in 1933 had been to save the commercial banking system. None of that seemed to matter to the members of the Liberty League.

There was something else going on in upper-class circles: an angry fear that some basic prerogatives of wealth were under assault or under threat. The regulation of Wall Street via the creation of the Securities and Exchange Commission, the confiscation of gold through the Gold

Reserve Act of 1934, the promise of support to organized labor, and the vilification of financiers as the people who were truly to blame for the Depression all corroded the sensibilities of those who, in the 1920s, were regarded by many as the pillars of modern society.

By 1934, certain magnates were calling FDR a traitor to his class. But this was just the beginning. An extravagant "hate Roosevelt" campaign was spreading in America's boardrooms and country clubs, a campaign that began to circulate obscene "Roosevelt stories" and "FDR jokes" that came to the president's attention. Many of these jokes (as recorded in memoirs from the period) were luridly sexual. This too began to push the president decisively leftward. He became extremely angry.

There were even allegations by Marine Corps General Smedley Butler that agents of some members of the Liberty League had approached him with blandishments and bribes in the hope that he would lead a fascist coup that would topple FDR and establish a dictatorship.

8

The Politics of Class Conflict
During 1935 and 1936

AFTER THE TURMOIL OF 1934, the politics of hard times veered into a prolonged confrontation between left and right that was reminiscent in some ways of what happened in the 1890s. The difference was the presence this time of a leader who was willing (at least on occasion) to act *on behalf* of the stricken instead of lashing back at protests as Grover Cleveland had done.

The prod of challenges from the left such as the gubernatorial candidacy of Upton Sinclair combined with the threat of a Huey Long presidential quest pushed FDR into a second round of legislation that was just as consequential (if not more so) than the first round had been. Rightwing attacks by the Liberty League (both explicit attacks and the underground hate campaign) combined with a Supreme Court decision that toppled a New Deal program (the NRA) made the ideological dialectics of Great Depression politics increasingly stark.

In 1936, the presidential election became a veritable plebiscite on FDR and the New Deal. The incumbent president defended his record and attacked his opponents with a populistic rhetoric worthy of Huey Long. And this was a consequential development, a new departure for FDR in a great many ways.

The point bears emphasis: there was a significant amount of conservatism in the New Deal, especially in its earliest and formative incarnation. FDR had sought to create a kind of "middle way" in his statecraft, a synthesis of conservative and liberal values, a fact that he acknowledged quite explicitly on at least one occasion in 1936.

But the conservative side of the New Deal—its dedication to fixing, repairing, and propping up the status quo instead of changing it radically—was invisible to conservatives in the 1930s and afterward. The tendency of American conservatism from the 1870s onward to embrace laissez-faire made people on the right almost blind to the ways in which FDR had been acting in the time-honored tradition of the faithful country squire, the Tory steward who averts revolutionary change by wisely adjusting the balances of power in society.

With right-wing assaults in full cry and with Huey conveniently dead and buried, FDR began to speak more and more in the tones of left-wing outrage, pouring out his defiance at conservative ingrates who had little or no understanding of what he had been doing for them and their interests.

He regarded them as vicious and malevolent fools. And he would make them pay the price for their folly.

THE EXPANSION OF THE NEW DEAL IN 1935

The huge burst of legislation in 1935 would change American life forever. Many books have been written on each individual item in this legislative wave. For the purposes of this study, a concise presentation will suffice, though a number of programs enacted in 1935 will bear on the question of how the Depression of the 1930s—this greatest of all episodes of hard times in American history—came to an end.

Some of the new legislation was aimed directly at promoting recovery. Other new laws passed in 1935 were designed to prevent depressions in the future. Others responded to the struggles of left versus right. Still others were reforms of different kinds that proponents pushed forward for a simple reason: they saw a chance to promote their favorite projects in this "now or never" climate of legislative opportunity.

THE WORKS PROGRESS ADMINISTRATION

In 1935, FDR and Congress decided to spend $5 billion on creating new jobs—jobs for three and a half million unemployed workers. Because the total number of unemployed in 1935 was roughly ten million (down from approximately thirteen million in 1933), this was obviously not an effort to achieve full employment immediately. It was a program to provide a significant amount of work relief in the hope that the wave of new hiring would act as an economic stimulator. There was great debate both in and out of Congress as to whether $5 billion was too much or too little.

In any case, the appropriation would be split between the existing Public Works Administration (PWA) that was headed by Interior Secretary Harold Ickes and a new agency that was dubbed the Works Progress Administration (WPA) to be run by Harry Hopkins.

The two programs would be run according to opposite strategies: PWA was a project-centered program, which is to say that Ickes would approve a certain capital project and then direct private contractors to hire as many men as they needed to complete it. WPA would be a jobs-centered program, in which Hopkins set out to enroll a predetermined number of men and then figure out creative ways to put them to work. To be sure, there was some programmatic overlap between the agencies because WPA workers did construct some capital projects (such as roads and buildings) that were similar in their nature to the projects of PWA. These projects were often undertaken in cooperation with state and local governments. But WPA also sponsored many improvised programs for certain professions that simply put the unemployed to work in temporary ways—programs that conservative critics down through the years have derided as "leaf raking."

WPA sponsored a series of projects designed to create quick work for unemployed people who were designated by their professions: the Federal Writers Project hired unemployed authors to write books (such as guidebooks on the history and geography of the forty-eight states), the Federal Art Project hired unemployed artists who would create murals and sculpture to adorn public buildings, and the Federal Theater Project hired unemployed actors, stage directors, and theater crews to present plays free of charge to the public.

Because Hopkins's approach to the challenge of job creation promised faster results, he got more of the 1935 appropriation, to the consternation of Ickes.

WPA was finally terminated in 1943.

SOCIAL SECURITY

Like FDIC, the Social Security program stands as one of the great long-term structures in the "New Deal safety net" put together in the 1930s to set up some long-range protection for American citizens and institutions through insurance.

Proposals for unemployment compensation and old-age pensions had been circulating in America since Theodore Roosevelt endorsed such principles in 1912. Supreme Court Justice Louis Brandeis generated behind-the-scenes support for such reforms. An American Association for Old Age Security offered responsible proposals well before the "Townsend Plan" frenzy began. A social security bill had been introduced in Congress by 1932 and an alternative proposal was introduced in February 1934. In June, FDR formed his "President's Committee on Economic Security," chaired by Labor Secretary Frances Perkins, to examine different options.

The Social Security Act encompassed old-age pensions, unemployment compensation, and welfare, the latter effort targeting families without a male breadwinner, families consisting of an unemployed mother and her children. The old-age pensions would be provided by the federal government directly to recipients, though the act provided for grants to the states for the same purpose. The other programs would be run entirely in conjunction with the states.

Agricultural workers and domestic workers were exempted from the program for political reasons.

FDR and his advisers designed Social Security as an insurance program to be supported by joint contributions by participants (through payroll deductions) and employers, contributions that would build up dedicated funds to be paid out over time under specified conditions. The rationale was to make these benefits "entitlements," vested rights that could not be taken away in the future through legislative cuts in spending. As FDR put it years later, "we put those payroll contributions there so as to give the contributors a legal, moral, and political right to collect their pensions and their unemployment benefits. . . . No damn politician can ever scrap my social security program."

One short-term problem of Social Security was that payroll taxes pulled money out of the economy, thus exerting some measure of "drag" on economic recovery. The taxes were collected for the first time in 1937 and some lump sum payments were granted in that same year. Then regular monthly payments began in 1940.

And because the program would cover American workers who were just about to retire as well as younger workers, the payroll deductions from the latter group were made even larger in order to establish the necessary short-term "reserve fund" that would subsidize the imminent retirements. This drastically increased the amount of purchasing power that would be pulled out of the economy.

THE WAGNER ACT

The National Labor Relations Act—better known as the Wagner Act for its sponsor in the Senate, Robert F. Wagner of New York—promised decisive federal protection to labor unions, protecting the right of employees to establish unions and engage in "collective bargaining" through tactics that might include strikes. The enforcement provisions gave an existing federal entity, the National Labor Relations Board (NLRB)—created at first to back up the section 7(a) promises of NRA— new power: the power to supervise elections for the creation of unions and to require companies to engage in collective bargaining by issuing cease and desist orders against "unfair labor practices," among which were actions to "interfere with, restrain, or coerce employees in the exercise of the rights" set forth in the law. The act did not include agricultural workers, domestic employees, government workers, or independent contractors. The cease and desist orders were subject to judicial review, but they were also to be enforceable through court orders and judicial sanctions as determined by federal courts.

This act, like other legislative provisions of the New Deal, would be challenged in court as to constitutionality, and the Wagner Act would be resisted fiercely by a number of companies and corporate leaders, as well as by the Liberty League, which urged an organized campaign of corporate resistance, including efforts to obtain court injunctions against the NLRB.

RURAL ELECTRIFICATION

One of the most far-reaching new programs in 1935, though not designed to promote economic recovery, was the Rural Electrification Administration, set up to make long-term low-interest loans to rural cooperatives to bring electricity to farms in areas that were not served by private utilities. Several other laws embodying reforms or services without a direct relation to economic recovery were pushed through in 1935, and a brief summary of each will be presented for a fundamental reason: these efforts shed light on the social and political mood of America as the Depression and the New Deal approached their mid-point.

GREEN TOWNS

A new agency, the Resettlement Administration (RA), was created in 1935 to help the displaced migrants (such as the "Okies"). It combined two existing agencies, both of them charged with creating small homesteads to alleviate rural poverty: the Subsistence Homestead Division in the Interior Department and the Rural Rehabilitation Division of FERA. Among the most notable provisions of the new RA, the agency was empowered to design and construct model suburbs around large cities. Granted, a modest amount of job creation was performed by the "Suburban Division" of RA, but its main purpose was to demonstrate "garden city" planning, the kind of planning that was set forth decades earlier by a visionary British planning advocate, Ebenezer Howard.

These model towns were meant to demonstrate how future urban expansion ought to happen, how low-density, village-like communities could harmonize the motor age and conservation of the natural landscape. Each town would be surrounded by a "green belt" of forestation that would limit the town's growth, preventing sprawl. Each town would also be designed to harmonize the flow of pedestrian circulation and automobile traffic.

This project was the brainchild of a member of the Brain Trust, Rexford Guy Tugwell, and a hundred of these new model suburbs were supposed to be built. But only three were funded and constructed: Greenbelt, Maryland, Greenhills, Ohio, and Greendale, Wisconsin. FDR visited

Greenbelt, Maryland, a suburb of the nation's capital, in 1936 during its construction. In FDR's second term, when the Resettlement Administration was replaced by the Farm Security Administration (FSA)—created to administer the Bankhead-Jones Farm Tenancy Act of 1937—the Suburban Division of RA was merged into the new agency.

NEW FORMS OF REGULATION

The New Deal impetus to increase the regulation of the private sector was augmented in 1935 by a bill to force the dissolution of electrical utility holding companies (the Wheeler-Rayburn Act), the Federal Power Act, which gave the preexisting Federal Power Commission the right to regulate interstate electrical rates, and by the Banking Act of 1935.

The Banking Act of 1935 made the Federal Deposit Insurance Corporation (FDIC) permanent, and it also set forth the long-term *quid pro quo* by which insured banks would have to submit to federal inspection and regulation. The new banking act also gave the Federal Reserve Board the power to set the "reserve ratios" for member banks. The reserve ratio represented the percentage of the bank's funds that would have to be placed off limits as the basis for fractional reserve money creation. Thus, if a cash depositor made a $100 cash deposit, and if the Federal Reserve's reserve ratio had been set at 20 percent, $20 of the $100 cash deposit would have to be classified a "required reserve" and it would be placed on deposit with the regional Federal Reserve Bank. The $80 that remained would be classified as an "excess reserve" and it could be lent.

Of course, according to fractional reserve principles, this $80 would be doing simultaneous double duty: the original depositor could draw on it at the very same time as it was being lent out, thus, via the hocus pocus of accounting sleight of hand, $80 would be added to the nation's money supply. Because the very same $80 could be used by two borrowers at once (through the writing of checks), $80 of brand new money had been pulled from thin air.

As long as the bank's incoming revenues from the repayment of loans (the assets on its balance sheet) were equal to or greater than its obligation to pay out cash when checks were presented at the teller's window and when loan funds had to be disbursed (the liabilities on its balance sheet), the bank was solvent, and the cash that it needed (Federal Reserve Notes) could be borrowed as necessary from the regional Federal Reserve Bank.

THE SUPREME COURT THREATENS THE NEW DEAL

On May 27, 1935, the Supreme Court struck down the NRA as unconstitutional. The court reasoned that Congress had improperly delegated its power to regulate interstate commerce to the executive branch in the National Industrial Recovery Act. The court also argued that Congress had exceeded its own power under the interstate commerce clause of the Constitution because the NRA codes went beyond the regulation of activity that "directly" affected interstate commerce, encompassing business activity whose effect on interstate commerce was so indirect that it was properly the jurisdiction of states rather than the federal government.

FDR denounced this decision as an antiquated and narrow interpretation of the Constitution, and the ensuing struggle between the administration and the Supreme Court would escalate in FDR's second term. Roosevelt reasoned that the same logic that was used to topple NRA could be used to strike down all or most of the New Deal, and indeed the Supreme Court would go on to use comparable logic in striking down AAA.

Court challenges to the Wagner Act and Social Security were launched with encouragement and aid from the Liberty League and thus the very old debate regarding broad versus strict construction of the Constitution—a debate as old as the Founding Fathers, a debate that began in the 1790s when Alexander Hamilton and Thomas Jefferson took opposite positions on the constitutionality of the first Bank of the United States—overlapped in the 1930s with the politics of left versus right. For conservatives generally applauded the Supreme Court's action, whereas liberals and radicals abhorred it.

THE ELECTION OF 1936: CONFLICT VERSUS MODERATION

The presidential election of 1936 was exciting at the time and it produced an unambiguous result: FDR was reelected in a landslide over his Republican opponent, Governor Alfred Landon of Kansas. Insofar as the election was seen at the time as a plebiscite on the New Deal, a huge majority of Americans obviously approved of FDR's general course of action and they wanted more of it.

But in other ways the politics of this presidential election were ambiguous and they were fraught with contradictory implications both for FDR's second term and for the economic forces at work in the Great Depression.

On the one hand, a centrist theme was present in this election in two different respects: (1) the Republican candidate, "Alf" Landon, was a moderate-to-progressive member of his party who attacked the New Deal more for its inefficiency than for its underlying principles and (2) some of FDR's rhetoric in this election embraced principles of national unity, optimism, sweet reason, and ideological synthesis.

On September 29, in a campaign speech delivered in Syracuse, New York, FDR quoted a dictum handed down by a famous nineteenth-century British historian and politician, Thomas Babington Macaulay: "Reform if you would preserve." Then he added the following potent formulation: "I am that kind of conservative because I am that kind of liberal." He thus emphasized his wish to blend dynamism with moderation, boldness with a caution that was grounded in decent common sense. He was seeking to save and to preserve—to render guardianship to the American people that would protect the institutions of free enterprise (banking, for instance) as much as protect the natural landscape, the most vulnerable members of society, and the nation's resources in general.

And there was a tone of joyous optimism in much of what he said, as in a speech that he made to young Democrats in April. He spoke of the new "pioneering" that Americans were launching, observing that again, as so often in the past, "the very air of America is exhilarating."

In his acceptance speech at the Democratic convention, he spoke in eloquent terms about the challenge posed by the Great Depression to Americans as a whole—a challenge comparable to others that Americans, united in resolve, had confronted together in the past: "There is a mysterious cycle in human events. To some generations much is given. Of other generations much is expected. This generation of Americans has a rendezvous with destiny."

But in the very same speech, he sounded the notes of class war. He was on the attack—not so much against Landon or Republicans as against the selfish and the greedy aristocracy. He was targeting the nasty members of the upper class who—unlike himself—scorned philanthropy, the members of the Liberty League who opposed relief for those who suffered, the scurrilous whisperers in boardrooms and country clubs who had smeared his own reputation with smutty stories, the sorts of people whom Huey Long had loved to vilify.

And so FDR transmuted Long's homely rhetoric—"every man a king" with a "kingfish" as leader—into sweeping Rooseveltian attacks on "economic royalists," the sort of people who were trying to roll back the legacy of the American Revolution, trying to roll it back and reinstitute "royalism" in America. The "privileged princes of these new economic dynasties," FDR asserted, were creating "a new despotism" that "sought to regiment the people, their labor, and their property." And "as a result the average man once more confronts the problem that faced the Minute Man."

He went on: "These economic royalists complain that we seek to overthrow the institutions of America. What they really complain of is that we seek to take away their power." The crowd at the Democratic convention loved it.

On Halloween at Madison Square Garden, FDR added a religious note to his indictment of the royalists: the sins of the greedy in the 1920s had brought down on the people a wrathful and providential judgment. For the crime of leading others to join them in their worship of the golden calf, these sinners had brought on their land a disaster of Old Testament proportions: "Nine mocking years with the golden calf and three long years of the scourge! Nine crazy years at the ticker and three long years in the breadlines!"

But a new leader had taken up the covenant, restoring the fundamental proverb of love thy neighbor. And those who refused to obey that command would now be brought under control. "I should like to have it said of my first Administration," FDR told the crowd, "that in it the forces of selfishness and lust for power met their match." The crowd roared. He stoked the fires a bit more: "I should like to have it said of my second Administration that in it these forces met their master!" The crowd went berserk.

As it was in the depression of the 1890s, when the rhetoric of William Jennings Bryan sent the Democratic convention into delirium—a delirium of joyous rage that was aimed against oppressors of the poor—so now, in a speech that Huey Long might have given, FDR aimed the same sort of rhetorical thunderbolts at the plutocracy. But unlike Bryan or Long, he was no mere challenger to the powers that sustained the status quo. He was the leader of a brand new order, the powerful incumbent president of the United States, and he would soon be reelected in the greatest landslide the country had ever seen.

Of course, many of the votes that were garnered by FDR in 1936 would probably have gone to Huey Long if he had lived.

These political facts would determine to a certain extent—for better or for worse—the course of hard times in the United States from 1937 to 1939.

9

Recovery and Recession, 1937–1939

CONSERVATIVES WHO CLAIM that the New Deal actually thwarted American recovery from the Great Depression have a heavy burden of proof, at least regarding the performance of the economy from 1933 through the first half of 1937. Unemployment dropped from approximately 13 million when FDR was sworn in as president to roughly 11 million in 1934, 10.5 million in 1935, 8 million in 1936, and 7.7 million in 1937. In other words, the level of unemployment had dropped by roughly a third by the time that FDR began his second term. It does not seem far-fetched to credit the drop in unemployment after 1935 to the gradual effects of WPA.

Furthermore, by 1937, the physical volume of American industrial production had risen to approximately the level of 1929 and so, in general terms, had profits and wages.

All of these indicators would appear to show that a recovery was under way. As to whether the recovery could have come faster, it is obviously possible to answer yes, though the case can be made very differently depending on the nature of other questions that are asked. For example, when many conservatives argue that New Deal "bureaucracy" stultified private sector action, it is possible to theorize that the cumbersome apparatus of NRA might indeed have bogged down private enterprise. But NRA was gone by 1935—thanks to the Supreme Court—and the record of AAA was mixed: it increased rural unemployment, while at the same time shoring up the income of the farmers and planters who survived the shakeout. At the other side of the ideological spectrum, the case can be made (on "Keynesian" terms) that recovery could surely have come faster if the New Deal had gone further, especially in job-creation efforts such as PWA in 1933 and CWA in the winter of 1933 and 1934.

But in 1937, everything changed. A great downturn occurred, and the critics of FDR called it the "Roosevelt recession." Controversies raged in regard to the causes of the economic downturn. And the controversies rage to this day.

It is possible to make the case that some mistakes committed by FDR in 1937 were to blame, mistakes of an overlapping political and economic nature. Many conservatives have argued that the negative effects on profits (and wages) caused when the new Social Security contributions by employers and employees kicked in, combined with the higher wages that some corporations had to pay as organized labor flexed its muscles, contributed to the recession by lessening the profit incentive of businessmen. They also cite a reduction in "business confidence" due to new labor violence. There can be little doubt that the new Social Security taxes, by cutting purchasing power, put a damper on sales. Some have argued that the Federal Reserve played a role in the recession because the reserve ratios of member banks were raised. Liberals and Keynesians blame fiscal austerity because FDR decided to cut relief spending in June 1937 to balance the budget.

MORE STRIKES

In January 1937, the United Auto Workers, founded in 1935 and operating under the aegis of the CIO, went on strike against General Motors. Though UAW workers went on strike at various GM plants, the most spectacular strike took place in Flint, Michigan, at GM's Fisher Body Plant Number Two, where workers invaded the plant and then shut down operations through a "sit-down strike." The tactic was different from the older picket-line technique through which strikers tried to keep strikebreakers out of a factory. In this case the strikers themselves went inside.

In subzero temperatures, the company turned off the heat. Then on January 11, an all-night battle broke out when police tried to prevent the delivery of food. As police beat picketers, strikers inside the plant hurled heavy objects at the police and sprayed them with freezing water from a fire hose. Michigan governor Frank Murphy alerted the National Guard, but he also consulted with John L. Lewis and decided not to break the strike. FDR got involved. The strike, which lasted over a month, was finally settled in a UAW victory: a contract with GM. A subsequent strike at Chrysler was also successful.

The last holdout was Ford, and Henry Ford was an adamant autocrat who not only refused to deal with unions but who also sought actively to prevent their formation through the use of company spies and a private security force. In May, the UAW called for a strike at Ford's River Rouge plant in Dearborn, and violence resulted. When UAW President Walter Reuther and others were distributing flyers on an overpass approaching Gate 4 of the plant, Ford's guards poured out and beat the strikers savagely. Photographs of the "Battle of the Overpass" show thugs beating a Reuther associate named Richard Frankensteen, whose face and clothes were drenched with blood after the beating. Subsequent action against Ford via NLRB procedures took several years.

But the violence by Ford was surpassed by the "Memorial Day Massacre" at Republic Steel in Chicago.

In June 1936 the CIO had formed a Steel Workers' Organizing Committee (SWOC), headed by Philip Murray. The first target of SWOC was U.S. Steel, and on May 2, 1937, CIO head John L. Lewis announced victory: a contract guaranteeing better pay, overtime pay, and an eight-hour day. Lewis himself played a role in the victory by meeting with Myron Taylor, the chairman of the board at U.S. Steel, and turning on the charm. Lewis's anger was often on display, but he was also well read, eloquent, and a marvelous conversationalist. This time he used his genteel powers to prevail.

But the victory with U.S. Steel only hardened opposition among the leadership of a cluster of corporations known as "Little Steel." Among the most militant of these corporate leaders was Tom Girdler of Republic Steel, another defiant autocrat like Henry Ford.

A strike at Republic had begun on May 26, though the workforce was divided and a substantial number of steelworkers stayed on the job. But on May 30, when a peaceful union march on the plant took place, Chicago police fired into the crowd, killing ten and injuring over ninety. As the marchers panicked and fled, some were shot in the back. Though the Chicago police called the incident a riot, films of the event that were shown at congressional hearings proved otherwise.

Violence against striking steelworkers occurred in other parts of the United States, and the Republic Steel strike collapsed in July. Union leaders turned to other tactics, not only the NLRB procedure—through which "Little Steel" was eventually ordered to recognize unions by the Supreme Court in 1942—but also through voter registration drives through which union members increased their clout with local and state elected officials, who of course were in charge of police and the National Guard.

FDR'S SECOND-TERM AGENDA AND THE COURT FIGHT

After his triumphant reelection in November 1936, FDR became the first president inaugurated in January because the Constitution was amended to shorten the lame duck interval between administrations and Congresses. In his second inaugural, he struck a visionary note and pledged bold action. He said "one third of a nation" was "ill-housed, ill-clad, ill-nourished," and he pledged to do something about it.

Visionary plans were in the works for a new legislative agenda, including Republican George Norris's proposal to replicate the Tennessee Valley Authority in other river valleys all over the country. FDR supported the concept of "seven little TVAs," though support for the proposal sputtered out in the administration, not least of all due to jurisdictional jealousies on the part of other agencies, especially the Army Corps of Engineers and the Interior Department's Bureau of Reclamation. The Corps of Engineers (with PWA funding) had built the Bonneville Dam (1933–1938) on the Columbia River, and the Reclamation Bureau had built the Grand Coulee Dam (1933–1942), also on the Columbia River, as well as Hoover Dam (1931–1935) on the Colorado River. (Originally named Boulder Dam in the legislation that authorized it, the dam was renamed Hoover Dam by Hoover's secretary of the interior, renamed Boulder Dam by Harold Ickes, FDR's interior secretary, and then renamed Hoover Dam by Republicans in Congress after World War II.) In any case, these dam-building agencies were not eager to be preempted by any more new and *ad hoc* river valley "authorities."

FDR did achieve some additional New Deal legislation during his second term, not least of all the Fair Labor Standards Act of 1938, which established a minimum wage in interstate commerce. But overall, his second term failed to come close to the legislative record of his first, and

Refugees from Tulsa, Oklahoma, by the side of a California highway in June 1936.
Photograph by Dorothea Lange.
Source: Courtesy of the Library of Congress.

many have ascribed this result to the "court-packing" fight that the president initiated as soon as he was sworn in.

FDR saw no reason to proceed with new legislation until the Supreme Court's opposition to his efforts had been quashed. In point of fact, the court was in a volatile and mutable state: before the toppling of NRA and AAA, a majority of justices upheld some New Deal legislation (along with reform laws at the state level) through broad construction of the Constitution. But the court was sharply divided into conservative and liberal factions, and the chief justice, Charles Evans Hughes, would frequently cast swing votes. The striking down of NRA was an occasion to unify the court because the liberal justice Louis Brandeis was opposed to central planning and thus opposed NRA. But the reasoning behind the court's decision in the case of NRA went beyond judicial politics. The language of the decision struck many as excessive and alarmingly reactionary.

FDR was anticipating Supreme Court obstruction in 1937 and afterward. So he proposed to change the Supreme Court's composition and to do it as his very first order of business. He proposed to expand the size of the court and appoint additional justices.

In February, FDR suddenly proposed a bill that would expand the number of justices on the Supreme Court, up to a maximum of six: for every justice over the age of seventy years and six months, the president could nominate an additional justice. Though FDR would claim in the months that followed that he simply intended to improve the court's efficiency and reduce an alleged case backlog, he made his true motivation clear right away.

At a March 4 Democratic Party victory dinner, FDR excoriated the court's obstructionism, its squinty and narrow "strict construction," and its power to "nullify" new laws that were necessary to modernize American democracy, to make America capable of solving its new problems.

In an oratorical incantation, the president spoke as follows: "Here are thousands upon thousands of farmers, wondering whether next year's prices will meet their mortgage interest—*now*! Here are thousands upon thousands of men and women laboring for long hours in factories for inadequate pay—now! Here are thousands upon thousands of children who should be in school, working in mines and mills—now! Here are strikes more far-reaching than we have ever known, costing millions of dollars—now! Here are spring floods threatening to roll again down our river valleys—now! Here is the dust bowl beginning to blow again— now! If we would keep faith with those who had faith in us, if we would make democracy succeed, I say we must act—now!"

In a radio fireside chat on March 9, Roosevelt said that "the Court has improperly set itself up as a third House of Congress—a super-legislature reading into the Constitution words and implications which are not there, and which were never intended to be there. We have, therefore, reached the point as a Nation where we must take action to save the Constitution from the Court and the Court from itself."

There was nothing technically wrong in constitutional terms with the court-packing bill. The Constitution gives Congress broad powers in regard to the composition of the Supreme Court and even its jurisdiction. Nothing in the Constitution gives the Supreme Court the power of judicial review regarding constitutionality: the court gave itself that power in the 1803 case of *Marbury v. Madison*. The size of the Supreme Court had been changed by Congress before. Even Lincoln, in the course of the Lincoln-Douglas debates, hinted that Republicans might be forced to pack the Supreme Court to overturn the hideous *Dred Scott* decision.

But FDR lost the court-packing fight. It got buried in committee by Senator William Fountain Ashurst, and its chief proponent in the Senate, Joseph Robinson of Arkansas, died. Conservatives thundered denunciation, arguing that FDR was trying to overturn American checks and balances and assume dictatorial powers—and to do it in 1937, the Sesquicentennial of the Constitution.

Critics at the time and in subsequent years concluded that FDR's gambit was maladroit, that his maneuver was botched, that the president did little or nothing in advance to line up the necessary support for the bill. Perhaps he was still in a fey and combative mood, overconfident after all of those speeches against the economic royalists and after his massive victory at the polls.

Importantly, however, FDR's attack on the court began to show big results right away in the court's behavior. For whatever reasons, but perhaps in response to the presidential threat, one justice who had previously opposed New Deal legislation, Owen Roberts, switched sides and began to uphold the most recent New Deal innovations. Another justice, Willis Van Devanter, retired. It was enough: a new era in American jurisprudence resulted when the court turned away from its previous strict construction of the interstate commerce clause, upholding the Wagner Act in 1937 (*NLRB v. Jones*), the Social Security Act in two cases during 1937 (*Steward Machine Co. v. Davis* and *Helvering v. Davis*), and the Fair Labor Standards Act in 1941 (*United States v. Darby*).

As the court began to alter its behavior, support for the court-packing scheme among Democrats and liberals in Congress plummeted. But long after it was obvious that the court was changing and that FDR's bill lacked sufficient support, the president kept pushing it, dividing the Democratic Party, burning up months' worth of legislative energy, and alienating erstwhile supporters. Perhaps he felt that his credibility and clout would diminish if he gave up the effort. But that was precisely what happened when he chose to persist.

THE "ROOSEVELT RECESSION"

FDR had always believed in balancing the budget, like Hoover. And his dedication to the principle was encouraged by his fiscally conservative treasury secretary, Henry Morgenthau Jr. After years of deferring the goal of bringing the budget into balance, FDR decided to reduce the federal deficit in 1937. In June, he slashed spending for both WPA and PWA, and he did this at the very same time that $2 billion in new Social Security taxes were being pulled out of the economy. In August, a steep economic decline began, and by 1938 the level of unemployment had climbed from 7.7 million to 10.4 million. Industrial activity declined, a wave of selling hit Wall Street, and, in essential terms, all the progress toward recovery since 1935 was wiped out.

Notwithstanding conservative claims at the time (and ever since) that business activity suffered because of the need to pay higher wages (on the part of those companies that made deals with unions), the cost of the new Social Security payments, and the loss of "confidence" due to FDR's "radical" behavior in the court-packing fight, the link between the spending cuts and the "Roosevelt Recession" is hard to ignore as a primary cause of the decline. Some commentators have also pointed to the Federal Reserve's decision to raise reserve ratios as a contra-inflationary measure. The records of the Federal Reserve Board show concern about inflation as early as 1935, perhaps especially in light of administration efforts to devalue the dollar and raise farm prices. Some have speculated that Fed Chairman Marriner Eccles supported raising reserve ratios as a way to preempt the pressure from bankers who were using the inflation issue as a way to agitate for higher interest rates.

In any case, Eccles regarded monetary policy as being less important than fiscal policy in fighting the depression. Eccles was an outspoken Keynesian—and a follower of William Trufant Foster. He declared that "the Government must be the compensatory agent in this economy; it must unbalance its budget during deflation and create surpluses in peri-

"Drought Refugees, California," 1936.
Photograph by Dorothea Lange.
Source: Courtesy of the Library of Congress.

ods of great business activity." (It bears noting that "deflation" at this time referred to more than just lower prices; it also denoted contraction of the overall money supply as well as economic contraction in more general terms.)

There is reason to believe that something else was occurring on the budgetary front: largely in response to the court-packing fight, a number of conservative Democrats such as Vice President John Nance Garner began to defect from the New Deal, joining hands with conservative Republicans in Congress to form a new bipartisan bloc in opposition to Roosevelt. In subsequent years, this bipartisan bloc would be increasingly consequential, not least of all when southern Democrats revolted against the espousal of black civil rights by such prominent figures in the New Deal as First Lady Eleanor Roosevelt and Interior Department Secretary Harold Ickes.

Among other things, many Democratic conservatives complained about deficits, and it seems possible that FDR's new budget-balancing efforts should be understood at least in part as a maneuver taking place within a much larger process of political give and take.

FDR continued to insist on balancing the budget during the autumn of 1937. Interestingly, however, he began to agree with some members of his administration such as Harry Hopkins, Harold Ickes, and Assistant Attorney General Robert Jackson who suggested that the recession might have been caused by an act of sabotage within the business community, a conspiracy by corporate leaders who were deliberately cutting back production in order to induce an economic slump that would spike further liberal reform and undermine FDR. The proposed remedy of these New Dealers: anti-trust action. In 1938, FDR convinced Congress to establish a "Temporary National Economic Committee" (TNEC) to investigate the extent of monopoly and oligopoly in the corporate world. Inconsistently, however, FDR at the very same time began to wonder whether a revival of NRA cartel-type planning might be in order.

In short, FDR was profoundly in doubt about which way to turn.

In April 1938, the president proposed renewed spending on job-creation efforts, and Congress responded to the tune of roughly $3.7 billion. By 1939, the unemployment level had shrunk by roughly a million, but the overall economic condition of the United States remained dire.

Some prominent New Dealers such as Harry Hopkins had been theorizing that the Great Depression of the 1930s might prove to be permanent, a new normality. A concept that had been circulating since 1932, the idea that the United States had reached an outer limit for economic expansion, was back on the table.

Few people could realize in 1939 how spectacularly wrong that idea would be proven to be within the next decade—indeed, within the next two to three years.

10

The Great Depression and American Culture in the 1930s

BEFORE PROCEEDING FURTHER with economic and political accounts, it is time to consider the overall effects of the Great Depression on America. To date, the Depression of the 1930s is nothing less than *the* event that epitomizes hard times in American memory. It was almost an all-pervasive presence in American culture while it lasted.

Of all the depressions in American history, the 1930s Depression left the most extensive historical record of its influence—and rich book-length accounts of Depression-era culture continue to be written. So vast was the reach of the Great Depression that a comprehensive account within the length of this chapter is impractical. Instead, some representative case studies of 1930s culture will be presented, studies that will show the different ways in which the Great Depression affected American cinema, visual arts and architecture, and music.

THE GREAT DEPRESSION AND 1930s CINEMA

Hollywood films of the 1930s came to grips with the Depression in different ways. Some ignored the Depression completely, while others sought to lift people's spirits by wafting them into fantasies that were vastly removed from their everyday cares and tribulations.

But many films of the era confronted the Depression, and films from the Hoover era were often suffused with social commentary. Much of it was bitter, though some of these movies were engaged with the Depression more directly than others.

A good representative example of an angry Hoover-era protest film is the 1932 Warner Brothers production *I Am a Fugitive from a Chain Gang*, starring Paul Muni and directed by Mervyn LeRoy. Based on a book by an escaped convict who claimed he was wrongly convicted, the film tells the story of a World War I veteran named James Allen, played by Muni. A depression connection is established right away by showing him wandering around from city to city seeking work in the short depression of 1919–1921.

In a flophouse, he meets a tramp who invites him to go panhandling. It turns out that the tramp is a crook who holds up a lunch wagon, and Allen, along for the ride, becomes an unwitting accomplice. Arrested, he is sentenced to ten years of hard labor on a chain gang. This chain gang is like a throwback to an antebellum Southern plantation; he is whipped and beaten by smirking guards, and after escaping and making good as a business executive, he is hunted down, brought back, and treated even worse.

This movie creates a mood of despair intermingled with outrage. The hero is relentlessly beaten down by a "system" that, in the name of "good government," generates horror. In Hoover's America, penniless wanderers who had once been solid citizens and breadwinners were treated by police too often like bums, striking workers were beaten or shot, and the marchers of the Bonus Army were gassed and driven away at sabre point.

Many film critics have seen indirect or subliminal Depression connections in other films of the Hoover era, especially the gangster films produced by Warner Brothers and other studios during 1931 and 1932—films such as *Little Caesar* (Warners, 1931), *Scarface* (United Artists, 1932), and *The Public Enemy* (Warners, 1932). Though the gangster protagonists in these movies were surely depicted as vicious—and they all went down in a hail of lead—it is possible to put aside for a moment the ugly character of the gangsters and wonder whether some viewers might have found a vicarious sort of fulfillment in the spectacle of characters going "outside the system" and taking whatever they wanted. Though the films were in some respects backward-looking commentaries on the gangsters and gangs of the 1920s—though it does bear noting that a new class of colorful lone wolf outlaws such as John Dillinger and "Pretty Boy" Floyd were gaining attention in the Hoover years—a Depression-era resonance seems possible.

Other film critics have suggested connections to Depression-era moods in what some have called the "shyster movies" of the Hoover era, films providing commentary on big city fraud, on the fleecing of "suckers," on corruption in general by parasitic hustlers—some of them lawyers, some of them tabloid journalists, some of them investors, some of them politicians—who mingle, collaborate, double-cross, and blackmail each other as well as assorted victims in a cynical skyscraper Babylon. Some of these films were adaptations of plays from the 1920s. Yet film historians such as Andrew Bergman have cited them as examples of an ongoing delegitimization of authority that was perhaps brought into even sharper focus in the Hoover years.

Of all the Hollywood studios during the Depression, Warner Brothers in particular specialized in tough-minded and gritty exposés, and some of them contained social protest.

Films like *The Mouthpiece* (Warners, 1932), the famous dark comedy *The Front Page* (United Artists, 1931)—based on the 1928 play by Ben Hecht and Charles MacArthur—and *The Dark Horse* (Warners, 1932) might be seen as commentaries on a society sent spiraling downward by people who believed in nothing. Or, even worse, by people who believed in nothing but the thrill of the moment, especially if that thrill derived from something dirty and fraudulent. It was all a matter of what you could get away with, for profit but also for fun. There were many in the 1930s who saw the Great Depression in religious terms as castigation of a deeply corrupt people.

One Hoover-era film that dramatized current events with an upbeat moral was the 1932 comedy-melodrama *American Madness*, directed by Frank Capra and produced by Columbia Pictures. This film is a commentary on banking, and the hero, a bank president named Tom Dickson (played by Walter Huston), is an altruistic businessman who struggles over policy issues with his board of directors. Dickson likes to make loans that give the little guy a break, as opposed to the members of the board, who urge caution and impersonal calculation. In a charismatic speech at a board meeting, Dickson preaches that investment, not retrenchment, is the key to economic recovery.

A gangster/shyster element is introduced in this film (a corrupt bank employee helps gangsters rob the bank) and as news of the robbery spreads, a catastrophic panic ensues. Capra used brilliant cinematic devices such as rapid-fire editing and splicing of telephone gossips who exaggerate and worsen the situation and overhead "crane shots" that depict the writhing crowd as it storms into the bank.

Dickson's bank is saved when some people whom he helped band together and show their confidence in the institution by making small deposits, thus slowing down the panic and shaming the members of the board into making some big deposits themselves.

In 1933, as the New Deal commenced, another film starring Walter Huston was produced as a Depression commentary. This one, *Gabriel Over the White House*, was political. Directed by Gregory La Cava and produced by Cosmopolitan Productions (a vehicle for William Randolph Hearst), the movie was distributed by MGM. Like *American Madness*— and like many other films of 1933, when the Hoover era ended and the New Deal began—this movie is a morality play that sent a message: America needed strong and visionary leadership in this national crisis.

Huston plays a president named Judson Hammond who, in the beginning, is merely a hack politician who reacts to the Depression with smugness. He and his political cronies are the worst kind of cynics: profane, amoral, unfit to hold public office. But after suffering a brain concussion in an auto accident, his recovery transforms him into a Lincolnesque visionary. Many physical but subliminal devices—his makeup, his gaunt demeanor, his rumpled hair—drive home the comparison. The film implies in many ways (through song and imagery) that the nation confronts its worst crisis since the Civil War.

The movie slowly reveals that the transfiguration of "Jud Hammond" has resulted from an angelic intervention: he is inspired by Gabriel, who guides him in words that he alone can hear.

A march of the unemployed takes place and invidious comparisons to Hoover are presented immediately; in an obvious reference to the treatment of the Bonus Army, Hammond's aides recommend a show of force to disperse the crowd. Hammond dismisses such advice and makes a personal appearance in the tent city of the marchers. He tells them he will induct them into a magnificent "army of construction." When Congress refuses to appropriate the necessary funds for this effort, Hammond quickly declares martial law, adjourns Congress, assumes dictatorial powers, and ends the Depression himself.

A whole series of films released by Warner Brothers in 1933 depicted tough-as-nails leaders who propelled economic expansion using bold, audacious, impatient, even ruthless techniques. A 1933 "B" film, *Employees Entrance*, that was produced by First National Pictures (by then a Warner Brothers subsidiary) and directed by Roy Del Ruth, portrays a hard-driving department store executive named Curt Anderson, played by Warren William. Like the bank president in *American Madness*— but without the benevolence and decency of that character—Anderson believes that investment, not retrenchment, is the proper way out of depression. He fights it out with myopic advisers who recommend layoffs. *Employees Entrance* possesses amusing thematic complexity. It is something of a dark comedy: while Anderson saves both his store and the jobs of the people who work there, he is also a misanthropic boss from hell, a workaholic who preys on women.

Warners used similar themes in a series of movie musicals in 1933.

The plots of *Forty-Second Street* and *Gold Diggers of 1933* were built around the challenge of finding some daring investors who would pay to reopen closed theaters, thus helping chorus girls, singers, dancers, and stagehands find employment. In *Forty Second Street*, another hard-driving and workaholic boss named Julian Marsh (played by Warner Baxter) is the protagonist. In *Gold Diggers* a comparably manic stage director is played by Ned Sparks.

Gold Diggers of 1933 contained production numbers that expressed the alternation of moods in the early New Deal—moods that could range from euphoric to somber. "We're in the Money," the film's opening song that was performed with insouciance by Ginger Rogers, expressed the giddy optimism that greeted the advent of FDR's administration in a way that was aligned with the theme of Roosevelt's 1932 campaign song "Happy Days Are Here Again." But the film concludes with a very different kind of number, another reminder of the Bonus Army and its rout: "Remember My Forgotten Man," a torch song presented by Joan Blondell. It bears noting that the phrase "forgotten man" came directly from an FDR speech, in which the candidate had pledged to do more for "the forgotten man at the bottom of the economic pyramid."

All of the songs in the Warner Brothers musicals were written by Harry Warren and Al Dubin. The dance numbers were created by the fabulously inventive Busby Berkeley.

Another Warners film from 1933, *Wild Boys of the Road*, was a melodrama that depicted the misery of the Depression in very stark terms.

Directed by William Wellman, the film depicts the journey of some teens who leave their homes in order to ease the economic burden on their families. As they ride the rails, they are constantly on the run from police who regard them as truants and vagrants.

One of them, a teenaged girl, gets raped by a railroad brakeman. Another stumbles in a railroad switching yard, and then, after trying desperately to crawl away from the path of an oncoming train, gets hit and loses his leg. This nightmarish exposé is given a relatively happy ending when a kindly judge dismisses the charges against one of the runaway teens and promises to help get him settled and employed.

All through the Great Depression, movies were produced that showed the plight of the newly impoverished and unemployed millions. One of the greatest was Charlie Chaplin's 1936 masterpiece *Modern Times* (United Artists) in which Chaplin's "Little Tramp" wanders around Depression America seeking work, getting caught up in strikes, and falling for a female wandering waif played by Paulette Goddard. Chased by cops, finding short-lived work on a monstrous assembly line, living in a shack by the edge of a lake somewhere in industrial America, Chaplin captured much of the period's pathos and turned it into gentle humor.

Some of the Hollywood films that addressed the Depression offered remedies. *Gabriel Over the White House* was one such film and there were others. In 1934, producer/director King Vidor filmed and released an independent production, *Our Daily Bread*, that tracked the lives of two characters who were familiar because they had appeared in a previous Vidor film: John and Mary Sims, the hero and heroine of *The Crowd*, a silent 1928 melodrama from MGM. In the new film, John and Mary abandon city life and try to survive on a shabby and abandoned farm, where they are joined by other displaced Americans. They set the farm up as a cooperative enterprise.

Many in election year 1934 probably saw in this film a thinly veiled depiction of the contemporaneous Upton Sinclair EPIC plan. Having fended off many hardships, these homesteaders confront the worst of all: a Dust Bowl–generated drought. But they manage to combine their skills in a heroic 'round-the-clock endeavor to draw water from a nearby river by digging a complicated irrigation canal. They work together in a rhythmic tempo that Vidor set up with a metronome: the pick axes all swing in unison. And this cooperative labor (by torchlight at night) saves the farm in a euphoric happy ending.

This film, it bears noting, contained an explicitly religious component: in an early scene, the people offer up prayerful thanks on the brow of a hill as the first shoots of corn break the earth.

A different version of the back-to-the-land idea was presented in the 1936 comedy/melodrama *Mr. Deeds Goes to Town*, a Columbia film produced and directed by Frank Capra. The stars were Gary Cooper and Jean Arthur. Cooper played a character named Longfellow Deeds who lives a contented life in a small New England town until he suddenly inherits a fortune from an uncle in New York City who had been a wealthy socialite. A firm of shyster lawyers who are handling the estate—lawyers who had previously bilked the rich uncle by co-mingling his funds with their own—bring Deeds to Manhattan in the hope of regaining the power of attorney they had tricked the uncle into giving them.

Deeds is naïve in a great many ways, though he also possesses inner toughness. He is also extremely eccentric, a fact that is noted by some predatory characters who seek to manipulate his quirks. He becomes the dupe of some tabloid journalists who dub him "the Cinderella Man," follow him all around the city, then write up his nocturnal antics as front-page coverage. They do their best to depict him as a fool on a spree, with the obvious implication that the money that he has inherited could be put to better uses.

Deeds comes to roughly the same conclusion: he really doesn't need the inheritance. So as he packs his bags and prepares to go home, he announces an altruistic venture: the "Deeds Plan," through which he will give all the money away to some down-and-out farmers and help them establish a model agricultural community. The shyster lawyers swing into action: they trump up a case to send Deeds to an insane asylum and transfer the estate to some other descendants of the wealthy tycoon, having first made a deal with these descendants. Their frame-up seems to be a sure thing at first because "Exhibit A" in the insanity hearing contains all the front-page coverage of Deeds's "Cinderella Man" behavior.

In the end, however, Deeds turns the tables on everyone.

Examples of Depression-era films of this type could be piled up indefinitely, but the plot variations were remarkable. In 1936, for instance, a Universal film, *My Man Godfrey*—starring William Powell and Carole Lombard and directed by Gregory La Cava—depicted the transformation of a down-at-the-heels aristocrat named Godfrey Parke (played by

Powell), who is living in despair in the aftermath of a tragic romance. He is living in rags with a community of unemployed men in a garbage dump by the edge of a river.

A neurotic and wealthy family, the Bullocks, are out on the town in the midst of an obnoxious and arrogant scavenger hunt: according to the rules of this game, the first participant to find an authentic "forgotten man" is the winner.

Godfrey gets "found."

Through some lengthy plot complications, he becomes the butler for this ridiculous idle-rich family—who of course have no idea that he is wealthy himself.

He endures the patronizing scorn of the spoiled eldest daughter, falls in love with the charming younger daughter (Lombard), and, through it all, gets a new and refreshing slant on life, finding many new kinds of inspirations, most of them comic. By the end, he has redeemed almost everything his life has touched. Using funds of his own, he rescues this undeserving family from Wall Street losses, teaches several people a thing or two about humility, marries the younger daughter, and, best of all, turns the Hooverville by the river into a swanky new nightclub that is given an appropriate tongue-in-cheek name: "The Dump." Of course he hires the unemployed inhabitants of the shacktown as waiters and cooks.

My Man Godfrey was a commentary on class relations, and the New Deal years were replete with memorable films that explored that potent theme from a number of angles.

But before proceeding further with the theme of class relations, a stand-alone example of a film series that managed in remarkable ways to reconcile visions of high society with everyday experience ought to be noted.

A symbolic fusion of democratic values and swanky surroundings can be found in the Fred Astaire and Ginger Rogers musicals produced from 1933 to 1939 by RKO Radio Pictures. Through all sorts of plot situations, these films presented Fred and Ginger in surpassingly elegant surroundings, not as members of the wealthy class but rather as two talented but otherwise representative Americans who somehow found their way into one ritzy environment after another.

Through gifted choreography and superb performances, this dancing couple swept moviegoers into a paradise of elegance in which almost any man sitting in a hometown movie theater might imagine himself wearing top hat, white tie, and tails while his female companion could imagine herself wearing Ginger's latest stunning gown. Some of these movies pushed the iconography to its outer limit, as when, in the 1936 film *Swingtime*, Fred is shown (for reasons that are far too complicated to explain) wearing formal wear as he jumps aboard a freight train to hitch a ride out of town. Social images of high and low were in an instant magically fused, and for reasons that the plot makes perfectly believable.

To be sure, the Astaire-Rogers series was a light form of commentary; the effects were achieved through iconography. But other films of the 1930s probed the issues of class relations, class conflict, and interclass reconciliation through their plot structures.

In 1934, Frank Capra's film *It Happened One Night*—a film that swept the Academy Awards—was built around romance between improbable lovers, a theme that was quickly becoming a near-standard feature of a new class of films that some critics were beginning to call "screwball comedy." The stars were Claudette Colbert and Clark Gable.

Ellie Andrews (Colbert), a charming but slightly spoiled daughter of a Wall Street banker, meets a hard-boiled reporter named Peter Warne (Gable), who proves in the end to be a sentimental guy, notwithstanding his wise guy persona. Ellie is running away from home, and so this romance across the class lines features a long and comic road trip—via Greyhound bus, hitchhiking, and sleeping out in the open (in haystacks). A panoramic glimpse of Depression America is presented throughout.

After a series of plot twists and misunderstandings, a happy ending is engineered by the girl's tycoon father, who, like Warne, is a tough but tender character. He is ready to bless his daughter's marriage to a common working-class "Joe" because Warne is refreshingly different from the typical phonies of upper-class society whom the father detests. Perhaps most importantly of all, Warne learns that wealthy people can turn out to be perfectly decent folks, at least some of the time.

Decent folks, like the charming aristocrat from Hyde Park who was reaching out a helping hand to those down below.

Another romance across class lines was the 1935 film *Alice Adams*, which was based on an older Booth Tarkington novel. An RKO Radio Pictures film, *Alice Adams* was directed by George Stevens and starred Katherine Hepburn.

Hepburn's character, Alice, is a sensitive but high-strung young woman who lives with her parents and brother in a smallish Midwestern city. She is trapped in a web of frustrations—trapped in a social milieu where she is constantly snubbed on account of her shabby home, her outdated wardrobe, and her lack of prospects. She is also trapped in a tense home environment; day after day she has to listen to her parents and their never-ending quarrels over money.

The poor girl becomes neurotic and she radiates a tense insecurity. She talks too much and too fast and her attempts to impress people backfire. Every day she becomes more self-defeating.

But a wealthy and deeply sincere prince charming, played by Fred MacMurray, solves everything: he falls ardently in love with Alice. He can see through her silly affectations and he knows exactly what she needs. He overlooks her aggravating family. He is immune to the pressure to conform to the conventions of class and status; his rebellion is nothing short of elegant.

Class, status, and family: this triad of overlapping themes played out in almost endless creative permutations in American Depression-era cinema.

The family—whether functional or dysfunctional—was perhaps the theme of greatest importance. And family dynamics played a fundamental role in the rise of a remarkable star who was for several years the greatest box office draw in America: the child star Shirley Temple.

Economic privation wrought havoc with American families. Marriages were under brutal strain. Fathers, unable to provide any longer, sank into demoralization, and they sometimes abandoned their families. In a great many cities in Depression America, statistics for alcoholism, child abandonment, and domestic violence were shocking.

Much of Shirley Temple's appeal in the 1930s was due not only to her cuteness but also to a brilliant plot device—largely the conception of Darryl F. Zanuck at 20th Century Fox—that reversed an understandable presumption that abandoned children were victims. Cast in film after film in the role of a forsaken little waif, this cheerful and dauntless little girl would not only survive, she would save the day for everyone else. She would bring her troubled parents back together. If cast as an orphan, she would somehow create a new family.

This theme of reuniting shattered families proved to have contagious appeal. In her 1936 debut, the child star Deanna Durbin and her sisters succeed in reuniting their divorced parents. *Three Smart Girls* was the film, Universal was the studio, and this film quite possibly went on to influence a later movie that is far more famous: *The Parent Trap*, which appeared in successive versions decades later.

The theme of reuniting a divorced couple was interwoven with commentaries on class relations in *The Philadelphia Story*, a sophisticated comedy of manners written by Philip Barry as a stage vehicle for Katharine Hepburn and then brought to the screen by MGM in 1940. This famous and complex concoction—featuring love triangles, plot twists, sharp repartee and absurdist humor, and, not least of all, some brilliant casting and superb direction by George Cukor—was played out in the high-society setting of Philadelphia's "Main Line."

As the story unfolds, the inner conflicts and unresolved emotional issues of each of the principal characters are plumbed, laid bare, worked over, and, with breathtaking wit, progressively resolved: all is redeemed. Two failed marriages are reestablished (on much better terms), generational bitterness is healed, immature personalities are coaxed into beautiful wisdom, and, not least of all, some characters from opposing social classes learn invaluable lessons about themselves, their opposite numbers, and class dynamics in general. A populistic tough guy reporter, for example, played by James Stewart—contemptuous at first of the idle rich—learns from a transformative direct experience that "in spite of the fact that somebody's up from the bottom, he can still be quite a heel. And even though somebody else is born to the purple he can still be a very nice guy."

Just as Warner Brothers was known in the 1930s for its gritty realism and populistic themes, MGM under Louis B. Mayer's assertively conservative leadership had a corresponding knack for portraying the wealthy as friendly, amusing, and fun to be with if you could somehow find your way into their proximity. These lessons were never better represented on screen than in *The Philadelphia Story*.

In the very same year, however—1940—the Depression as experienced directly by the desperately poor was presented on screen by 20th Century Fox with a vivid power that could rival almost any Warner Brothers production of the preceding decade. The 1940 film version of John Steinbeck's 1939 novel *The Grapes of Wrath* was directed by John Ford and starred Henry Fonda. Though the novel's apocalyptic conclusion was replaced in the film with a trite happy ending—not least of all due to the constraints of the Production Code—the movie as a whole portrayed the westward migration of the Joads, a displaced family of struggling "Okies," with nightmarish clarity. Not the least of the considerations regarding this film was the continued timeliness of its content: as late as 1940, the effects of the Great Depression continued to be all too vividly on display in many parts of the United States.

THE EFFECTS OF THE DEPRESSION ON ART, ARCHITECTURE, AND DESIGN

Did the Depression affect the *aesthetics* of motion pictures as well as their subject matter?

The question could be posed for almost any of the visual arts in the 1930s—from the studio arts of painting and sculpture to applied arts such as industrial design and architecture (the latter making occasional use at the time of ornamental elements drawn from the world of studio art such as murals and sculpture)—and photography, which occupied something of a mid-way position between studio art and applied art, at least in the case of the *documentary* photography produced in the Great Depression.

Whether the Depression *as such* affected camera aesthetics during the 1930s is debatable. But the *subject matter* of 1930s camera work was obviously shaped by the Depression. As we have seen, Hollywood films of the 1930s addressed Depression-related issues, though in different ways depending on the plot and "message" of the film. One fact that should not be overlooked is that Hollywood films were largely *fiction*.

That was not the case with still photography, with the exception of a few avant-garde experiments.

In any case, documentary camera work depicting the Depression was fraught with *messages*: themes of suffering, heroic effort, and endurance were integral to the work of the photographer. They were integral to the photographer's state of mind, and the finished work could elicit corresponding emotional effects in the viewer.

The same thing could be said about the so-called documentary films of the period that sought not only to record Depression-era themes but to *comment*, often through a narrative script that accompanied the imagery.

"Migrant Mother."
This famous photograph taken by Dorothea Lange in 1936 depicts migrant workers in California.
Source: Courtesy of the Library of Congress.

Several famous documentary films of this type were produced: *The Plow That Broke the Plains* (1936), *The River* (1938), and *Power and the Land* (1940). The first two films were produced by Pare Lorentz, initially a writer and film critic who produced an illustrated book about FDR's first year in office. Lorentz was commissioned by Rexford Guy Tugwell to make a documentary film about the Dust Bowl under the aegis of the Resettlement Administration. The result, with narration and a musical score by Virgil Thomson, was released in 1936 as *The Plow That Broke the Plains*. While the Hollywood studios that owned large chains of movie theaters turned down the film for presentation, an independent theater owner in New York, Arthur Mayer, accepted it for his Rialto Theater. The film was sufficiently well reviewed in New York to prompt other independent theater owners to present the film around the country.

The film prompted Tugwell to commission Lorentz to produce a second film about conservation, *The River*, which presented commentary on the themes of deforestation, soil erosion, and flooding in the Mississippi Valley, contrasted to the beneficial work of TVA.

Lorentz headed an agency, the U.S. Film Service, that proved to be short lived. Later, under the auspices of the Rural Electrification Administration (REA), he participated in producing another film, *Power and the Land*, that was directed by Joris Ivens and released in 1940. The film depicted the transformation in the world of an Ohio farm family when electrification lifted immense physical burdens from their everyday lives.

These films provided documentation, but they were also films with a message, with a point of view that was meant to be persuasive and convincing. Some would relegate all such films to the category of "propaganda." But surely all documentary films, from the 1930s to the present, contain one or more points of view, some of them presented in (or embedded in) narration and others presented explicitly through interviews with "talking head" experts, a method pioneered decades later. In any case, the New Deal documentary films showed suffering and natural disaster during the Depression, and these themes were presented more directly than was possible in most commercial feature films produced in Hollywood.

The art of camera work in general during the 1930s was certainly affected by hard times, and the art of still photography reflected this as much as the art of motion pictures. American photography was shaped by the Great Depression for the simplest of reasons: many gifted American photographers fanned out across the country to document all the human misery.

Some of these photographers were sent out by New Deal agencies, such as the Resettlement Administration (RA) and its successor, the Farm Security Administration (FSA).

Photographers such as Dorothea Lange, Walker Evans, Arthur Rothstein, John Vachon, Marion Post Wolcott, Margaret Bourke-White, and Edwin Rosskam documented the Depression. Their work was sometimes published in mass circulation magazines, especially in features that covered natural disasters that worsened the conditions of American life even more. On February 15, 1937, for instance, a photograph by Bourke-White led off a feature in *Life* magazine on the devastation of Louisville,

Unemployed "bums" on the road after police chased them out of Los Angeles in 1936.
Photograph by Dorothea Lange.
Source: Courtesy of the Library of Congress.

Kentucky, by an Ohio River flood. The picture showed African Americans lining up for food and clothing in front of a Chamber of Commerce billboard that flaunted the following ironic slogan: "World's Highest Standard of Living: There's No Way Like the American Way." This photograph became famous for obvious reasons.

Like the photographs of Matthew Brady that were taken during the Civil War, these photographs sent graphic evidence of horror over long distances. Many of the images, such as Lange's portrait *Migrant Mother* (1936), achieved iconic status in American cultural memory.

In the course of their travels, the photographers also took pictures of everyday life. And this work continued during World War II when the Office of War Information (OWI) paid some of the FSA photographers to go on depicting "the American way of life"—democracy—in contrast to life in the Axis nations. In all, the federal government during these years created a documentary record of over 145,000 images, many of which are on deposit at the Library of Congress.

The photographers came from different sorts of backgrounds, but most of them had significant artistic interests beyond photography. Dorothea Lange, after studying photography at Columbia University, opened a portrait studio and married a studio artist, Maynard Dixon. In the course of a second marriage to economist Paul Schuster Taylor, the husband-wife team studied poverty among California sharecroppers through a collaboration that paired Taylor's interviews with Lange's photographic images. The result was the book *American Exodus*.

To cite another example, Walker Evans in his youth was a member of a literary circle and he contributed three photographs to *The Bridge*, a book of poetry by Hart Crane. After he began working for the Resettlement Administration, his photographs caught the attention of *Fortune* magazine, and the editors hired him to take pictures of poverty in Alabama for a feature story to be written by James Agee. Even though the editors decided not to run this story, Agee's prose and the photographs of Evans were published together in a 1941 book, whose title—*Let Us Now Praise Famous Men*—proved apt as well as ironic because the book itself became famous later on after decades of neglect. Evans eventually turned to writing, signing on as a staff writer for *Time* magazine in 1945.

Just as Evans linked the artistic realms of photography and writing, his work provided an important (though by no means unique) connection between the worlds of photography and studio art. In particular, Evans influenced the painter Ben Shahn, prompting him to expand his work beyond brush and canvas and to take up the camera as well.

Shahn, a Lithuanian-born Jewish immigrant, was a figure of great importance in an international artistic movement known as "social realism," a movement that affected the world of sculpture as well as painting. Indeed, some art historians stretch the term "social realism" to encompass the aforementioned trends in American 1930s documentary photography as well as studio art.

Self-consciously "modern," the social realists rejected abstraction, insisting on representational work to comment on social conditions from a generally left-of-center perspective. The painting was done in a manner that might well be described as deliberately "proletarian," a style that drew from traditions in folk art, including so-called primitive art.

A representative example of this latter trend was Philip Evergood's *American Tragedy* (1937), a portrayal of the infamous "Memorial Day Massacre" at Republic Steel. The people are depicted by the artist in child-like strokes, perhaps to convey (or imply) the destruction of childish innocence among those who had presumed that the police were incapable of such deeds.

Some of the most famous of these social protest paintings were the twenty-three gouache paintings that were created by Shan to memorialize and protest the 1921 trial of Sacco and Vanzetti—a case whose verdict and sentence were widely decried at the time as a gross injustice. This series of paintings was exhibited in 1932 to great acclaim.

Among the other international figures to achieve fame in this movement was Diego Rivera. Shahn worked with Rivera on a mural project for Rockefeller Center, but his career expanded when his friendship with Walker Evans led him to participate in photographic projects under federal auspices—at the same time that he produced major murals under federal sponsorship for public buildings.

Shahn was an iconic figure, but he was also one of many dozens of social realists who sought to record the effects of hard times in the 1930s. A number of painters in America achieved individualistic results that drew on the social realist conventions in some ways while departing from them in others. One of the most important was Reginald Marsh, whose work depicted both everyday American life and also famous/notorious events, such as the gunning down of the outlaw John Dillinger, events that took on an aura of folklore in the artist's portrayals.

The Great Depression served as a tremendous impetus to social realism, especially under the sponsorship of government from the federal level to the local. At the federal level, much of this work took place through the Public Works of Art Project in the Treasury Department—it bears noting that according to a now-defunct tradition, the Treasury Department's "supervising architect" oversaw design and construction of many federal buildings at the time—and the Federal Art Project created under the leadership of Harry Hopkins in the Works Progress Administration (WPA).

Social realist paintings were produced in great volume all over America. In the nation's capital, murals of this type were created for federal office buildings that were nearing completion—the Department of Justice and Department of the Interior buildings in particular.

The former building (1931–1935) is part of the Federal Triangle project built directly north of the National Mall on Constitution Avenue. Murals adorn many public spaces within this building, even stairwells. Some of these murals were quintessentially social realist by dint of the fact that they depicted not representations of justice but *injustice*—they were murals of social protest.

But others—such as a series of murals by Henry Varnum Poor—depicted heroic construction. The link to "justice" in these paintings might be taken to imply that new forms of modern pioneering, such as the New Deal and its programs, were required to achieve a decent context for justice by removing or reforming certain situations that made life "unjust."

Murals that depicted New Deal construction, such as William Gropper's *Construction of a Dam* in the Interior Department building, were often juxtaposed with murals showing earlier forms of pioneering in American history (covered wagon days, for instance), thus grounding New Deal visions of progress in American tradition as much as innovation.

The murals that portrayed heroic effort had their counterpart in sculpture. At the sides of the Federal Trade Commission building (1936–1938) in Washington, D.C., are matching sculpted groups that show muscular heroes reining in wild horses. *Man Controlling Trade* was the title that the sculptor, Michael Lantz, conferred on this work. In the model New Deal suburb of Greenbelt, Maryland, the community and school building was adorned with bas-relief sculpted panels produced by WPA artist

Lenore Thomas Strauss. Each limestone panel illustrates a clause from the Constitution's preamble, but the figures of the people who act out the content of each clause are rendered in a simplified manner that shows the possible influence of Shahn.

Overlapping social realism was a related movement known as "regionalism." Its painterly qualities—the color palette and the brushwork employed by the artists—had much in common with social realist aesthetics. And like social realism, regionalism was under way before the Depression began, though both movements accelerated in the decade of hard times.

Rejecting big city imagery, the regionalists depicted life in the hinterland, thus to some extent partaking of the influential "back-to-the-land" movement. John Steuart Curry was a major figure in regionalism, and several of his paintings such as *Tornado Over Kansas* (1929) and *Line Storm* (1934) became famous. So did the work of Grant Wood, who lived and worked in rural Iowa. Another regionalist was Thomas Hart Benton, who used themes from American history—both factual history and imagery from legends and "tall tales"—along with contemporaneous themes in his paintings, murals, book covers, and other creations. The influence of these painters can be sensed in much of the artwork produced for WPA and other New Deal agencies.

Regionalist and social realist qualities were sometimes fused in the work of certain artists. Alexandre Hogue's *Drought-Stricken Area* (1934), for instance—a painting that shows an abandoned farm half-buried in sand dunes blown across the prairies in the Dust Bowl—can be related to both of America's representational schools in Depression-era studio art. Some commentators simply classify regionalism and social realism as one single movement.

The last of the visual arts to be considered here are the so-called plastic arts of industrial design (the design of manufactured products) and architecture. The effect of hard times on industrial design was straightforward: designers strove to counteract hard times by creating "streamlined" products that exuded the symbolism of progress, optimism, speed toward a brighter tomorrow, and harmony through planning. In regard to the latter item, *Design This Day* (1940), a major book manifesto that was written by designer Walter Dorwin Teague, bore a title that possessed a potent double meaning for those who could discern it.

The world of architecture in the 1930s was more complex because converging and diverging movements were competing for the allegiance of architects who were rising within the profession. For example, an ideological war was raging at the time between architects who espoused traditionalism (especially Greco-Roman classicism in the case of public buildings) and modernists who preached abstract form in the manner of the work that had been done (before Hitler) in Germany by the designers of the Bauhaus school.

But one common element linked the worlds of industrial design and architecture: the streamlining fad was embraced with enthusiasm by a number of architects, especially those who designed commercial buildings, as well as industrial designers.

Industrial design, as such, was a rising new profession in the 1920s. Manufactured articles had of course been shaped and adorned for centuries to achieve what the craftsmen hoped would be appealing ornamental effects. But the emphasis of the new sales psychology that was pitched by the industrial designers was *industrialism as symbolism*. It became a sales theme, a form of packaging for products that was meant to convey an appealingly modern and futuristic quality.

"Streamlining" began as a functional idea to achieve certain benefits in moving vehicles: the rounding of outward contours would lead to beneficial results. In airplanes, locomotives, and automobiles, the smoothing of outward surfaces would increase speed, decrease wind resistance, and reduce fuel consumption.

But the "look" of streamlining caught on in the 1930s because of the perceived message: these products were seen by many as the vanguard of progressive changes that would soon propel society forward out of economic stagnation, that would smooth out the chaotic ups and downs of the jagged business cycle, and that would harmonize the flow of social interactions in a way that could usher in a brave and beautiful tomorrow.

And so the streamlined look became rapidly applied to a range of products that were never intended to move through space (refrigerators, toasters, radios) or else to move at such low rates of speed (vacuum cleaners) that the functional advantages of streamlining were nonexistent. It didn't matter: as the fad took hold, it was patently pointless to look for any logical justification.

An elite group of celebrity designers rose to prominence: men such as Raymond Loewy, Henry Dreyfuss, Donald Deskey, Norman Bel Geddes, and Walter Dorwin Teague. Locomotive design, in particular, increased the fame of the designers: Dreyfuss was known far and wide as the man who had designed the locomotive for the Twentieth-Century Limited. Even more dramatic—even sexier—was Loewy's design for the Pennsylvania Railroad's S-1 steam locomotive.

Architects had been experimenting with rounded contours as a design theme since the 1910s. But in the 1930s streamlined buildings were designed and built all over the United States, and in staggering profusion. Certain building types in particular—for instance, roadside diners—used streamlined effects to achieve an emblematic or iconic effect on viewers, especially motorists who (of necessity) would often have to look at the building for a fleeting instant and size it up for what is was.

Perhaps the streamlining fad in architecture reached its apex when the illustrious Frank Lloyd Wright used it as the theme for the headquarters complex of the Johnson Wax Company in Racine, Wisconsin. The complex, which encompasses two buildings—the administration building and the "research tower"—was built between 1936 and 1939.

Streamlined architecture figured largely in two great public expositions that captured the public's imagination in the 1930s: the 1933 Century of Progress Exposition in Chicago and the 1939 New York World's Fair.

Organized in 1928 by a Chicago nonprofit organization, the Century of Progress Exposition featured streamlined structures and exhibit halls with a multicolored scheme to contrast it with the "White City" of Beaux Arts classical buildings featured at the 1893 World's Columbian Exposition in Chicago. The 1933 fair featured exhibits and novelties of different kinds. But its overall theme was scientific progress through applied industrial design. In addition to corporate displays of automotive design, an influential exhibit was the "Homes of Tomorrow Exhibition," which was dominated by corporate displays of new household conveniences.

The 1939 New York World's Fair was far more influential: it captured the imaginations of millions of people, even people who could not afford to visit it. An international exposition, its theme was futuristic progress; its official literature stated that "the eyes of the Fair are on the future—not in the sense of peering toward the unknown nor attempting to foretell the events of tomorrow and the shape of things to come, but in the sense of presenting a new and clearer view of today in preparation for tomorrow; a view of the forces and ideas that prevail as well as the machines."

Planning for the fair began in 1935 when a committee of New York businessmen and officials—including Mayor Fiorello La Guardia—decided that a bold exposition of this type might lift the spirits of Depression America, much as the dramatic construction of Rockefeller Center in the midst of the Depression was viewed by many as a bold act of faith in the future. The New York World's Fair Corporation rented a suite at the top of the Empire State Building. Its board elected Grover Whalen, a former chief of police who had gone into public relations, as its president.

New York City Parks Commissioner Robert Moses created a vast site for the exposition in Flushing Meadows (Queens). To the chagrin of some, the fair was heavily dominated by corporate pavilions, especially the streamlined pavilions of Ford and General Motors in the "Transportation Zone." The GM pavilion featured a "Futurama" designed by Norman Bel Geddes. Visitors were carried in suspended seats above a massive diorama showing an entire future region of America with streamlined highways and gorgeous new skyscrapers. At the end of the ride, visitors would walk into a life-size city intersection of the future.

Other types of corporations offered a range of enticing exhibits purporting to predict the "World of Tomorrow" and also to present emergent products such as nylon, dishwashers, air conditioning, fluorescent lighting, and television. Television technology was displayed (in the form of some actual television sets) and explained (in brochures) by RCA; indeed NBC took advantage of the World's Fair to initiate regular television broadcasting in the New York area and FDR's opening speech was telecast as well as broadcast.

Over sixty nations participated and built their own pavilions. Nazi Germany did not participate, but the Soviet Union did.

A pair of large, white, and abstract symbolic buildings, one triangular and one circular—respectively the Trylon and Perisphere—constituted the fair's universally recognized motif. They were linked by a spiraling pedestrian walkway called the "Helicline." Inside the Perisphere was yet another "model city of tomorrow."

And the World's Fair had a theme song—performed posthumously after the tragic and untimely death of the composer, George Gershwin—*Dawn of a New Day*. The lyrics had been written, as always, by Ira, the composer's brother and partner.

THE EFFECTS OF THE GREAT DEPRESSION
ON AMERICAN MUSIC

In a great many ways, the hard times of the 1930s affected American music in a manner that correlated directly with the visual arts: the imagery of suffering recorded in films, photographs, and paintings had its counterpart in melodies and lyrics of expressive songs, and the optimistic symbolism of dynamic *flow* in the streamlining fad had its audible counterpart in swing music. Even regionalism (and the back-to-the-land movement generally) correlated with the orchestral music composed by Virgil Thomson, Aaron Copland, and others.

The American musical world encompassed movements as diverse as the grassroots-inspired traditions of blues and jazz (the latter encompassing popular dance culture, and especially so by the time of the "big band" era in the 1930s), the show tunes of Broadway plays and Hollywood musicals, the sheet music of "Tin Pan Alley," the worlds of folk music and rural string band music (the latter evolving into the overlapping realms of country music, bluegrass, and western swing in the 1930s), and the high-art orchestral compositions of people like Gershwin and Copland, some compositions for opera and others for ballet.

The preexisting movements of blues and folk music were admirably suited for commentary both on the hardship of the Depression and the themes of class conflict that overlapped it. The blues classic "Nobody Knows You When You're Down and Out," written by Jimmy Cox in 1923 and performed by the superb Bessie Smith only months before the stock market crash in 1929, expressed in a haunting manner the plight and the feelings of America's desperately poor and its melody and lyrics would resonate throughout the 1930s.

Folk ballads associated with the struggles of the labor movement—some of them satirical, such as "The Preacher and the Slave," written by Joe Hill in 1911, with its famous line about "pie in the sky when you die"—along with rural string band songs about the life of "hobos" laid the groundwork for a repertoire of songs composed and performed in the 1930s by Woody Guthrie.

Born in Oklahoma, this musician became known as the "Dust Bowl Troubadour." He traveled with migrant Okies, learned much of their song repertoire, and added to it with compositions of his own. Avowedly left-of-center—and allegedly a Communist sympathizer—Guthrie composed songs of commentary on the labor management confrontations of the 1930s, songs such as "Vigilante Man" and "When the Curfew Blows." His song "Pretty Boy Floyd" portrayed the Dust Bowl bank robber as a kind of Robin Hood. His song "Tom Joad" was built around the central character in Steinbeck's *Grapes of Wrath*. And he wrote many songs about the miseries of the Dust Bowl, songs such as "Dust Can't Kill Me" and "Dust Pneumonia Blues."

Some famous songs composed for shows and/or sheet music by Tin Pan Alley songwriters became Depression-era classics. Perhaps the most famous was "Brother, Can You Spare a Dime?" written in 1930 by E. Y. "Yip" Harburg and composer Jay Gorney. It became famous in recordings and radio performances by singers such as Bing Crosby and Rudy Vallee. Written mostly in a somber minor key, it became a great signature melody of hard times. Its lyrics contained elements of social protest, such as commentary on the sad condition of many World War I veterans fully two years before the march of the Bonus Army gripped the nation's attention.

Songs such as these had their optimistic counterparts in tunes like "We're in the Money," written by Harry Warren and Al Dubin for the film *Gold Diggers of 1933*. Other songs that could be associated with the Depression-era moods were emotionally equivocal, half-somber and half-optimistic. Irving Berlin's "Let's Face the Music and Dance" was written for the 1935 Astaire-Rogers film *Follow the Fleet*. The dance number, superbly choreographed by Astaire, tells the story of a man and woman who make separate decisions to end it all after losing everything in a gambling casino. But when they meet—and dance—the result is the reverse of a suicide pact: they resolve to carry on and face the hardships of life together. A light-hearted version of the overall idea was Jerome Kern's "Pick Yourself Up" from the 1936 Astaire-Rogers film *Swingtime*.

Major trends in American music that developed during the New Deal years seem expressive of mid-1930s optimism. And these trends seem stunningly related to some corresponding trends in the visual arts. The emergence of swing as an offshoot of jazz is an excellent example, for the flowing "lilt" of swing might be seen as a neat musical counterpart to the symbolism of streamlining.

In swing, the fast-paced rhythms of jazz in its earliest versions are somehow—and without losing dynamism, tempo, or rhythmic pace—"stretched out," as it were, smoothed out into graceful patterns of *flow*. Famous literary counterparts exist: Shakespeare in *Julius Caesar* constructed some extraordinary lines of oratory that use one-syllable words to gain a rolling momentum and a forward-thrusting power that sweeps listeners (or readers) along. So swing music could stretch out staccato rhythm and pack it full of onward-flowing power. To be sure, the technique can be seen in a rudimentary form as early as the 1920s. But Depression-era swing brought the trend to its apex of development.

One of the pioneers of this method was the composer and band leader Fletcher Henderson, whose orchestra frequently performed in the New York ballroom and dance emporium "Roseland." Compositions by Henderson such as "Down South Camp Meeting" helped usher in the new age of swing. Henderson became an arranger for the Benny Goodman band after Goodman's spectacular rise in 1935 launched the "Big Band Era."

The sheer "sweetness" of swing was enhanced even more when accompanied by the "close harmony" performances of vocalists such as the Boswell Sisters (who hailed from Louisiana and gave their singing a slight southern drawl) and, later on, the Andrews Sisters.

Swing had a great many variations, but one of the most interesting was its infiltration of evolving country music. Country music, in its formative years, was developing a number of subgenres such as bluegrass. In "western swing," the converging elements of "Country and Western" were given a strong *melodic* emphasis that drew directly from patterns in mainstream swing. Western swing was perhaps inspired to some extent by novelty stars like the cowboy singers Gene Autry and Patsy Montana. Close-harmony singing for western swing was provided by groups like the dulcet-voiced duo Girls of the Golden West.

As to the "western" side of country western music, the high-art compositions of Aaron Copland and his peers can be seen as a musical counterpart to regionalism in painting. Copland's music exuded lyrical qualities of the sort that many people beheld in American rural life, and they were given a distinctively "western" emphasis at times by the composer's use of nineteenth-century cowboy ballads as themes. Composer Virgil Thomson's compositions used the same technique. Thomson's score for the Lorentz film *The Plow That Broke the Plains* made heavy use of the cowboy ballad "Old Paint." And the score that was written by Dimitri Tiomkin for the 1939 Frank Capra film *Mr. Smith Goes to Washington* used cowboy songs such as "Red River Valley" and "Bury Me Not on the Lone Prairie" as leitmotifs. Here was a musical counterpart to depictions of covered wagon days in some of the murals produced by the WPA artists during the 1930s—commentary on the need for Americans to embrace new forms of pioneering in order to confront new challenges as formidable as those that confronted their hardy forbears.

The western fad was sufficiently pervasive to prompt gentle parody in the mainstream swing hit "I'm an Old Cowhand (From the Rio Grande)," written by Johnny Mercer for performance by Bing Crosby in the 1936 film *Rhythm on the Range*.

Such were the affinities and cross-alignments of Depression-era music in relation to a great many other trends in 1930s American culture.

11

How the Great Depression Ended

The Keynesian School of Thought

THE GREAT DEPRESSION ENDED for one of two possible reasons: (1) it ended because of the federal spending in World War II or else (2) it ended *at the same time* but for reasons that had no cause-and-effect link to the federal spending.

For one and for possibly two generations after the Second World War, an enormous consensus existed among Americans who had lived through the back-to-back depression and global war, a consensus that the first of these explanations was correct—that World War II did the trick by replacing all the jobs that the Depression had destroyed. Anybody in America during World War II who wanted a job had a job. In fact, there was a labor shortage so significant that housewives were brought into factories to keep the production lines rolling.

Many who were versed in economic theory concluded that John Maynard Keynes had been correct in 1932 when he predicted that only spending on the scale of total war (or its peacetime equivalent) would end the Great Depression.

The underlying principle was this: when an out-of-control contraction in an economy wipes out enough purchasing power, what is left of the functioning economy sinks downward, stabilizes at a very low level, and *stays there*.

Too much of the energy—the financial energy consisting not only of money but of *money that will actually be spent*—had been destroyed. The financial energy that propels investment requires spending to sustain itself. When this fails to occur, the economy contracts.

Quantum leaps upward or downward can reach a certain level that ushers in a "new normality." In the case of a collapse like the Great Depression, the condition continued until such time as an entity with sufficient financial power and sufficient independence—enough distance—from market forces intervened to replace what had been lost. This entity was government.

In the United States this happened through democratic methods. In Nazi Germany it happened through totalitarian power. Then Germany and other totalitarian nations caused a war that forced the American economy to start functioning (at last) at its full potential through democratic processes. But if the war had never come along, the corollary question is unanswerable: Would America have ever emerged from the Great Depression through democratic processes?

DOUBLING THE AMERICAN MONEY SUPPLY AND GNP

The election of 1940 was dominated by controversies about the war, which had broken out in Europe when Hitler attacked Poland in 1939. The world had been drifting toward war in both Europe and Asia since the early 1930s. Americans had been overwhelmingly isolationist throughout most of that period.

In 1940, Hitler's Blitzkrieg overran Denmark, Norway, Holland, Belgium, and France, which capitulated in June. German bombing of England, beginning right after the fall of France, was a prelude to a planned cross-channel invasion in the fall. Britain's new prime minister, Winston Churchill, sought assistance from FDR, who was running for a third term.

Isolationists in both parties insisted that America must at all costs avoid war. But interventionists began to pose a question that even isolationists found hard to avoid: How would America survive if a Nazi triumph led to an Axis-dominated world? What if America, alone in such a world, were attacked?

Thus cornered, some isolationists began to agree to a fast-paced defense buildup that began in mid- to late 1940. This mobilization continued into 1941, after FDR won reelection. Aid to Britain, via the "Lend-Lease" program that was instituted early in 1941, won formal approval from Congress.

Based on the facts and figures, this spending can be correlated with a drop in unemployment. This certainly does not mean that the Depression was eradicated by December 7, 1941, when the Japanese attacked Pearl Harbor. But it does appear to demonstrate that the Depression was beginning to vanish. Moreover, the trend laid the groundwork not only for recovery but also for a stupendous period of economic growth, perhaps the greatest in the nation's history.

In 1938—in the middle of the "Roosevelt Recession"—unemployment had climbed to approximately 10 million. By 1939, after Congress had reversed the earlier spending cuts of 1937 and restored roughly $3.7 billion in federal public works spending, unemployment shrank to roughly 9.5 million. In 1940, with significant defense spending, unemployment dropped to roughly 8 million, the lowest figure since 1931, during the Hoover years.

Then in 1941, when federal spending climbed to the level of $13.3 billion, much of it for military spending, unemployment shrank to 5.6 million. In 1942, when the declaration of war propelled America into a fast-tracked economic mobilization, unemployment fell to 2.5 million.

By 1943, unemployment was substantially wiped out.

But that was just the beginning: war necessities and the job market brought work to an additional 3.9 million new job seekers who had just reached employment age as well as to another 7.3 million Americans—people such as housewives—who would seldom have sought work in the decades before World War II.

Federal spending rose through the following steep progression: in 1942, the first year after the Pearl Harbor attack and the declaration of war, federal spending more than doubled from its 1941 total, reaching the level of $34 billion. Federal spending more than doubled again in the next year, 1943, reaching $79.4 billion. By 1944, the level of federal spending stabilized (on an annual basis) in the $90 billion range. Uncle Sam spent $95.1 billion in 1944 and then another $98.4 billion in 1945.

In any given year of the Great Depression, federal spending for public works had never exceeded roughly $5 billion.

These facts and figures appear to speak for themselves.

Wartime austerity and rationing limited short-term consumer spending, but the salaries that Americans were earning both in and out of uniform were building up tremendous purchasing power, regardless of whether the savings from salaries were deposited in bank accounts or invested in war bonds. And even with the shortages and rationing, the American standard of living was transformed with breathtaking speed, as the following reminiscences testify.

A shipyard worker in Portsmouth, Virginia, said that "going to work in the navy yard, I felt like something had come down from heaven. I went from forty cents an hour to a dollar an hour. . . . At the end of the war I was making two seventy an hour. . . . I was able to buy some working clothes for a change, buy a suit. . . . It just made a different man out of me." A native of Portland, Oregon, recalled years later that during the war "for the first time we began to have money. You started to think you could do things. We used to go out to a restaurant now and then, where we would never do that before the war. We hardly ever went to the picture shows during the Depression; now I did all the time. . . . My mother saved enough money to buy a modest home. That was the first home we ever bought."

By 1944, this transformation caused many Americans, including leading politicians, to conclude that a state of full employment ought to remain the "new normality" for the United States and that the federal government should assume responsibility for ensuring this state of affairs. In 1944, Republican presidential candidate Thomas Dewey declared that "if at any time there are not sufficient jobs in private employment to go around, then government can and must create additional job opportunities because there must be jobs for all in this country of ours." On January 11, 1944, President Roosevelt called for a "second bill of rights," an economic bill of rights. The first of these new rights would be "the right to a useful and remunerative job in the industries or shops or farms or mines of the nation."

In 1944, as a first step, FDR and Congress created the "G. I. Bill of Rights," a program to guarantee education and other benefits for veterans after victory had been achieved. Not the least of the motivations behind this program was the desire to prevent any repetition of the ill-planned (or unplanned) demobilization following World War I, which had led to unemployment for veterans during 1919 and 1920 and had also contributed to the short postwar depression. But for many, the G. I. Bill was nothing less than a demonstration of what the federal government should sooner or later be doing for everybody.

An overall generational lesson was emerging, along with a conclusion about the Depression of the 1930s from the standpoint of hindsight: if

America could generate full employment in war, there was no inherent reason why the same thing could not have been done in the Depression. So all the suffering had been needless. Keynes had been right back in 1932 when he said that "we should be ready to spend on the enterprises of peace what the financial maxims of the past would only allow us to spend on the devastations of war."

The "financial maxims of the past" had dictated budget balancing except in wartime. Keynes had recommended deficit spending as the preferred method for financing a fiscal stimulus to propel economic expansion because finance via taxation would be counterproductive: the taxes would represent funds *withdrawn* from the economy instead of being injected into it.

To be sure, there was an important third alternative to taxes and deficit spending: the direct creation of sovereign fiat money by government, the "Greenback" method that was still on the table (for some) in the 1930s. By the 1940s, however, that method was being forgotten.

In any case, deficit spending was employed on a massive scale to finance America's participation in World War II. FDR's treasury secretary, Henry Morgenthau Jr., preferred to raise roughly half of the necessary revenues through taxation and the other half through the sale of war bonds. Eight successive bond drives brought in revenue so vast that the accumulated national debt that was piled up during World War II ($258.7 billion) exceeded America's gross national product by 1945 ($213.4 billion). But the results seemed to justify the method. For America's GNP had been doubled during World War II, to the profound benefit of all. From $100.4 billion in 1940, GNP had surged to over twice that amount through the economics of wartime superabundance.

Many Americans probably understood the fact that the bond sales represented borrowing by Uncle Sam, that is, deficit spending. But how many Americans might have wondered where all the money was coming from in the first place? Indeed, it would be interesting to know what was going through President Roosevelt's mind when he made those wartime quips about the inexplicable nature of money ("the stock argument of the stars. . . . The possessor of money is entitled to . . . worth as divided by money. Now don't forget that, divided by money").

The truth: the methods of deficit spending were grounded in fractional reserve banking, whereby money is created by banks out of nothing. By

World War II, the Federal Reserve played a primary role in this process. These facts were made available to the public; in 1939, the Federal Reserve produced a guidebook explaining its operations for lay readers. And this book, *The Federal Reserve System: Its Purposes and Functions*, included the following statement: "Federal Reserve Bank Credit . . . does not consist of funds that the Reserve authorities 'get' somewhere in order to lend, but constitutes funds that they are empowered to create."

But how many during World War II (including FDR) understood that fact in clear terms? How many understand it today? One has to understand it to have any clear conception of the way in which World War II was financed.

The financing depended on revenue, streams of funding that were brought into government coffers through taxation or bond sales. But in order to create the monetary base that would produce the necessary funds in the first place, the money supply of the United States was doubled during World War II, and it was done by the Federal Reserve. A vast number of war bonds were purchased with *borrowed money*, and the money had been newly created by the banking system, with the Federal Reserve in the lead. It was no exaggeration when economist Seymour Harris once said that "in World War II . . . the task of the Federal Reserve was to manufacture money."

This doubling of America's money supply has been confirmed by any number of economists and economic historians. Allan H. Meltzer, in his definitive two-volume history of the Federal Reserve, has stated that America's "monetary base doubled in the four years ending fourth quarter 1945." Economic historians Gary M. Walton and Hugh Rockoff concur: "The stock of money in 1939 was only slightly higher than in 1929, but by 1944 it had more than doubled."

THE NEW KEYNESIAN CONSENSUS

John Maynard Keynes (1883–1946) lived to see his own worst-case prediction come true: it took spending to fight a total war (instead of peacetime spending conducted on the scale of total war) to end the Great Depression of the 1930s, at least in the United States and the other democracies.

He did not live to see his own name canonized in a school of thought that would dominate the economics profession and public policymaking for several decades. In the year of his death, however, the essential "Keynesian" lesson was written into law by Congress in the form of the Employment Act of 1946, which created the Council of Economic Advisers and vested the federal government with permanent responsibility for maintaining high levels of employment (more on that later).

Keynes's teachings regarding the fundamentality of purchasing power and fiscal stimulation (as related to depressions) were not new in the twentieth century. Not only had the British economist John A. Hobson said much the same thing in the 1890s, but American politicians and policy advocates had done likewise from the days of John Quincy Adams and Henry Clay in the 1830s to Jacob Coxey two generations later. Job creation through "internal improvements" or "public works" had been proposed as an antidote to economic depressions for a very long time.

But this school of thought had always constituted the path not taken until the Second World War seemed to validate its premises and thereby ushered in "the New Economics" as economists such as Seymour Harris and others dubbed it by the 1950s.

All sorts of commentaries poured forth in the 1950s regarding the lesson that World War II had forced on America. New Dealer Thurman Arnold, in memoirs written during the 1950s, declared that "we did not learn the real nature of our economic difficulties until the tremendous spending of the Second World War pulled us out of our static economy and made us the richest nation that the world had ever known." Economist Alvin Hansen—like Harris, a key figure in the promulgation of Keynesian principles after the war—wrote in 1957 that "the war put the American giant to work, and once fully employed, we found that we were able to raise our standard of living . . . beyond any level previously achieved at the very same time we were fighting a total war. This no one would have believed until it actually happened."

People outside of the economics profession were equally convinced, and not the least of them was President Dwight D. Eisenhower. Early in Eisenhower's first term a recession had begun and the president's economic report to Congress in 1954 pledged the government to use its "vast powers to help maintain employment and purchasing power." In October 1954, Ike declared that "so long as any citizen wants work and cannot find it, we have a pressing problem to solve. This administration is working vigorously to bring about a lasting solution."

What the president hoped would be a "lasting solution" was a public works program designed to be sped up or slowed down to even out the peaks and valleys of the business cycle and counteract recessions. According to journalist Robert J. Donovan, Eisenhower at a cabinet meeting in 1954 announced he had instructed adviser Arthur F. Burns to "co-ordinate reports from the various departments and agencies on their plans for public works projects." Ike said it was essential "to have planning advanced sufficiently to insure that men would be put to work quickly. Too often, he said, preliminary planning, testing, and surveys delay start on work. . . . Projects actually under way, he noted, gave the government flexibility in speeding them up or stretching them out, as conditions required."

The result was the Interstate Highway System, the details of which were hammered out in deliberations and congressional negotiations in the two subsequent years. Eisenhower commissioned a blue ribbon task force chaired by Gen. Lucius D. Clay to study the concept and offer alternative methods for its implementation. The administration sent its recommendations to Congress in 1955, and then the system was created the following year in the Federal Aid Highway Act of 1956.

Authors William Trufant Foster and Waddill Catchings had recommended this sort of thing back in 1927 and 1928: public works to be used as discretionary antidotes to short-term slumps in purchasing power. Few people paid much attention at the time.

But times had changed.

Eisenhower, to be sure, was averse to deficit spending, which was Keynes's preferred fiscal method. Though willing to put the budget out of balance, he was staunchly committed to reversing course with a budgetary surplus as soon as conditions permitted it, not least of all to preempt or counteract inflation. In essence, however, his position (though liberals often gave it short shrift at the time) was not very far from the position that Keynes himself had adopted.

Keynes argued that fiscal and monetary policies should be used as compensatory balance wheels to adjust the macroeconomy. In his best-known work, the 1936 *General Theory of Employment, Interest, and Money*, Keynes had characterized his vision of compensatory government action as "moderately conservative in its implications." Like Eisenhower, Keynes believed in capitalism and he wanted to preserve it. Both men, being realists, declared that any economic or social system could break down, wherefore a system of alternating "fixes" was advisable.

In order to avert the threat of inflation, Eisenhower cut spending significantly in his second term. The case can be made that he might have overdone it because a recession began in 1958. Democrats took advantage of this with their calls to "get the country moving again" in the elections of 1960. And it was during this election that candidate John F. Kennedy made Paul Samuelson, a Keynesian economist, his adviser on economic policy.

The policies of the Kennedy administration were grounded in the "New Economics." Kennedy appointed a number of Keynesians to the Council of Economic Advisers, not least of all the chairman, Walter Heller. To sustain both economic growth and high employment while avoiding inflation, JFK and his advisors created a system of "wage and price guideposts." These were standards that—subject to periodic review—would be put forward by the administration as recommendations both to "big business" and to "big labor," the latter represented by the then powerful AFL-CIO (the two erstwhile rival organizations had merged after World War II).

As a matter of law, the guideposts were voluntary propositions. But there were also some discretionary coercive methods at the administration's disposal if compliance were not forthcoming. In 1962, when U.S. Steel, the industry leader, hiked prices in defiance of administration policy, Kennedy angrily condemned the corporation in public (in televised press conferences) and threatened anti-trust action in private.

The price hike was rolled back.

With inflation averted, Kennedy made flexible and eclectic use of tax cuts and deficit spending to stimulate the economy. In a commencement address that he delivered at Yale in 1962, JFK condemned the doctrine of budget balancing as simplistic. The federal budget, he asserted, "in relation to the great problems of Federal fiscal policy which are basic to our economy in 1962, is not simply irrelevant; it can be actively misleading." Debts, he argued, whether public or private, "are neither good nor bad, in and of themselves." What mattered, he said, were the economic *results* when debts were incurred.

That general conclusion was sufficiently widespread by the 1960s for economic writer Edwin L. Dale to contend in 1965 that "the big majority of economists, and a growing number of businessmen, bankers, and labor leaders, believe that the recent deficits in the Federal Budget have been good, not bad, for America."

Such was the Keynesian consensus on the eve of the Vietnam and Watergate era, which began to change everything, both in political and economic terms.

12

The Revolt Against Keynes

FROM THE 1970S ONWARD, the Keynesian consensus that prevailed for two decades after World War II broke down on the intellectual front and in popular culture.

The philosophy that Keynes represented was never completely wiped out as a force to be reckoned with. But the shattering of the consensus ushered in the fragmented and angry mood that prevails on economic policy matters to this day.

It began in the Vietnam and Watergate era—the Nixon era—when a period of economic troubles commenced that did not originate in any clear-cut pattern emanating from the financial sector. These economic troubles coincided with political transformations, with shocks to American civic culture that triggered an ideological sea change in public life. In particular, the Vietnam and Watergate era launched a new wave of "government bashing" on the left and the right that gave laissez-faire ideology a new lease on life.

"STAGFLATION" AND THE ANTI-KEYNESIAN BACKLASH

In the Nixon era, the American economy got sluggish. And this happened at precisely the same time that an inflationary trend became a problem so serious that by the end of the 1970s it ranked at the top of America's problem-solving agenda.

Economists, politicians, and citizens disagreed in regard to their diagnoses of the economic ailments during these years. And the disagreements among the economists regarding the 1970s continue to this day. Inflation was perhaps the most obnoxious of the economic woes of the

1970s. But the lapse in America's overall economic performance since the peak years of the late 1950s and early 1960s was also apparent.

During World War II and the Korean War, wage and price controls had been imposed to contain the economic dislocations on the home front that wartime conditions (especially shortages of goods) might create. When the Vietnam conflict was escalated by Lyndon Johnson after John F. Kennedy's assassination, the expectation in administration circles was that American victory would be easy to attain. So no serious provision was made for any worst-case economic developments. Even JFK's wage and price guideposts began to fall by the wayside.

By the time of the Nixon presidency, economic dislocations were so obvious that Nixon briefly imposed wage and price controls. But the inflationary trend that would continue to dog the American economy throughout the 1970s had started.

The condition was aggravated, not only in America but all over the world, when the OPEC oil cartel began to jack up the price of oil in a manner that increased the cost not only of fuel but of products whose creation involved petroleum by-products, and the higher price of oil raised prices of other commodities and services as providers had to cover the higher fuel cost in the price that they charged to their customers. It bears noting that this increased cost of doing business began to constitute something of an overall economic "drag." The phenomenon of "stagflation" was in the offing.

In addition to the obvious effect of the "oil shock" in creating inflation, commentators argued along ideological lines regarding other possible causes. Conservatives blamed new federal regulations for environmental protection and workplace safety for adding to the overhead of businesses in a manner that was passed along to consumers in the form of higher prices. Liberals often blamed corporate profiteering, abetted by oligopolistic conditions in certain industries.

In any case, by mid-decade inflation had established itself as a self-sustaining trend, complete with an inner logic and momentum. People paid higher prices to avoid paying *higher* prices, which many presumed were over the horizon. And in acting this way, they made the expectation of higher prices self-fulfilling. After Nixon was forced from office in the Watergate scandal, his pleasant but hapless successor, Gerald Ford, wore a button with an acronym slogan that he hoped would catch on with the

American people: his button said "WIN," which meant "Whip Inflation Now." The effect of course was nil.

Meanwhile, a number of economic indicators—especially productivity—began declining in a way that was symptomatic of deeper structural problems in the American economy. Among its other effects, World War II had obliterated (through bombing) many of the industrial plants in the nations that constituted America's Axis enemies: Germany and Japan. As America's erstwhile enemies rebuilt, with American assistance, after the war, they built plants that were far more up to date than their older American counterparts.

By the 1970s, American industries were getting hit hard by some serious competition in the form of Japanese and German imports that were better by far than their American counterparts. And American consumers responded. U.S. firms that could not keep up with this competition went under, so "rustbelt" factory closings and layoffs began to occur in many parts of America's manufacturing sector. Here was yet another drag on the American economy.

Such were the contributing causes to "stagflation," an economic slump in the 1970s that combined an economic slowdown with higher prices. Though hardly a depression, it constituted a case of hard times (in relative terms) that added to a range of political and social discontents: assassinations and other forms of domestic violence, the success of America's Communist enemies in Vietnam, and the shame of Richard Nixon's abuse of power and the ignominious result: he became the first American president to resign in disgrace. By 1976, when America celebrated its Bicentennial (1776–1976), the national mood was ironically gloomy and disgusted.

The victorious candidate in the presidential election of 1976, Jimmy Carter, presented himself to the American people as an antidote to—as a dialectical antithesis of—the "imperial presidency" that had led the American people astray under Richard Nixon. For this and other reasons, Carter helped to initiate a broad-based trend on the left ("neoliberalism" as some called it) that sought to counteract and repudiate the "arrogance of power" as it manifested itself in government.

"Government cannot solve our problems," said Carter in his 1978 State of the Union address. It was Carter (and not his successor Ronald Reagan) who initiated policies of federal deregulation, principally in the airlines industry and in banking. Carter in his way, from an authentically left-of-center perspective, helped usher in the revival of laissez-faire that Reagan intensified enormously in the 1980s.

But the revival of laissez-faire had deeper roots in conservative thought. Ever since the days of the Liberty League in the 1930s, there were plenty of conservatives (many in the business community) who were never reconciled to the "big government" implications of the New Deal and its legacy. During World War II, a pair of Austrian economists, Ludwig von Mises and his acolyte Friedrich Hayek, wrote and published laissez-faire manifestos that American conservatives would later canonize, especially because Mises had taken up residence in the United States. In addition, an American economist, Milton Friedman, began in the 1950s to push his own brand of laissez-faire economics.

These thinkers had little to no influence in mainstream economic circles until the 1970s. But by the middle of the decade they attained a new respectability, both within the economics profession and outside of it. Their influence was magnified by the action of wealthy donors who established new conservative "think tanks," such as the Heritage Foundation and the Cato Institute, in Washington, D.C. In addition, conservative-minded publications such as the *Wall Street Journal* began in the 1970s to intensify their longstanding opposition to government regulation by advocating new (or new sounding) theories such as "supply side" economics.

Like most of the advocates of "pure" free market principles, the economists and theoreticians who opposed the Keynesian consensus tended to think and argue in all-or-nothing terms. Mises, for instance, in his 1944 book *Bureaucracy* asserted that "contrary to a popular fallacy there is no middle way, no third system possible" as an alternative to a choice between the free market and "statism."

With due respect, one might easily argue that Mises was the one who succumbed to a fallacy: what the logicians call the "fallacy of the excluded middle," the denial that a range of possibilities exists along a spectrum of conceptual choices between dialectically opposite extremes. In any case, the rhetoric of Mises was a challenge to one of the central tenets of New Deal and Keynesian statecraft, namely the principle that capitalism and government are reciprocally necessary components of a "mixed economy," which in turn is the best available alternative to totalitarian systems.

A comparable attack on one of the central tenets of Keynesianism, the principle that consumer purchasing power is a necessary precondition for prosperity, was conducted in the 1970s by a bevy of economist-journalists, some of them *Wall Street Journal* editors. Arthur Laffer, Paul Craig Roberts, and Jude Wanniski pushed a creed called "supply side" economics, reviving the old nineteenth-century doctrine ("Say's Law") that production will always generate sufficient "demand" to sell the goods.

In his 1978 manifesto *The Way The World Works*, Wanniski claimed that "the supply of goods creates a demand for goods and . . . the supply of goods can be increased by removing government impediments to production and commerce."

One final factor in the 1970s contributed to the critical mass of challenges to the Keynesian consensus: a widespread notion that the very existence of "stagflation" proved that the "Keynesian model" was wrong.

For a long time, an oversimplification of economic life had distorted many people's understanding and even shaped the views of economists: the frequently unexamined notion that economies move in one general direction—either expansion or contraction—but will not unfold in ambiguous patterns that defy simple visualization. Consequently, "inflation" and "deflation" were terms that oversimplified a great many overlapping trends that deserved much better analysis. Take the term "inflation," which is still in our own day and age quite familiar to most of us, and we understand the term in general to mean a certain and very specific thing: higher prices. But for years, the term was also widely understood to denote a simultaneous increase of *all* major economic indicators: prices, money supply, and economic activity in general. So it stood to reason that many presumed that expansion of the money supply must lead *inherently* to higher prices, that is, "inflation," because expansion of the money supply and an increase in prices were different facets of the same unitary process.

But that is not necessarily the case.

By the same token, "deflation" was often understood as the flip-side proposition: it was understood as comprehensive economic "contraction," that is, lower prices, smaller money supply, and less market activity.

It is very important to understand that these sets of conditions may *sometimes* go together in the course of everyday economic life: *sometimes* an increase in economic activity goes along with an increase in the size of the money supply and an increase in the overall price level.

But these things do not *always* go together.

Due to widespread imprecision of terminology, grounded in an over-simplification of ideas, it was not unusual for "Keynesianism" by the 1970s to be understood (or misunderstood) as a system designed to regulate two *and only two* alternative sets of economic situations with ready-made policy prescriptions, to wit: when "deflation" gets harmful, the policy of government should pump up expansion; when "inflation" gets out of control, it is the duty of government to "put the brakes on" an "overheated" economy.

This principle of "contra-cyclical" action by government applied as much on the monetary front as on the fiscal front; in the 1960s, for instance, William McChesney Martin, the chairman of the Federal Reserve, declared that "our purpose is to lean against the winds of deflation or inflation, whichever way they are blowing."

Once again, there are times when such visualizations do give an accurate description of the economic forces in play and Keynes certainly did recommend a program of compensatory "balance wheel" government action. But there are also times when economic life becomes more complex and Keynes was an extremely flexible and sophisticated thinker. And sadly enough, many influential commentators in the 1970s failed to understand these facts.

And so it came to pass that the very existence in the 1970s of "stagflation"—the existence at one and the same time of a slump (recession or "deflation") and higher prices ("inflation") suggested an anomaly that the Keynesian "model" was powerless to "explain." Therefore, many people concluded, the "Keynesian model" was flawed.

Willy-nilly, many commentators began to reject the teachings of Keynes and instead turned to Hayek, Friedman, or Laffer as alternative gurus.

But there are numerous examples of stagflation in economic history. One obvious example is the short depression that followed World War I. The conversion of wartime industries to civilian production required many factories to close for retooling. One result of this process was layoffs, resulting in unemployment, contraction, and "deflation." At the same time, the shortage of consumer goods led to higher prices, "inflation." There it was: a demonstration of the fact that two processes that were supposed to be mutually exclusive could exist at one and the same time, that is, stagflation.

The decline in the reputation of Keynesianism by the 1970s was hardly universal. Many people on the left (especially those who had lived through the 1930s and 1940s) were convinced that the overall concepts of Keynes retained validity. But economists were increasingly divided, and a cleft between the schools of thought that are currently known as "salt water economics" and "fresh water economics" began to develop.

The "salt water" term was a shorthand reference to the fact that in the academic departments of economics in East Coast and West Coast universities, adherence to the Keynesian school remained strong. In the heartland, however, an increasingly insistent avowal of free market principles prevailed, with the Department of Economics at the University of Chicago in the lead.

Once launched, the campaign to discredit the teachings of Keynes gained momentum, and it led to some revisionist conclusions regarding the relationship between the Great Depression and World War II. In 1986, historian Robert Higgs declared that "the war had taught the American people many lessons, some true, some false. Of the latter sort, a leading example was the Keynesian illusion. . . . The notion that wartime 'full employment' had resulted from the huge federal deficits was false. Quite simply, unemployment fell mainly because of the buildup of the armed forces. . . . Any government that can conscript prime workers by the millions can eliminate unemployment."

This must surely stand as one of the great *non sequiturs* in the writing of economic history. For unless the soldiers were to serve *without pay*, it must surely stand to reason that a financial method of one sort or another would have to be used by the federal government to pay them. As it was, the level of deficit spending during World War II was so massive that by 1945 the accumulated national debt was actually greater than America's gross national product.

DIFFERENT KINDS OF RECESSIONS

In 1979, in anticipation of a tough reelection campaign in 1980, Jimmy Carter confronted the twin economic evils of recession and inflation and decided that inflation was by far the worse problem. And so Carter appointed as chairman of the Federal Reserve Board Paul Volcker, an

economist and banker with a reputation as a tough maverick. It was generally understood that Volcker would use the powers of "the Fed" to get
inflation under control.

And he did. Under Volcker's leadership, the Federal Reserve Board in
1979 and 1980 contracted the money supply, and it was done with such
tenacity and severity that it worsened the economic slump of the 1970s—
worsened it to the point that unemployment levels reached the highest
point (at that time) since the 1930s.

Instead of worsening the slump by raising interest rates, the board
inflicted its draconian measures through indirection: it raised the reserve
ratios instead, which meant that banks would have to put more funds
off limits as the basis for fractional reserve money creation. In 1980, at
the Fed's request, Congress gave the Federal Reserve the power to set
reserve ratios for all "depository institutions" that benefitted from federal deposit insurance, which meant that the Fed would now control not
only the ratios of commercial banks but also the ratios of savings and loan
institutions and credit unions as well.

This severe recession within a recession lasted through 1982, when
inflation had at last been driven down to the point at which Volcker
declared victory and eased up on the policy, much to the relief of advisers
to the new president, Ronald Reagan, who feared that hard times would
cast a pall over his presidency.

This severe economic downturn was notable and interesting for a
number of reasons.

For one thing, it was a trial by fire of the New Deal safety net, for it
tested the long-term efficacy of unemployment compensation, which had
not existed when the Great Depression of the 1930s began. Unemployment
compensation eased the suffering for many people who were thrown out
of work because of Volcker's anti-inflation campaign. But because unemployment compensation was set up as a partnership between the federal
government and the states, lost income was usually not replaced in full
because many state policies did not make provisions for that.

It bears noting that when Volcker initiated his campaign, the legal
mandate set by the Employment Act of 1946, which had vested the
federal government with responsibility for maintaining high levels
of employment, had fallen by the wayside. That act had been recently
superseded—gutted, in effect—when Congress passed the Humphrey-

Hawkins Act in 1978. This newer legislation downgraded the mainte-
nance of employment to the status of merely one among a number of
economic goals for federal policy.

It is also notable that this recession within a recession started as an
emanation from the financial sector, but this time the contractionary
dynamics derived from regulatory action by a part of the sector with an
overriding public responsibility, mandated by government—the Federal Reserve, which serves in effect as America's central banking institution—rather than from a speculative panic on Wall Street.

The next recession to strike America began within a decade and its
origins were very different.

The hard times of the 1970s were chased away to some extent in the
1980s, when a trend that some proclaimed to be an economic boom (more
on that momentarily) appeared and the inflationary problems of the
1970s were banished. Volcker, of course, could take much (perhaps most)
of the credit for eradicating the inflationary trend, but it also bears noting
that the OPEC cartel became weaker in the 1980s.

As to the "boom," however, the elements of economic recovery in the
1980s were combined with all kinds of problems. One genuine benefit
was certainly due to the policies of Ronald Reagan: an enormous defense
buildup, financed by a huge increase in federal spending, injected dynamism into certain segments of the private sector. The result was to some
extent Keynesian, a fact that conservative supporters of Reagan were
averse to acknowledging.

Even Keynes's financial method, deficit spending, was employed by
Reagan indirectly. It is perfectly true that Reagan was a putative foe
of deficit spending and an advocate of balanced budgets. But Reagan's
own budgetary calculations were flawed from the beginning, as one of
his chief economic advisers, David Stockman, admitted a few years later.
Reagan, a believer in "supply side" economics, pushed through enormous
tax cuts for the wealthy in the first year of his presidency, confident that
these tax cuts would pay for themselves. But that never happened.

So to make up for the enormous gap between tax revenue and Reagan's
defense spending, the budget was thrown out of balance and "into the red."

Stockman later confessed that he had never believed in the best-case
assumptions of supply side finance and that his own computer modeling
had been based on severely flawed premises.

More telling was the fact that despite the economic stimulus of the defense spending, American manufacturing continued to decline in the 1980s. Other sorts of decline became apparent with the rapid emergence of "downsizing," "outsourcing," and globalization, devices that corporations started using for the purpose of cutting down labor costs and breaking down the power of labor unions.

The outsourcing of services meant that employers could cut back on pensions, medical insurance, and other important fringe benefits that labor unions had won during previous contract negotiations. The exporting of production to foreign countries—accompanied by a diversion of investment to those countries—made it hard if not impossible for American unions to employ the leverage of threatening to strike, for there was no practical way for the AFL-CIO to flex its muscles overseas.

For these and related reasons, the earning power of American middle-class and working-class families started to stagnate or even decline in the 1980s, thus initiating a long-term trend that has continued right down to the present. This diminution in purchasing power would weaken America's economic strength over time. By the 1980s, many middle-class families found that it suddenly took two incomes to approximate the standard of living that the earnings of a single "breadwinner" had provided in the Eisenhower years.

This underlying weakness may well have contributed to the next recession, which began in the administration of Reagan's successor, the elder George Bush. But a major trigger point for this recession was—as had been so often the case in the past—a speculative frenzy in America's financial sector, in this case a frenzy that combined the "S & L crisis" with the craze for leveraged buyouts of companies by the means of "junk bonds."

In 1980, under Jimmy Carter, the savings and loan industry had been partially deregulated. This trend continued under Reagan via the Garn-St. Germain Act that was passed by Congress in 1982. Savings and loans, which were lending institutions set up to grant home loan mortgages, had been regulated to some extent for a long time (since the Hoover era) by a Federal Home Loan Bank Board. And the deposits of savings and loans were insured during FDR's administration by an agency designed to serve as an S & L counterpart to FDIC: the FSLIC, or Federal Savings and Loan Insurance Corporation. The same quid pro quo that governed the insurance of deposits in commercial banks was established for S & Ls:

in return for the federal insurance, participating banks would have to submit to some regulation in order to ensure that sound banking practices prevailed.

The 1980 and 1982 deregulation acts undercut this federal oversight. Specifically, the S & Ls were permitted in the 1980s to make riskier investments. They were also permitted to pay higher interest rates at the very same time that the upper limit of their deposit insurance was increased. These policies within a few years caused the "S & L crisis" (or "S & L scandal") that bankrupted FSLIC, caused a multibillion dollar taxpayer bailout in 1990, and led to the crash of the junk bond market, with severe ramifications for the stock market as well.

S & Ls began to attract huge brokered deposits from investors who were after the higher interest rates. Simultaneously, S & Ls were purchased by well-connected hustlers who proceeded to make all kinds of risky investments in ill-grounded real estate projects.

Some of these investments were buy-and-flip (or build-and-flip) schemes in which developers would acquire or build office buildings in areas where the rental market was volatile. The idea was to build the tower quickly, then sell it for a profit and eject before the rental market was exhausted, whereupon the last in the series of owners would be stuck with a property full of unleasable office space. "See through" (that is, empty) office buildings were all too prominent in areas of ill-grounded real estate speculation by the end of the decade.

Once-reputable S & Ls were acquired by hustlers through junk bond deals. Junk bonds were high-risk and high-interest borrowing instruments. Investment firms such as Drexel Burnham Lambert helped manipulators buy control of S & Ls, often at prices far above their net worth. The new S & L owners would pay themselves enormous salaries and enormous bonuses. They would give themselves enormous "perks": Rolls-Royces, vacation homes, and private aircraft. Then in return for the help of the investment firms that helped them gain control of the S & Ls, the new owners would buy huge amounts of junk bonds from such firms.

Junk bonds were sometimes used in connection with "corporate raids." Put simply, the raiders' technique was to buy enough stock to take over once-reputable firms, then strip them (for short-term profit) of long-term assets by means of downsizing, service cutbacks, and other shoddy practices. In the name of "efficiency," the raiders ruined the long-term business plans of a great many firms in the 1980s. Prominent businesses such as department stores with a long-term loyal clientele were run into the ground by these raiders, who of course would sell the companies well before they went (predictably) bankrupt.

All of this led to some macroeconomic consequences that were equally predictable.

Many risky investments went sour after those who had perpetrated them had bailed out and left the scene. In due time, the bottom fell out of the junk bond market and the stock market crashed in 1987. As the Federal Home Loan Bank Board shut down more and more insolvent savings and loans, FSLIC had to pay out deposit insurance on a scale so staggering that the agency itself ran out of funds. A huge taxpayer bailout had to be orchestrated by Reagan's successor, George Herbert Walker Bush, who was left holding the bag after winning the election of 1988.

There was at least a little bit of institutional and personal accountability in the course of this tawdry experience: Drexel was hit by an insider trading scandal in 1986 and one of its executives, Michael Milken, went to jail, as did arbitrager Ivan Boesky.

A recession set in after Ronald Reagan left the White House. It was arguably caused by all or most of the earlier referenced economic trends. It made the elder George Bush a one-term president because the in-house campaign slogan of the Democratic presidential nominee Bill Clinton, who won the election of 1992, was "It's the economy, stupid."

Clinton was in general a "neoliberal" who therefore applauded and abetted the overall trends of deregulation and globalization. But it does bear noting that in 1993 he proposed a definitively Keynesian "stimulus package" consisting of $16.3 billion of infrastructure spending. This stimulus package, however, was filibustered to death by Senate Republicans.

The recession slowly abated. Yet the underlying economic problems that developed in the previous decade, especially the drop or stagnation of middle-class and working-class earning power, grew apace in the 1990s as more and more wealthy investors sent their dollars overseas instead of spending them on job-creating ventures here in America. The result was a "jobless recovery," with corporate earnings and stock prices surging even as job growth remained stagnant. Ironically, this economic situation was hailed by many in the 1990s as a great economic "boom" at the very same time that middle-class and working-class Americans struggled harder than ever to stay afloat. This situation represented a reversion to conditions of the 1980s. It also reflected the growing predominance of the financial sector, which grew prodigiously while manufacturing declined. The "boom" accelerated further in the final years of the decade when the so-called Dot Com Boom began—an investment frenzy in the new technologies of "Silicon Valley" accompanied by the advent of the internet and its related new technological wonders.

But the short-term frenzy played out. The Dot Com Boom became deflated during the first presidential term of George W. Bush into the "Dot Com Bust." The result was a major recession. And as economic conditions sank back into their preexisting state, the younger Bush continued the Reagan tradition by persuading Congress to institute the largest tax cuts to date.

Supply side theory died hard. But the economic windfall for superwealthy Americans, who benefitted the most from this latest round of tax cuts, was dispersed with great speed through investments all over the globe that did nothing to put the American people to work.

13

The Great Recession

THE GREATEST ECONOMIC CONTRACTION in American history since the 1930s began in 2008 and its effects have continued ever since. "The Great Recession" is what many people have called it, though some, like the Princeton economist Paul Krugman, have labeled it a full-scale depression.

It would surely have become a depression that everyone would label as such were it not for the fact that the New Deal safety net, especially via FDIC and unemployment compensation, contained its worst effects, and this containment was increased by two funding actions on the part of the federal government: (1) the Troubled Asset Relief Program (TARP) created by Congress and George W. Bush in the final months of his administration (augmented by action of the Federal Reserve to prop up lending institutions) and (2) the creation by Congress and President Barack Obama of a stimulus/spending package in the early months of 2009.

There is no question as to how this recession/depression began: it began because of practices in the financial sector that got out of control and then started to drag down the whole "brick-and-mortar" economy, in much the same manner that so many previous episodes of hard times in American history had played out.

THE "SUBPRIME" REAL ESTATE CRISIS

The first cause of the Great Recession arose in the real estate industry. Mortgage brokers seeking quick commissions started packaging "adjustable rate mortgages" or "ARMS." These were mortgages whose interest rates would shift. Initially low rates of interest would balloon

and soar upward after an initial grace period that would get the payments flowing. These mortgages were sold to low-income home buyers whose earning potential should never have qualified them for the
long-term payment burden that these mortgages would impose. Many
of these people were first-time buyers who did not fully understand the
implications of what they were doing. They were veritably destined to
lose the houses they were buying through foreclosure.

A member of the Federal Reserve Board, Edward Gramlich, perceived the danger and tried to get the Fed to intervene. Under the terms
of the 1968 Truth in Lending Act, the Federal Reserve had some power
to curb the worst of these practices. But the chairman, Alan Greenspan,
was a free marketeer and his preference was to keep hands off. Reagan
had appointed him to succeed Paul Volcker in the 1980s. In the 1990s,
Bill Clinton had renewed Greenspan's term at the Fed.

Greenspan was a believer in the "pure" free market. And his faith was
abetted by pseudoscientific certitudes within the economics profession.
Some of these certitudes involved the misuse of mathematics—math that
was corrupted at its very source by some very false premises.

Finance economists, for instance, had developed a so-called capital
asset pricing model (or CAPM) grounded in the premise that investors typically base their decisions on rational calculations and that, in
the aggregate, their decisions are typically right on target, as supposedly
demonstrated by statistics.

On close examination, however, such statistics were obviously drawn
from a limited evidence base.

Some of the "fresh water" economists hedged their bets; in the 1970s, a
prominent member of the tribe, Robert Lucas, acknowledged that recessions result sometimes from *confusion* among investors. But he went on
to argue that attempts to rectify the situation by external interventions
would worsen things by making it harder for investors to learn from
their bad experience (survival of the fittest) and become more successful
in their chosen craft.

Is it any wonder in an intellectual climate like this that the plight
of inexperienced buyers who fell into the trap of adjustable rate
mortgages could be shrugged away by a person such as Alan Greenspan—shrugged away as an eyes-open calculation of short-term versus
long-term contingencies?

Ironically, the common presumption (conscious or unconscious, stated or unstated) among economists that economic behavior is "rational"—and thus easy to measure or predict—according to mathematical models was subjected to a stunning challenge by psychologist Daniel Kahneman, who won the Nobel Prize for economics in 2002, the first noneconomist to win it. Kahneman suggested that all kinds of economic choices are irrational, and he and his followers gave these forms of behavior common sense names: "overconfidence," that is, the tendency to make overoptimistic generalizations from small amounts of information; "confirmation bias," that is, the reflex of discounting information that contradicts what we want to believe; and "weak self-control," that is, the tendency to let short-term impulses override the sense that would guide us to recognize bad risks for what they are.

The fact that this common sense as amplified by "social science" had (and still has) minimal influence with so many ideologists is itself a sad commentary on what Kahneman called "confirmation bias."

In any case, Greenspan refused to intervene in the increasingly dangerous real estate market, so the "subprime" lending, as people were beginning to call it circa 2005, ran its course. In the meantime, some other financiers were working out a method that would spin this situation into spectacular profits.

CREDIT DEFAULT SWAPS

In financial jargon, a "derivative" is a form of security (an investment vehicle) that takes the form of a contract. It is set up to deliver specific results that depend on the performance of underlying assets.

In 2000, President Bill Clinton, on his way out of office, signed a piece of legislation, the Commodity Futures Modernization Act, that was supported and recommended by economic advisers such as Robert Rubin and Lawrence Summers. This legislation exempted from regulation a certain type of derivative known as a "credit default swap." Clinton also signed legislation repealing a key provision of the 1933 Glass-Steagall Act, the provision separating commercial banking from investment banking, thus eliminating a firewall set up to prevent the bad results of bad investments in stocks, bonds, and other securities from wreaking havoc on commercial banks, where so much of the nation's money supply originates.

As the twenty-first century commenced, the New Deal's firewall was ripped down.

As the adjustable rate mortgage crisis played out, the bad mortgages were repackaged and sold to different banks and investment houses. In the process, these doomed-to-fail mortgages—doomed to fail because the borrowers would default at some point—were wrapped into larger securities known as "collateralized debt obligations," or CDOs. These investment packages were dangerous because of their complexity: it was often hard for investors to understand everything that was in them, and especially so in the rapid-fire, high-turnover world of high finance.

But some operators on Wall Street and elsewhere perceived that the predictable failure of the ARMs within the CDOs could provide them with a golden opportunity to make profits. They created and sold some credit default swaps—derivatives—that amounted to insurance policies on the CDOs. If the CDOs plunged in value, the firm that issued and sold the credit default swaps would have to pay out a great deal of money.

Again, there were people who perceived the danger right away; investor Warren Buffet, for instance, who got rich through the time-honored method of acquiring companies with track records of producing excellent products and selling them in great volume, warned that the credit default swaps were "financial weapons of mass destruction." And the destruction would play out in global terms because the sellers and the buyers of these credit default swaps were located all over the world.

In January 2009, in an article published in the *Village Voice*, attorney and writer James Lieber declared that the credit default swap disaster was "the worst financial scandal in history." He also wrote that its perpetrators ought to be prosecuted—brought to justice.

He pointed out that the payoff value of the credit default swaps sold by people at the huge insurance firm of AIG was "worth more than three times the value of the parent company"—the company that would have to pay out when the CDOs failed and the credit default swaps were invoked. And the people who were selling the credit default swaps knew exactly what would happen, Lieber claimed, because they knew perfectly well that the CDOs were full of bad debt. That was precisely the point of creating these insurance policies and then selling them—selling them to people who did not even own the CDOs in the first place.

"Imagine," wrote Lieber, "if a ring of cashiers at a local bank made thousands of bad loans, aware that they would break the bank. They would be prosecuted for fraud and racketeering under the anti-gangster RICO Act."

Early in 2008, as the rate of defaults on the ARMs became obvious, investment raters started downgrading the CDOs that contained the bad mortgages to junk investments, and the race to dump them was on. Many of the CDOs that were full of bad debt had been tucked away in the portfolios of some of the largest banks in the country. The result was a massive financial panic that spread to international dimensions.

The alarms prompted action by three key figures in America: Ben Bernanke, the chair of the Federal Reserve Board; Henry Paulson, treasury secretary under George W. Bush; and Timothy Geithner, who was serving at that time as president of the Federal Reserve Bank of New York. All through 2008, these men would collaborate on strategies to keep the nation's top banks from failing. Their efforts were attacked at the time from both the left and the right: by liberals outraged by the rescue of Wall Street investors who were over their heads in bad securities and by conservative hardliners who would brook no interference whatsoever by government in "free enterprise."

The "bailout," as its friends and its foes alike would quickly call it, proceeded from March 2008—when $29 billion of government financing was extended to rescue the firm of Bear Stearns—to September, when the Treasury Department saved the government-backed mortgage agencies Fannie Mae and Freddie Mac. Then the task of saving Lehman Brothers from falling into bankruptcy commenced.

Journalist James B. Stewart interviewed the various participants in this drama, then wrote up the results for the *New Yorker* magazine. He reported on a week's worth of frenzied efforts by Bernanke, Paulson, and Geithner, together with the CEOs of all the Wall Street firms that were threatened. The rescue of Lehman Brothers proved impossible. But the nightmare was only beginning. On Saturday, September 13, Paulson was reportedly just about to leave the latest crisis session when a billionaire CEO named Christopher Flowers turned to him and said, "have you been watching AIG?"

AIG was the huge insurance firm whose super-salesmen had been selling massive credit default swaps on the endangered CDOs. "Why, what's wrong with AIG?" Paulson asked. Then Flowers pulled out the previous day's spreadsheet from AIG and showed it to Paulson. Paulson reportedly stared at the document and said, "Oh my God!"

Paulson had formerly been the CEO of Goldman, Sachs. His successor at the firm, Lloyd Blankfein, told him that if AIG were not rescued quickly, Goldman Sachs would lose $20 billion and then go under.

AIG was rescued to the tune of $85 billion.

If the biggest banks in the United States had indeed toppled in 2008—even worse, if the upper limits of FDIC deposit protection had been exceeded—this crisis might very well have ushered in another Great Depression on the scale of the 1930s calamity. Already, by the autumn of 2008, the vast economic contraction set in motion by the widening financial crisis was causing millions of Americans to lose their homes through mortgage foreclosures. In total, more than four million homes would be foreclosed before the crisis abated.

And the steady losses in the banking sector—as the frenzy to dump the CDOs continued—exerted an enormous contractionary pressure on the overall economy. Without any firewall in place to stop the chain reaction from spreading from investment banking to commercial banking, which of course plays its own decisive role in the network that links the financial sector to the "real-world economy" of companies that sell real products and services, the onset of a huge recession was all but inevitable.

So Paulson and Bernanke prevailed upon George W. Bush, himself a free marketeer, to go to Congress and request one of the largest federal interventions in the private sector in American history: the $700 billion "Troubled Asset Relief Program" that would lend enough money to the "troubled" banks to permit them to work themselves out of trouble over time and (perhaps) reform the way they did business.

Additional billions were created by the Federal Reserve—through the legerdemain of fractional reserve banking—and extended to the threatened banks (as loans) through the Fed's emergency liquidity program. Given the economic stakes, such banks were deemed "too big to fail," that is, too big to be *allowed* to fail.

It looked for a very fleeting moment as if the whole world of "fresh water economics" was about to be purged by a wholesome flood of fresh air, clear thinking, and true-to-life reality therapy as Alan Greenspan confessed to an irate congressional committee that he was "shocked" by the way the disaster had played out. Late in 2008, Henry Paulson proclaimed that "raw capitalism is dead."

THE MISCALCULATIONS OF OBAMA

The new president, Barack Obama, sensed that a major intervention—Keynesian action—was required to prevent this disaster from ushering in a new depression.

All over the world, the financial chain reaction was causing a decline in manufacturing. By March 2009, European manufacturing was down 12 percent from the previous year, according to the *New York Times*. In China, exports had fallen off by 25 percent and millions of workers were being laid off. In Taiwan, manufacturing had fallen off by 43 percent.

Time was of the essence: Obama and his team would have to move very fast, and he knew it.

But the case can be made that he blew it.

His first questionable move was the appointment of Lawrence Summers, an economist who had been one of the people complicit in the deregulation of credit default swaps back in 2000, as his chief economic adviser. He could have appointed the already-famous Paul Krugman. But he didn't.

Many critics of the bailout started saying that things were even worse under Obama. Columnist Frank Rich, for example, complained in the *New York Times* about what he called "the perennial and bipartisan revolving-door incestuousness of Washington and Wall Street," adding that as recently as 2008, Summers "made $5.2 million . . . from a hedge fund, D. E. Shaw, for a one-day-a-week job" and went on to earn "$2.7 million in speaking fees from the likes of Citigroup and Goldman Sachs."

Rich then raised the issue of conflict of interest, asking whether Summers could "be a fair broker of the bailout when he so recently received lavish compensation from some of its present and, no doubt, future players."

In a similar vein, Paul Krugman (a newspaper columnist as well as a Princeton professor) complained about how Timothy Geithner, whom Obama had appointed as his treasury secretary, was administering the

TARP program. No significant reforms were apparent, Krugman charged, in the way that investment banks did business. And this was outrageous: "Given all the taxpayer money on the line," Krugman wrote, "financial firms should be acting like public utilities, not returning to the paychecks and practices of 2007."

In the spring of 2009, Summers reported to Obama that an economic stimulus package of $787 billion worth of federal spending, slightly more than the TARP program that was already up and running, would do the trick. Krugman counter-argued in his newspaper column that the sum fell woefully short of what was needed, and a great many other "salt water economists" concurred. The situation, wrote Krugman, was roughly comparable to the tepid rate of New Deal spending as compared to the vast amount of spending it would finally take to pull America out of the Depression in World War II.

But Obama and his team sent the $787 billion program to Congress, which the Democrats controlled. Some observers in Washington whispered that Obama's political strategists were worried that a larger appropriation might get filibustered by the Republicans. And the very idea of getting Democrats to scrap the Senate's filibuster rule was off the table for all kinds of reasons.

So the bill went through, Obama signed it, and Vice President Biden got the task of reviewing applications from state and local governments—applications for funds to be spent on infrastructure projects that would put people to work. Biden worked slowly and carefully, fearful of giving Republicans a basis for claims that the spending was somehow wasteful.

Harold Ickes did much the same thing when he administered the newly created PWA back in 1933.

And the results were eerily (or quite predictably) similar. A slow recovery started in 2009 and it continued to inch along. But the pace was so slow that many millions were suffering—and impatient—as unemployment soared to its highest point since the 1930s and the termination of unemployment benefits was visible over the horizon. Supporters of the administration worried that Obama was being too judicious and too "responsible" in a situation that called for heroic audacity. In the summer of 2009, writer Kevin Baker mused that Obama was moving "prudently, carefully, and reasonably toward disaster."

The economy being what it was, the corporate sector was able to show some profits in ventures that did little or nothing to put people back to work. Before long, the phrase "jobless recovery" was making the rounds and Obama was confronted with a choice: Should he go back to Congress for a second, larger, and fast-tracked job creation program— or not?

He did not. Instead, he put health care reform at the top of his legislative agenda.

Meanwhile, grassroots rage was exploding and it turned in a right-wing direction with the founding and growth of the ultra-libertarian "Tea Party" movement that gained tremendous strength in the Republican Party. Tea Partiers said that hard-working Americans were being taxed to the point of bankruptcy by an arrogant federal regime that should give the people some authentic relief by simply getting off their backs. The complicated nature of the health care legislation, whose procedures seemed occasionally bewildering even to sophisticated observers, worsened this climate of opinion.

As the mid-term elections of 2010 approached, over eight million people had lost their jobs, though the administration claimed credit for saving approximately 3.3 million jobs—as well as for saving the auto manufacturers Chrysler and GM, which might otherwise have gone bankrupt. But as Rich observed in October 2010, "the dark cloud cast by undiminished unemployment" was giving millions a "fatalistic sense that the stacked economic order that gave us the Great Recession remains not just in place but more entrenched and powerful than ever."

In the mid-term elections of 2010, the Democratic Party lost control of the House of Representatives. The new Republican majority was rife with Tea Partiers, many of whom had little to no experience in the world of political give and take. They were extremists.

And their hostility was such that they were determined to resist—even to the point of outright sabotage—almost anything Obama proposed. In 2011, they embarked on a course that became a repetitive routine far into Obama's second term. They would clamp down on federal funding at the end of each fiscal year. They would refuse to "raise the debt ceiling," that is, pass appropriations sufficient to redeem the bonds of Uncle Sam, thus risking an unprecedented federal default, unless sweeping across the board cuts in federal spending occurred.

A stalemate between the White House and Capitol Hill set in and it paralyzed the Obama presidency in a great many ways from then on. The fiscal brinksmanship of the Tea Party resulted in repeated government shutdowns that lasted until some weak compromises were engineered by moderate Republicans.

Meanwhile, Americans were divided by increasingly shrill debates as to whether Uncle Sam had done too little or too much since the election of 2008. The anger on both sides of this debate was to a large extent emanating from the misery of millions who were trying to pay the rent and support their families during this stubborn spell of hard times. Millions of young adults were graduating from college only to find themselves in menial jobs paying salaries so pitifully small that they had no other choice but to go on living at home with their parents. Their short-term futures were stultified.

A few economists asserted as early as 2009 that the recession was officially "over." But other economists (better economists, in truth)—along with millions of distressed Americans and their elected leaders—knew that such claims were farcical due to the nature of the ongoing "jobless recovery."

A wide range of indicators must support any characterization or labeling of economic trends. The mere fact that corporate profits and stock values go up does not in any way support the conclusion that the real-life well-being of American citizens has necessarily improved. If the recession was "over" in 2009, then economists need to get busy and revise their definition of recession.

Put bluntly: The case can be made that in light of the damage that was done in the chain reaction of 2008, the size of the recovery/stimulus package was much too small and it was spent too slowly by far.

But economists working in free market circles have disputed every inch of this contested ground, and they go on to assert that most (if not all) forms of federal intervention in the economy since 2008 have worsened the situation rather than improved it.

But what else would such people tend to say?

A steady sequence of op-ed columns in the *Wall Street Journal* throughout the recession sought to spin the situation in ways that would discredit proposals for reforms to hold Wall Street accountable. As late as April 15, 2016, Phil Gramm and Michael Solon wrote that while "candidate Barack

Obama weaponized the crisis by blaming greedy bankers," it was "Washington that propped up subprime debt and then stymied recovery."

Government bashers across the board came to similar conclusions: "Washington" was to blame. And so it stood to reason that "Washington" (that is, government) needed to refrain from making things worse. Instead, "Washington"—ashamed of itself—should retrench, pinch pennies, and practice self-discipline.

And policymakers listened to such pronouncements all over the world. Instead of fiscal stimulation, one government after another was turning to financial austerity as orthodox budgetary scolds pushed them on to impose ever-greater doses of fiscal "discipline" in societies that were spiraling downward.

As Obama faced the challenge of reelection in 2012, some twenty-four million Americans were either unemployed or severely underemployed according to the bleakest estimates. Krugman had no hesitation in proclaiming that the Great Recession should have been classified as a full-fledged depression. The title of his latest book—*End This Depression Now*—made this obvious in 2013.

And the depression was global. Doubters who might hesitate about using the term should "talk to the Greeks, the Irish, or even the Spaniards, who have 23 percent unemployment—and almost 50 percent unemployment among the young," Krugman wrote. It was essentially "the same kind of situation that John Maynard Keynes described in the 1930s: 'a chronic condition of subnormal activity for a considerable period without any marked tendency either towards recovery or towards complete collapse.'" Austerity would make the problem worse.

He pointed out that researchers at the International Monetary Fund had identified "no fewer than 173 cases of fiscal austerity in advanced countries over the period between 1978 and 2009," and every one of these austerity episodes was "followed by economic contraction and higher unemployment."

Yet instead of coming to the obvious conclusion that "now is the time for the government to spend more, not less, until the private sector is ready to carry the economy forward again, . . . job-destroying austerity policies have instead become the rule" all over the world.

Even if Obama had come to the same conclusion by 2013, there was little he could do about it because Congress—by then completely controlled by the Republicans—refused to go along with almost anything he suggested.

The result of the election of 2016, the upset victory (in the Electoral College) of Donald Trump, a billionaire with no political experience, resulted at least in part from economic grievances in the "rustbelt" states where many suffered from the seemingly interminable hard times. Trump promised them job-creating infrastructure spending, together with a tougher policy toward trade competitors and American businesses that continued to ship jobs overseas.

As of this writing (autumn 2017), he has yet to make good on those promises.

When Election Day 2016 approached, the outgoing vice president, Joe Biden, reflected that the Democrats should have done much more to promote a full-employment recovery when they had the chance. In October 2016, as he watched some television coverage of a Trump rally near Wilkes-Barre, Pennsylvania, he felt a rush of panic and regret. "Son of a gun," he reflected, "we may lose this election." The chanting crowd was full of "the people I grew up with" or "their kids." It was suddenly obvious to Biden that the Democrats for years had "made a mistake of not speaking to the fears, aspirations, and concerns of middle-class people."

Just before leaving office, Obama came to similar conclusions. "In 2010," he said—when the Democrats began to lose control of Congress— "there were a lot of folks who were still out of work. There were a lot of folks who had lost their homes or saw their home values plummet, their 401(k)s plummet. . . . Whoever is president at that point is going to get hit, and his party's going to get hit."

This made the electoral outcome of 2010 sound almost inevitable. But Obama went on to say that "I take some responsibility." He admitted that he, like Biden, looked back on it all with regret.

Quite right: he did bear a major share of the responsibility, and so did Lawrence Summers.

The parlous state of our politics today is the direct result of hard times. Only time will tell if our historical experience can help us create better times.

Let us fervently hope that it can.

A Note on Sources

CHAPTER 1: HARD TIMES FROM COLONIAL
TO POSTREVOLUTIONARY AMERICA

Though new scholarship has added much to our knowledge of hard times in early America, a great deal of valuable material can still be gleaned in some older sources. An excellent account of the seventeenth-century Virginia tobacco economy may be found in *American Slavery, American Freedom: The Ordeal of Colonial Virginia* by Edmund S. Morgan (New York: W. W. Norton, 1975). Bernard Bailyn's book *The New England Merchants in the Seventeeth Century* (Cambridge, MA: Harvard University Press, 1955) is also very useful. A pathbreaking study of Pennsylvania's colonial monetary experiment of the 1720s is Richard A. Lester's article "Currency Issues to Overcome Depressions in Pennsylvania, 1723 and 1729," *Journal of Political Economy* 46 (June 1938): 325. Good coverage of the depression in the 1780s is easy to come by, and a vivid older account that was written for a general audience may be found in *American Economic History* by Broadus and Louise Pearson Mitchell (Boston: Houghton Mifflin, 1947). *Shays's Rebellion: The American Revolution's Final Battle* by Leonard L. Richards (Philadelphia: University of Pennsylvania Press, 2002) is a very fine recent account.

CHAPTER 2: HARD TIMES AND THE
FINANCIAL PANICS OF 1819 AND 1837

A good older account of American monetary history, written for laymen, is Arthur Nussbaum's *A History of the Dollar* (New York: Columbia University Press, 1957). For an effective account of the development of fractional reserve banking, see Glyn Davies, *A History of Money: From Ancient Times to the Present Day* (Cardiff: University of Wales Press, 1994). A good account of Alexander Hamilton's economic thought, in a biographical context, may be found in Forrest McDonald's *Alexander*

Hamilton: A Biography (New York: W. W. Norton, 1982). On the politics surrounding the Second Bank of the United States, see Bray Hammond's *Banks and Politics in America, From the Revolution to the Civil War* (Princeton, NJ: Princeton University Press, 1957) and "Jackson, Biddle, and the Bank of the United States," in *Essays on Jacksonian America*, edited by Frank Otto Gattell (New York: Holt, Rinehart and Winston, 1970), 1–23. On the Panic of 1837 and the ensuing depression, see Alasdair Roberts, *America's First Great Depression: Economic Crisis and Political Disorder after the Panic of 1837* (Ithaca, NY: Cornell University Press, 2012), and Jessica M. Lepler, *The Many Panics of 1837: People, Politics, and the Creation of a Trans-Atlantic Financial Crisis* (Cambridge: Cambridge University Press, 2013).

CHAPTER 3: THE PANICS OF 1873 AND 1893—
AND HARD TIMES IN BETWEEN

For coverage of the "Greenback" experiment, see E. G. Spaulding, *A Resource of War—The Credit of Government Made Immediately Available: History of the Legal Tender Paper Money Issued During the Great Rebellion, Being a Loan Without Interest and a National Currency* (Buffalo: Express Printing, 1869), and Wesley Clair Mitchell, *A History of the Greenbacks with Special Reference to the Economic Consequences of their Issue, 1862–1865* (Chicago: University of Chicago, 1903). On the shift from bank notes to checking accounts in commercial banking and fractional reserve lending, see Arthur Nussbaum, *A History of the Dollar* (New York: Columbia University Press, 1957), Irving Fisher, *100% Money: Designed to Keep Checking Banks 100% Liquid; to Prevent Inflation and Deflation; Largely to Cure or Prevent Depressions; and to Wipe Out Much of the National Debt* (New York: Adelphi Publications, 1935), and Stephen Quinn and William Roberds, "The Evolution of the Check as a Means of Payment: A Historical Survey," *Economic Review* (Federal Reserve Bank of Atlanta), November 4, 2008. On the Panic of 1873, see Nicolas Barreyre, "The Politics of Economic Crisis: The Panic of 1873, the End of Reconstruction, and the Realignment of American Politics," *Journal of the Gilded Age and Progressive Era* 10 (October 2011), and Scott Reynolds Nelson, "The Real Great Depression: The Depression of 1929

Is the Wrong Model for the Current Economic Crisis," *The Chronicle of Higher Education*, October 17, 2008, accessible via http://chronicle.com/article/The-Real-Great-Depression/23394. For detailed coverage of the Tompkins Square protest in New York, see Herbert G. Gutman, "The Tompkins Square 'Riot' in New York City on January 13, 1874: A Re-Examination of Its Causes and Its Aftermath," *Labor History* 6, no. 1 (1965): 43–66. On Social Darwinism, see Richard Hofstadter, *Social Darwinism in American Thought* (Boston: Beacon Press, 1944). For sympathetic accounts of the National Farmer's Alliance and the Populist Party, see John D. Hicks, *The Populist Revolt: A History of the Farmers' Alliance and the People's Party* (Minneapolis: University of Minnesota Press, 1931), and Lawrence Goodwyn, *The Populist Moment: A Short History of the Agrarian Revolt in America* (New York: Oxford University Press, 1978). On the 1890s depression, see Charles Hoffman, *The Depression of the Nineties: An Economic History* (Westport, CT: Greenwood Publishing, 1970), and Frank B. Latham, *The Panic of 1893: A Time of Strikes, Riots, Hobo Camps, Coxey's Army, Starvation, Withering Droughts, and Fears of Revolution* (New York: F. Watts, 1971). For an early study of the Panic of 1893, see William Jett Lauck, *The Causes of the Panic of 1893* (Boston: Houghton Mifflin, 1907). There is a very rich literature on the subject of "Coxey's Army"; see Donald L. McMurry, *Coxey's Army: A Study of the Industrial Movement of 1894* (Seattle: University of Washington Press, 1968), Carlos A. Schwantes, *Coxey's Army: An American Odyssey* (Lincoln: University of Nebraska Press, 1985), Franklin Folsum, *Impatient Armies of the Poor: The Story of Collective Action of the Unemployed, 1808–1942* (Niwot, CO: University Press of Colorado, 1991), and Benjamin F. Alexander, *Coxey's Army: Popular Protest in the Gilded Age* (Baltimore: Johns Hopkins University Press, 2015).

CHAPTER 4: DEPRESSIONS AND POLICY
DISPUTES IN AMERICA, CIRCA 1720–1928

For studies of laissez-faire doctrine as intellectual and economic history, see Jacob Viner, *Intellectual History of Laissez Faire* (Chicago: University of Chicago Press, 1961), and Richard Striner, "Political Newtonianism: The Cosmic Model of Politics in Europe and America," *William and*

Mary Quarterly 52 (October 1995): 583. On the creation of the Federal Reserve, see Allen H. Meltzer, *A History of the Federal Reserve* (Chicago: University of Chicago Press, 2009), vol. 1. For an account of the 1920–1921 depression from a free marketeering perspective, see James Grant, *The Forgotten Depression, 1921: The Crash That Cured Itself* (New York: Simon and Schuster, 2014).

CHAPTER 5: THE ONSET OF THE GREAT DEPRESSION

One of the best descriptive and analytical accounts of the 1929 crash and its relation to the Great Depression is John Kenneth Galbraith's *The Great Crash, 1929* (Boston: Houghton Mifflin, 1954). A more recent revisionist account is Maury Klein's *Rainbow's End: The Crash of 1929* (New York: Oxford University Press, 2001). For analysis and commentary, see also Christina Romer, "The Great Crash and the Onset of the Great Depression," *Quarterly Journal of Economics* 105 (1990): 597, and Benjamin Bernanke, "Nonmonetary Effects of the Financial Crisis in the Propagation of the Great Depression," *American Economic Review* 73 (1983): 257. For a superb overview of the Hoover years, see Arthur Schlesinger Jr., *The Crisis of the Old Order, 1919–1933* (Boston: Houghton Mifflin, 1957). For an excellent interpretive biography of Herbert Hoover, see David Burner, *Herbert Hoover: A Public Life* (New York: Knopf, 1979).

CHAPTER 6: THE EARLY NEW DEAL AND THE DEPRESSION

For good one-volume overviews of the entire New Deal, see Carl Degler, *The New Deal* (Chicago: Quadrangle, 1970), William Leuchtenburg, *Franklin D. Roosevelt and the New Deal* (New York: Harper and Row, 1963), and Joseph P. Lash, *Dealers and Dreamers: A New Look at the New Deal* (New York: Doubleday, 1988). Early treatments of FDR and the New Deal are still illuminating; see in particular the standard works: Robert E. Sherwood, *Roosevelt and Hopkins: An Intimate History* (New York: Harper and Brothers, 1948), Arthur Schlesinger Jr., *The Coming of the New Deal, 1933–1935* (Boston: Houghton Mifflin, 1958), James MacGregor Burns, *Roosevelt: The Lion and the Fox, 1882–1940*

(New York: Harcourt, Brace and World, 1956), Frank Freidel, *Franklin D. Roosevelt: The Triumph* (Boston: Little, Brown, 1956), and Freidel, *Franklin D. Roosevelt: Launching the New Deal* (Boston: Little, Brown, 1973). On individual members of the Brain Trust and FDR's cabinet, see George McJimsey, *Harry Hopkins: Ally of the Poor and Defender of Democracy* (Cambridge, MA: Harvard University Press, 1987), George Martin, *Madame Secretary: Frances Perkins* (Boston: Houghton Mifflin, 1976), T. H. Watkins, *Righteous Pilgrim: The Life and Times of Harold L. Ickes, 1874–1952* (New York: Henry Holt, 1990), and Bernard Sternsher, *Rexford Tugwell and the New Deal* (New Brunswick: Rutgers University Press, 1964). On the Civilian Conservation Corps, see Leslie Alexander Lacy, *The Soil Soldiers: The Civilian Conservation Corps in the Great Depression* (Radnor, PA: Chilton, 1976).

CHAPTER 7: 1934—A YEAR OF FEAR AND RAGE IN AMERICA

A pathbreaking comparison of recovery from the Great Depression in Nazi Germany and the United States was provided by John A. Garraty in his article "The New Deal, National Socialism, and the Great Depression," *American Historical Review* 78 (October 1973): 907. On the Dust Bowl, see James Noble Gregory, *American Exodus: The Dust Bowl Migration and Okie Culture in California* (New York: Oxford University Press, 1989). On the California waterfront strikes and the San Francisco general strike, see David F. Selvin, *A Terrible Anger: The 1934 Waterfront and General Strikes in San Francisco* (Detroit: Wayne State University Press, 1996). On Upton Sinclair's 1934 bid for the California governorship, see Greg Mitchell, *The Campaign of the Century: Upton Sinclair's Race for California Governor and the Birth of Media Politics* (New York: Random House, 1992). On Huey Long, a definitive though still controversial (because largely positive in its coverage) biography is T. Harry Williams's *Huey Long* (New York: Knopf, 1969). On the Liberty League, see George Wolfskill, *The Revolt of the Conservatives, the American Liberty League, 1934–1940* (Boston: Houghton Mifflin, 1962). On the long-term conservative campaign to roll back the New Deal, see Kim Phillips-Fein, *Invisible Hands: The Making of the Conservative Movement from the New Deal to Reagan* (New York: W. W. Norton, 2009).

CHAPTER 8: THE POLITICS OF CLASS
CONFLICT DURING 1935 AND 1936

On the New Deal safety net, see Edward Berkowitz and Kim McQuaid, *Creating the Welfare State: The Political Economy of Twentieth Century Reform* (New York: Praeger, 1980), and Kirstin Downey, *The Woman Behind the New Deal: The Life and Legacy of Frances Perkins, Social Security, Unemployment Insurance, and the Minimum Wage* (New York: Random House, 2010). On the CIO during its years of institutional independence, see Robert H. Zieger, *The CIO: 1935–1955* (Chapel Hill: University of North Carolina Press, 1995). On the conservative side of the New Deal, see Barton J. Bernstein, "The New Deal: The Conservative Achievements of Liberal Reform," in *Towards a New Past: Dissenting Essays in American History*, edited by Barton Bernstein (New York: Pantheon Books, 1968). For mid-twentieth-century commentary by a conservative writer on the conservative side of FDR's statecraft, see Peter Viereck, *Conservatism Revisited: The Revolt Against Revolt, 1815–1949* (New York: Charles Scribner's Sons, 1949), and Viereck, *Conservatism, From John Adams to Churchill* (New York: D. Van Nostrand Company, 1956). On the election of 1936, see Mary E. Stuckey, *Voting Deliberatively: FDR and the 1936 Presidential Campaign* (University Park: Penn State University Press, 2015). For outstanding coverage of the period in question, see Arthur Schlesinger Jr., *The Politics of Upheaval, 1935–1936* (Boston: Houghton Mifflin, 1960).

CHAPTER 9: RECOVERY AND RECESSION, 1937–1939

The most prominent recent critique of the New Deal as an affront to free enterprise and an impediment to economic recovery is *The Forgotten Man: A New History of the Great Depression* (New York: HarperCollins, 2007) by Amity Shlaes, a *Wall Street Journal* writer whose book is essentially a Reaganesque counter-narrative of the 1930s. On Walter Reuther and the UAW, see Nelson Lichtenstein, *The Most Dangerous Man in Detroit: Walter Reuther and the Fate of American Labor* (New York: Basic Books, 1995). On the Memorial Day Massacre, see Michael Dennis, *The Memorial Day Massacre and the Movement for Industrial Democracy* (New

York: Palgrave Macmillan, 2010). A recent study of the court-packing fight is journalist Burt Solomon's *FDR v. The Constitution: The Court-Packing Fight and the Triumph of Democracy* (New York: Walker, 2009).

CHAPTER 10: THE GREAT DEPRESSION
AND AMERICAN CULTURE IN THE 1930s

Two books by T. H. Watkins offer rich coverage of American social and cultural history during the Great Depression: *The Great Depression: America in the 1930s* (Boston: Little, Brown, 1993) and *The Hungry Years: A Narrative History of the Great Depression in America* (New York: Henry Holt, 1999). Many excellent books have offered commentary on American films of the 1930s, but interesting points about the Depression as it figures in such films can still be gleaned from an early study, Andrew Bergman's *We're in the Money: Depression America and Its Films* (New York: New York University Press, 1971). A more recent and insightful study of gender issues as they figure in Depression-era films is Maria DiBattista, *Fast-Talking Dames* (New Haven, CT: Yale University Press, 2003). Excellent commentary on the Astaire-Rogers partnership may be found in Arlene Croce's *The Fred Astaire and Ginger Rogers Book* (New York: Outerbridge and Lazard, 1972). A brilliant new study of Shirley Temple as a Depression-era icon is John F. Kasson's book *The Little Girl Who Fought the Great Depression: Shirley Temple and 1930s America* (New York: W. W. Norton, 2014). On the life and career of Dorothea Lange, see Milton Meltzer, *Dorothea Lange: A Photographer's Life* (New York: Farrar, Straus and Giroux, 1978), and on Walker Evans, see James Mellow, *Walker Evans* (New York: Basic Books, 1999). Excellent compilations of FSA photographs with commentary may be found in *Documenting America, 1935–1943*, edited by Carl Fleischhauer and Beverly Brannan (Berkeley: University of California Press, 1988), and in Michael Lesy's *Long Time Coming: A Photographic Portrait of America, 1935–1943* (New York: W. W. Norton, 2002). On Ben Shahn, see Susan Chevlowe, *Common Man Mythic Vision: The Paintings of Ben Shahn* (Princeton, NJ: Princeton University Press, 1998). On social realist art, see David Shapiro, ed., *Social Realism: Art as Weapon* (New York: Frederick Ungar, 1973). Good commentary on regionalism may be found in James M.

Dennis's *Grant Wood: A Study in American Art and Culture* (New York: Viking Press, 1975). An early study of the streamlining movement in 1930s architecture and design is Donald J. Bush, *The Streamline Decade* (New York: George Braziller, 1975). More comprehensive coverage of industrial design and the decorative arts during the period can be found in Richard Guy Wilson, Dianne H. Pilgrim, and Dickran Tashjian, *The Machine Age in America* (New York: Harry N. Abrams, 1986). On the music of Woody Guthrie, see Mark Allan Jackson, *Prophet Singer: The Voice and Vision of Woody Guthrie* (Jackson: University Press of Mississippi, 2008). On swing music, see Gunther Schuller, *The Swing Era: The Development of Jazz, 1930–1945* (New York: Oxford University Press, 1989), and David Stowe, *Swing Changes: Big Band Jazz in New Deal America* (Cambridge, MA: Harvard University Press, 1994).

CHAPTER 11: HOW THE GREAT DEPRESSION ENDED: THE KEYNESIAN SCHOOL OF THOUGHT

A good comprehensive account of the generational experience during the Depression and World War II is David Kennedy's *Freedom from Fear: The American People in Depression and War, 1929–1945* (New York: Oxford University Press, 2001). An influential book that contributed to the rise of Keynesianism after World War II was Seymour Harris's edited anthology *The New Economics: Keynes's Influence on Theory and Public Policy* (New York: Knopf, 1947). A good primary source account of the essentially Keynesian thinking behind the Interstate Highway System may be found in Robert J. Donovan, *Eisenhower: The Inside Story* (New York: Harper and Brothers, 1956). A famous mid-century book in the Keynesian tradition advancing an argument for greater public sector as opposed to private sector investment was John Kenneth Galbraith's *The Affluent Society* (Boston: Houghton Mifflin, 1958).

CHAPTER 12: THE REVOLT AGAINST KEYNES

Good contemporaneous coverage and analysis of economic trends from the 1970s through the 1990s can be found in a number of books from the period, some of them admittedly polemical. John Kenneth Galbraith's *Money: Whence It Came, Where It Went* (Boston: Houghton Mifflin, 1975) offers thought-provoking commentary on monetary issues spanning centuries but concluding in the 1970s. William Greider's *Secrets of the Temple: How the Federal Reserve Runs the Country* (New York: Simon and Schuster, 1987) provides in-depth coverage of the Volcker era at the Federal Reserve and the economic contraction that accompanied his anti-inflation campaign. Conservative commentary by a Nixon Republican who found himself appalled by Reagan-era economic trends may be found in two books by Kevin Phillips: *The Politics of Rich and Poor: Wealth and the American Electorate in the Reagan Aftermath* (New York: Random House, 1990) and *Boiling Point: Republicans, Democrats, and the Decline of Middle Class Prosperity* (New York: Random House, 1993). On the financial mechanics of the S & L crisis, see Lawrence J. White, *The S & L Debacle: Public Policy Lessons for Bank and Thrift Regulation* (New York: Oxford University Press, 1991), and James K. Glassman, "The Great Banks Robbery: Deconstructing the S & L Crisis," *New Republic*, October 8, 1990. On globalization, see William Greider, *One World, Ready or Not* (New York: Simon and Schuster, 1997), and Jeff Faux, *The Global Class War: How America's Bipartisan Elite Lost Our Future— And What It Will Take to Win It Back* (New York: Wiley, 2006). On the Dot Com Boom and Bust, see the prophetic article by Joel Kotkin and David Friedman, "As Wall Street Pats Itself on the Back, Trouble Lurks Behind the Boom," *Washington Post*, May 24, 1998. Paul Krugman's *The Great Unraveling: Losing Our Way in the New Century* (New York: W. W. Norton, 2004) is a Keynesian commentary on many issues pertaining to the recent past in American economic history.

CHAPTER 13: THE GREAT RECESSION

The literature on the subject of the ongoing recession is enormous. In particular, see Charles Morris, *The Trillion Dollar Meltdown: Easy Money, High Rollers, and the Great Credit Crash* (New York: Public Affairs, 2008), James Lieber, "What Cooked the World's Economy," *Village Voice*, January 27, 2009, Michael S. Rothberg, *Greed: A Personal and Professional Look at How Greed Caused the Great Recession of 2008*

(Bloomington, IN: Author House, 2010), David B. Grusky, Bruce Western, and Christopher Wimer, eds., *The Great Recession* (New York: Russell Sage Foundation, 2011), Paul Krugman, *The Return of Depression Economics and the Crisis of 2008* (New York: W. W. Norton, 2009), and Krugman, *End This Depression Now!* (New York: W. W. Norton, 2012). Especially interesting is Sheila Bair's *The Bullies of Wall Street: How Greedy Adults Messed Up Our Economy* (New York: Simon and Schuster, 2015), a book for children that was written by the former head of FDIC. See also John Cassidy, "Anatomy of a Meltdown: Ben Bernanke and the Financial Crisis," *The New Yorker*, December 1, 2008, Nelson B. Schwartz, "Rapid Declines in Manufacturing Spread Global Anxiety," *New York Times*, March 19, 2009, Frank Rich, "Awake and Sing," *New York Times*, April 11, 2009, Paul Krugman, "Money for Nothing," *New York Times*, April 27, 2009, James B. Stewart, "Eight Days: The Battle to Save the American Financial System," *The New Yorker*, September 21, 2009, and Frank Rich, "What Happened to Change We Can Believe In?" *New York Times*, October 23, 2010.

Index

About the Author

Richard Striner is professor of history at Washington College in Chestertown, Maryland. The author of over ten books, he specializes in interdisciplinary studies and intellectual history. Among his specialties are political and presidential leadership, economic history, monetary theory, literary history, architectural history, and the history of cinema. His most recent book on economic theory is *How America Can Spend Its Way Back to Greatness* (2015). He has also written about economics for *The American Scholar* magazine and the *Washington Post*.